POLITICS, GENDER, AND THE MEXICAN NOVEL, 1968–1988

T0349894

The Texas Pan American Series

POLITICS, GENDER, AND THE MEXICAN NOVEL, 1968–1988

Beyond the Pyramid

Cynthia Steele

University of Texas Press, Austin

First Edition, 1992

Requests for permission to reproduce material from this work
should be sent to Permissions, University of Texas Press, Box 7819,
Austin, Texas 78713-7819.

⊚ The paper used in this publication meets the minimum
requirements of American National Standard for Information
Sciences—Permanence of Paper for Printed Library Materials,
ANSI Z39.48-1984.

The Texas Pan American Series is published with the assistance of
a revolving publication fund established by the Pan American
Sulphur Company.

Library of Congress Cataloging-in-Publication Data
Steele, Cynthia.
    Politics, gender, and the Mexican novel, 1968–1988 : beyond
the pyramid / by Cynthia Steele. — 1st ed.
        p.   cm. — (The Texas Pan American series)
    Includes bibliographical references and index.
    ISBN 0-292-77661-6 (pbk. : alk. paper)
    1. Mexican fiction—20th century—History and criticism.
2. Politics in literature.   3. Sex role in literature.   4. Women in
literature.   5. Social problems in literature.   I. Title.   II. Series.
PQ7203.S74   1992
863—dc20   91-30491

For my parents,
Ned and Lorraine Steele,
and
in memory of
Joseph Sommers

Contents

Acknowledgments

The ideas explored here are the product of more than a decade of visits to Mexico City, involving conversations with numerous Mexican writers and critics, notably Margo Glantz, José Emilio Pacheco, and Elena Poniatowska. Various sections of the manuscript have benefited from comments by Elena Urrutia and the members of the Programa Interdisciplinario de Estudios de la Mujer (PIEM) at the Colegio de México; Carlos Blanco-Aguinaga of the University of California, San Diego; Grínor Rojo and Leslie Adelson of Ohio State University; Jean Franco of Columbia University; and Lauro Flores, Anthony Geist, and Yvonne Yarbro-Bejarano of the University of Washington. George Potratz thoughtfully critiqued nearly every chapter of the manuscript. Any errors and omissions that might remain in the text are, of course, my own.

Teresinha Bertussi and Agustín Cueva, Margo Glantz, Antonio Lazcano Araujo, and Elena Poniatowska opened their homes in Mexico City to me and offered books, journals, and invaluable introductions. Elva Macías, Masha and Eraclio Zepeda, and Juan Antonio Ascencio have been generous with information and hard-to-find publications regarding recent Mexican narrative. Russell Cluff shared his collection of reviews of *Las batallas en el desierto*, and Marco Antonio Campos and Hugo Verani provided me with copies of out-of-print books. My understanding of contemporary Mexican literature has also been enhanced by interviews and discussions with Jorge Aguilar Mora, Inés Arredondo, Arturo Azuela, Juan Bañuelos, Margarita Dalton, Luis González de Alba, Ethel Krause, Mónica Mansour, David Martín del Campo, George McWhirter, Javier Molina, Silvia Molina, Cristina Pacheco, Federico Patán, Aline Pettersson, María Luisa Puga, Luis Arturo Ramos, Jorge Ruffinelli, and Guillermo Samperio.

The four authors whose works I have chosen to analyze in depth have graciously submitted to lengthy interviews (or, in the case of

Pacheco, informal conversations). In 1982 Fernando del Paso responded in writing to my queries regarding *Palinuro de México*, which we discussed during brown-bag lunches on the lawn of the Hemeroteca Nacional (where I was reading about the student movement while he conducted research on Maximilian and Carlota). He also provided me with copies of articles about *Palinuro* published in European journals. José Agustín granted me an extensive interview regarding *Cerca del fuego* in September 1988 at his house in Cuaútla, Morelos (forthcoming in *Nuevo Texto Crítico*).

My many conversations over the years with José Emilio Pacheco and Elena Poniatowska have been fundamental to my understanding of contemporary Mexican culture. I began reading José Emilio Pacheco's works in 1978, when he and I were colleagues in the Departamento de Investigaciones Históricas of the Instituto Nacional de Antropología e Historia. The following year, as a visiting professor at Ohio State University, he wrote *Las batallas en el desierto* on the same typewriter, in the same office, where I, as an assistant professor at Ohio State, would later write my analysis of his novel. Pacheco took me on a walking tour of the Colonia Roma, the setting for *Las batallas*, in 1983, before the 1985 earthquake devastated the neighborhood. Yet even then it was a tour of a ghost town, of a "city of memory."

Elena Poniatowska has fed and sheltered me and has submitted to half a dozen taped interviews since 1981, in her homes in San Angel and Chimalistac, in my apartment in Seattle, and twice on the highway from Mexico City to Cuaútla (to visit José Agustín). A synthesis of these latter conversations appeared in *Hispamérica* 53–54 (1989). Elena graciously has given me free access to her library and archives, including notes for various of her projects, clippings of reviews and criticism of her books, drafts of *Hasta no verte Jesús mío*, and transcripts of many of her oral-history interviews with Josefina Bórquez. Also, she helped me to secure most of the photographs for this book.

Graciela Iturbide gave me a copy of *Marcha política* (*Political March*), her remarkable portrait of Hermila, the widow of a disappeared political leader from Juchitán; and Héctor García provided the striking photographs of the student movement of 1968, as well as of Elena Poniatowska and Josefina Bórquez. I would also like to thank the *Revista de Crítica Literaria Latinoamericana* and *Studies in Twentieth Century Literature* for granting permission to publish expanded versions of my articles on Elena Poniatowska and José Agustín.

Research and travel funds and release time were granted by the College of Humanities and the Graduate School at Ohio State University, as well as by the College of Arts and Sciences and the Graduate School of the University of Washington. The University of Washington Department of Romance Languages and Literature, particularly its chair and associate chair, Douglas Collins and George Shipley, have consistently supported my work over the past four years.

Theresa May has been any author's dream of an editor; her enthusiasm and great efficiency have played no small part in bringing the manuscript to completion.

This book is for my parents, who encouraged their middle daughter's passion for reading and writing and who once spent the night in a Stockton bowling alley so that she could discover Mexico. I also dedicate it to the memory of Joseph Sommers (1924–1979), who had faith in my potential and who continues to be my model for democratic teaching and for responsible, committed research on Mexican culture.

POLITICS, GENDER, AND THE MEXICAN NOVEL, 1968–1988

1. Of Pyramids and Fleas: Mexican Narrative and the Crisis, 1968–1985

Extremos de México: no se conoce un justo medio entre las pirámides y las pulgas vestidas. Como dice Octavio Paz, desde el punto de vista de la perfección no existe diferencia entre la pulga y el elefante. Nadie puede llevarse la pirámide del Sol a su casa; pero sí contemplar extasiado su boda de pulgas con mariachi en los cuatro paneles de una cáscara de nuez.

(Extremes of Mexico: There is no happy medium between pyramids and dressed fleas. As Octavio Paz says, from the point of view of perfection there is no difference between fleas and elephants. No one can take the Pyramid of the Sun home with them; but they can contemplate in ecstasy their flea wedding, complete with mariachi band, in the four panels of a walnut shell.)

—JOSÉ EMILIO PACHECO, "CIEN AÑOS DE JULIO TORRI" (1989)

Yoli se había reído despreocupada, igual que siempre, tomando las cosas así nomás, porque le daba miedo hablar en serio, con el lenguaje de papá, el lenguaje de los monumentos, riéndose porque la vida es un chiste y lo importante es saber contarlo.

(Yoli had laughed, unconcerned, as usual, taking things lightly, because she was afraid to talk in earnest with Papa's language, the language of monuments, laughing because life is a joke and what matters is knowing how to tell it.)

—JUAN VILLORO, "LA NOCHE NAVEGABLE" (1980)

In Mexico the novel has always been intimately linked with processes of political and social change, particularly the Revolution and its consequences, and with attempts at "modernization" beginning in the late 1940s. For the past two decades, this tendency has per-

Student rally at the National Autonomous University of Mexico (UNAM), 1968. Photograph by Héctor García.

Demonstrators and tanks in the streets of Mexico City, 1968. Photograph by Héctor García.

sisted alongside less referential strains of narrative. During the 1970s novels often took as their focus the student movement of 1968, generally considered a turning point in the hegemony of the PRI (Party of the Institutionalized Revolution), which has ruled Mexico since the Revolution of 1910 to 1920. In the late 1970s and early 1980s, this theme gave way to the "novel of the city," which examined the deterioration of the metropolis under dependent capitalism and the economic crisis. Following the devastating earthquake of 1985, the organization of grassroots social movements and a powerful political opposition front have provided renewed impetus for political literature. These two decades have also witnessed the emergence of middle-class and popular women's movements, along with an unprecedented number of women writers, many of whom question or subvert traditional gender roles and stereotypes in their works.

Poetry in the Streets, Blood on the Pyramid

In June 1989 the U.S. electronic and print media were flooded with coverage of the Chinese government's violent repression of the student movement in Beijing. The massacre of June 4 and its aftermath claimed the lives of hundreds of unarmed civilians in Tienanmen Square, which student participants in the "Democratization Movement" had occupied for three weeks. There was widespread speculation that victims' bodies had been burned; meanwhile, the Chinese government engaged in a national campaign of disinformation. The very extensive coverage that we had of the events in China can be attributed to U.S. foreign policy interests, as well as to foreign journalists being housed in a hotel located on Tienanmen Square at the time of the massacre. More important, it was part of an increasing trend toward grassroots democratization movements in totalitarian nations of both the socialist and capitalist worlds, not only in China but also in several Latin American and Eastern bloc countries.

In reporting the Chinese massacre, the U.S. media, unlike their Mexican counterparts, failed to notice the parallel with the one that took place at Tlatelolco, Mexico City, on October 2, 1968. Two decades ago European and U.S. journalists who were in Mexico to cover the Olympics were witness to a similar state military action against a peaceful civilian gathering in another Third World nation rocked by a student movement: at Tlatelolco, or the Plaza of the Three Cultures, the site of an Aztec city (of which part of a pyramid remains), a Colonial Spanish church, and a low-cost, high-rise housing development. The Mexican party in power in 1968, like Chinese authorities in 1989, took drastic measures to quell a democratization movement that represented a threat to their longstanding hegemony.

On September 28, 1968, Mexican soldiers, like their Chinese counterparts twenty years later, used tanks to forcibly remove students who had briefly occupied the main square, or *zócalo*, of the capital, located below the National Palace, the civic space *por excelencia.* Then, on October 2, state violence against the student movement escalated into a carefully orchestrated massacre when thousands of people attending a peaceful rally were mowed down by soldiers and police armed with tanks and machine guns.[1]

The Mexican government thus achieved two objectives: It paved the way for the upcoming Olympics to be held in Mexico City without incident, and it brought to a halt Mexico's first significant middle-class social movement. That movement was fueled by discontent springing from a rapidly changing economic panorama during the second half of the sixties, in which the middle-class dream of class mobility and achieving security through education was vanishing before high unemployment rates, and in which concrete instances of police violence and invasion of university autonomy inflamed indignation toward authoritarianism in all spheres. Collective outrage led 100,000 students from middle- and working-class schools to stage a strike, under the supervision of the National Strike Council, which was itself an experiment in direct democracy. Over a period of seventy-two days, as many as 500,000 sympathizers took to the streets and plazas of the capital, in addition to the smaller movements in provincial cities. The list of demands drawn up by the strike council included the release of political prisoners (leaders of the railroad workers' movement of 1958 were still in jail), the dissolution of the riot police, and the repeal of Article 145 of the penal code, which provided the legal basis for police action against acts of "social dissidence." After two months of refusing to speak with the students, the government finally agreed to begin negotiations with two of their leaders on October 2, the same day that it ordered the army, police, and riot police to encircle and open machine-gun fire on a rally of 10,000 people—workers, housewives, and students, including most of the 200 members of the National Strike Council— at Tlatelolco. An indeterminate number of people were killed (most nongovernment estimates are between 300 and 400), thousands were probably wounded, thousands more were arrested, many students were exiled, and over 300 of them were tried and imprisoned for a period of months or years.[2]

It was European, particularly French and Italian, journalists who sounded the alarm over the massacre, while U.S. reporters, perhaps wary of alienating an ally and publicizing a movement that had its worrisome counterpart on the home front, covered the event to a limited extent. Mexican newspapers, like the Chinese media today, drastically underestimated the death count and blamed the victims, charging the students with plotting against the nation and with provoking the ambush.

In this atmosphere of repression and intimidation, with their leaders removed, most participants were stunned into inaction. On December 4 the strike was called off and the National Strike Council was dissolved, ending the student movement. In subsequent years many people completely withdrew from political activism, some of them embittered (at least one prominent figure, who documented the movement on film, committed suicide), while others formed leftist political parties or worked within labor unions, and a few went underground to start the guerrilla movement of the 1970s. The effect of Tlatelolco on participants in the movement, then, tended to be either (at least temporary) depoliticization or radicalization.

The Mexican student movement, like those in France, Italy, and West Germany, was a spontaneous, independent, fundamentally middle-class phenomenon. One of its weaknesses, according to its Mexican critics, was its failure to establish broad connections and to collaborate in a systematic and nonpaternalistic manner with sectors of the popular classes (as local student movements had done in provincial cities during the early and mid-1960s). The movement focused on issues of state authoritarianism and repression, although anti-imperialist sentiment (particularly against U.S. intervention in Vietnam) and concerns with socioeconomic inequality were also present in the demonstrations and the brigades that were active in factories and working-class neighborhoods. Gilberto Guevara Niebla, one of the former leaders, has characterized it as a "crisis in authority" in the Gramscian sense, in which "important sectors of civil society polarize against political society."[3]

At the heart of the problem was the monopolization of political power, at the national, state, and local levels, by the PRI. During the half-century since the Revolution, the PRI had effectively suppressed all opposition and maintained political hegemony through a rhetoric appealing to a desire for modernization and social justice while pursuing economic policies that exacerbated class differences and made the nation profoundly dependent on the United States.

The pyramidal economic and social structure of Colonial society, with the masses of people at the base of the pyramid and a small intermediary group separating them from a tiny ruling class, has been reproduced by dependent capitalism in the nineteenth and twentieth centuries. Economists and other social scientists continue to use the pyramid to describe the structure of contemporary Mexican society. As Octavio Paz argues in *Posdata*, it is a model which has entered a crisis which began to be apparent in 1968.

During the two ensuing decades, an oil boom in the late 1970s resuscitated the dream of self-determination and plenty, only to destroy it when a crisis in the world market brought Mexico to the verge of bankruptcy. Subsequently, the external debt crisis has kept the situation grim, precipitating a major monetary devaluation, a stock market crash, and high levels of inflation and unemployment. The crisis of the 1980s has seriously lowered the standard of living and has curtailed already limited opportunities for social mobility for the vast majority of Mexicans who belong to the lower and middle classes.

This situation has fueled grassroots social movements which have increasingly challenged the political structure of postrevolutionary Mexico. In 1971 the student movement in the capital revived briefly, on a much smaller scale, only to be violently repressed again, definitively, this time not by uniformed soldiers but by *halcones*, or lumpen death squads, in the government's employ. These paramilitary groups killed about fifty participants in a peaceful march on October 10, Corpus Christi. The early 1980s saw the emergence of a new, less militant student movement in Mexico City and of two important social movements in the provinces: the organization of elementary school teachers in the poor southern states of Oaxaca and Chiapas, and the formation of the COCEI (Committee of Workers, Peasants, and Students from the Isthmus [of Tehuantepec]). This popular front movement, which began in 1975, won the municipal elections of Juchitán, Oaxaca, in 1980, only to be forcibly removed by the government in 1983 and replaced by representatives of the PRI.

A protest movement also emerged in Mexico City in 1984, when gas tanks exploded in San Juanico, a working-class neighborhood, due to the negligence of the government oil company, PEMEX. The explosions killed between 500 and 2,000 people, wounding some 2,000 more and leaving 10,000 people homeless.[4] Moreover, the early 1980s also saw a revitalization of labor union activities, especially by the telephone and electrical workers and the STUNERM, the university clerical workers' union. It would not be until 1985, however, that government mishandling of a natural catastrophe, the earthquakes, would mobilize broad sectors of the urban population. We will have occasion to look at this crisis, as well as the electoral crisis of 1988, in chapter 6.[5]

The Novel of Tlatelolco

The student movement and its repression are widely considered to mark a turning point in Mexico's literary production, especially narrative. Most writers and critics who are now reaching intellectual maturity were personally affected by 1968, through either direct participation or identification and support. It was, after all, an exhilarating and shocking series of events, investing hundreds of thousands of Mexicans with a sense of having claimed a certain degree of power over their own lives and of having had that power brutally ripped away from them by an authoritarian state. Moreover, this collective trauma coincided with a psychological turning point in most participants' lives—their entrance into adulthood.

Tlatelolco has inspired some thirty novels during the ensuing years, most of which were published during the 1970s. Two of the most eloquent interpretations of the student movement and the tragedy that truncated it were testimonial novels published within two years of the massacre: *La noche de Tlatelolco* (*Massacre in Mexico*, 1971), by Elena Poniatowska (b. 1932); and *Los días y los años* (*The Days and the Years*, 1971), by Luis González de Alba (b. 1944). For twenty years *La noche de Tlatelolco*, which appeared in spite of bomb threats against the publishing company, has been the definitive account of 1968 and the massacre. Poniatowska was moved to write the documentary novel by the testimony of women friends who lived in Tlatelolco and whose children were missing after October 2. Thus, her novel textualizes the sort of female solidarity that has characterized much testimonial literature, and many grassroots protest movements, in Latin America during the two ensuing decades. (The closest political analogy is to the mothers of disappeared political prisoners who have pressured and denounced repressive governments throughout Latin America, including Mexico, during the 1970s and 1980s.) When Poniatowska was awarded the prestigious Xavier Villaurrutia Literary Prize for her book, she declined it, asking who was going to offer a prize to the dead. Luis González de Alba was among the four top student leaders and one of their two most eloquent spokespersons. He, along with most of the 200 members of the National Strike Committee, was arrested at Tlatelolco and imprisoned; subsequently, he was exiled to Chile.

Following his reintegration into national life after a presidential pardon, he has become a well-known scientific journalist and an articulate spokesperson for gay rights. *Los días y los años* is a skillful first novel that captures the freshness of lived experience from an insider's perspective.

Outside the realm of documentary narrative, the two best fictional representations of Tlatelolco are relatively brief segments of two novels published a decade after 1968, both of them written in Europe: *Palinuro de México* (*Palinurus of Mexico*, 1977), by Fernando del Paso (b. 1935); and *Si muero lejos de ti* (*If I Die Far from You*, 1979), by Jorge Aguilar Mora (b. 1946).[6] Del Paso uses the traditional characters and style of the commedia dell'arte to narrate the protagonist's death at Tlatelolco. With the exception of Poniatowska's testimonial recreation, Aguilar Mora's is the most eloquent realist depiction of the atrocity, although it is framed within a highly experimental narrative framework. His text is structured around an implicit dialogue between the narrator and the other victims: "Where were you?" Since the author, a member of the National Strike Council, was present at the massacre, this episode also has a testimonial dimension. Aguilar Mora's novel was the first to explore the subjectivity of nonparticipants (those who remained on the sidelines or went into self-exile), as well as of *halcones*. While *Si muero lejos de ti* includes some exploration of female experience, it was not until twenty years after the student movement that women writers would continue Poniatowska's early attempt to interpret this turning point in history from a woman's perspective and would, in addition, include a critique of gender relations within the movement. Two examples are Emma Prieto's *Los testigos* (*The Witnesses*, 1985) and Vilma Fuentes' *Ayer es nunca jamás* (*Yesterday Is No More*, 1988).

The Post-1968 Mexican Novel: Decline or Democratization?

During the early 1970s Mexican writers and critics tended to see this outpouring of fiction about 1968 as a literary signpost, an indication that the Mexican novel was being renovated by another historic series of events, and that the Novel of Tlatelolco would displace the Novel of the Revolution and the Novel of the City as the principal genre of Mexican fiction. With the appearance of new publishing houses during the 1970s, an enormous number of books began to appear. Because of the particular interest in *novísimos escritores*, many of them were first novels. Still, disillusionment with the quality of novelistic production quickly set in. By the early

1980s there was widespread sentiment that the Mexican novel, unlike the short story and poetry, was in decline. On the one hand, it seems to be true that writers are frequently publishing works before they are ready; the quality of new novels has varied widely. Yet the more interesting of these young authors have been establishing patterns for narrative discourses capable of addressing the complex crossroads at which Mexico finds itself. With regard to this situation, Margo Glantz cites Carpentier: "Puede producirse una gran novela en una época, en un país. Esto no significa que en esa época, en ese país, exista realmente *la novela*. Para hablarse de una novela es menester que haya una novelística" (A great novel can be produced in an epoch, in a country. This does not mean that in that epoch, in that country, *the novel* really exists. In order to speak of a novel it is necessary that there be a novelistic tradition).[7] On the other hand, this outpouring of narrative is a symptom of an increasing democratization of Mexican culture, as are the recent proliferations of book presentations (free events involving the participation of the author and other writers and critics, often major figures) and of writing workshops, in both Mexico City and many state capitals. However, recently some of these activities, notably publishing, have been endangered by economic conditions. Over the past year or two, some publishing houses have disappeared, and those that have survived have been much more reluctant to take chances with first novels by unknown writers, preferring to reissue works by established authors. The crisis has also made books much more expensive and, in a context in which libraries are much less accessible and well stocked than in the United States, this has diminished the number of potential readers that a book may have. Elena Poniatowska estimates that there are currently about 2,000 authors in Mexico writing for some 3 million readers.[8]

Critics also complain that the writing workshops that have proliferated during the past two decades have tended to produce large quantities of poor literature and to suppress the literary differences among their participants. If larger numbers of people are writing, it stands to reason that there will be more poor writing, along with many works that are interesting but not transcendental, as well as, occasionally, very good or even great works. Yet the workshops are a key symptom of the expanding opportunities for access to and participation in areas of culture that formerly had been considered elite. Moreover, in sponsoring these activities without increasing their support for education, the government and the private sector are subscribing to a sort of trickle-down theory of culture. In order for these experiments to bear fruit and not perpetuate elitism, a broad spectrum of the Mexican population must have access to good education at the primary, secondary, and postsecondary levels. The consensus is that, at present, the quality of the public school system is inadequate; and, what's worse, many Mexicans do not have access to even poor schooling.[9]

Finally, critics often limit their judgments to a very narrow definition of the novel, failing to take into account new innovative discourses which draw on other traditional literary genres, as well as on oral history, the chronicle, and the essay. There has been such an interpenetration of various modes of narrative that it is misleading to examine the more traditional novels in isolation from the short story and from the hybrid relatives of both fictional genres. In fact, many of the best Mexican novels of the past twenty years are situated squarely at these perplexing generic crossroads.

The Writer as Witness and Social Agent

Elena Poniatowska and Carlos Monsiváis (b. 1938) have been largely responsible for converting the testimonial novel and the social and political chronicle into the quintessential narrative genre of the seventies and eighties;[10] at the same time, they have perpetuated José Revueltas' model of the committed writer as public figure. Poniatowska points to Tlatelolco as a turning point in her own political development. Her novel about Tlatelolco was, however, not her first excursion into advocacy of the powerless; in 1963 she had published *Todo empezó en domingo (It All Began on Sunday)*, a series of vignettes of how the popular classes spend their leisure time, especially in Mexico City. This was followed in 1969 by *Hasta no verte Jesús mío (Here's Looking at You, Jesus)*, to which chapter 2 will be devoted. This novel, based on the oral history of a poor woman, is another groundbreaking work that represented a further stage in the development of testimonial narrative, as pioneered by Ricardo Pozas (*Juan Pérez Jolote/Juan the Chamula*, 1949) and by Oscar Lewis, with whom Poniatowska had briefly collaborated on the research for *Pedro Martínez* (1964). In the years following the publication of these three books, Poniatowska's writing has been characterized by a commitment to representing powerless, marginalized, and oppositional members of society who lack access to self-representation in print and the media: the handicapped, AIDS victims, earthquake victims, women artists and writers of the past, political performers, political prisoners, trade-union organizers, opposition leaders, servants, garment workers, Indian women, servants. Particularly noteworthy in this vein are Poniatowska's lengthy prologue to *Se necesita muchacha* (*Maid Needed*, 1983) and the collection *Fuerte es el silencio* (*Strong Is the Silence*, 1980), about child street vendors, political prisoners, a hunger strike by mothers of the disappeared, and a peasant squatters' movement. Carlos Monsiváis achieved recognition with his first book, *Días de guardar* (*Days to Remember*, 1971). This collection of social chronicles, written in the vein of the irreverent New Journalists of the United States, examines the sixties and the student movement.

Like the New Journalists in the United States, both authors have constructed testimonial narratives that are aural collages or mosaics, orchestrated from images of their cultural milieu and excerpts from interviews with social actors, interspersed with the authors' reactions and interpretations. Their works incorporate elements of slang and popular dialects into a literary discourse characterized, in each author, by a distinct voice. Poniatowska's works, in particular, extensively incorporate *campesino* and working-class Mexican speech and ingeniously counterpose and blur literary genres. Even in her somewhat more traditional novels and short stories, the boundaries between documentary or autobiographical sources and fiction are difficult to define.

The influence of this literary project and style, and of the political commitment underlying it, on younger generations of writers has been considerable. For instance, numerous works published during the 1980s follow one of Poniatowska's literary models in representing the points of view of lumpen or impoverished working-class characters in an approximation of their own language. The writers may label their works "chronicles," or else "short stories" or "novels," but it is often difficult to tell from their discourse which label is more appropriate; that is, whether the characters are actual people who have told the writers their stories (and if so, to what degree the text has been modified by the writer) or whether they are fictional characters based loosely on real people, as in a traditional novel or short story. This is the case with *Las glorias del Gran Púas* (*The Glory of the Great Púas*, 1978), by Ricardo Garibay; *La última noche de "El Tigre"* (*"El Tigre"'s Last Night*, 1985) and several other books by Cristina Pacheco (b. 1941); and *Borracho no vale* (*It's No Good Drunk*, 1988), by Emiliano Pérez Cruz (b. 1955). Other recent narrative works that incorporate marginal perspectives include *Chin-Chin el teporocho* (*Chin-Chin the Wino*, 1978) and subsequent bestsellers by Armando Ramírez (b. 1954); *Violeta-Perú* (*The Violeta-*

Perú Line, 1979), by Luis Arturo Ramos (b. 1947); *Calles como incendios* (*Streets like Fires*, 1985), by José Joaquín Blanco (b. 1951); "La Gertrudis" ("Gertrude"), by Guillermo Samperio (b. 1948); and numerous other short stories by younger authors, especially those associated with the writing workshop that Miguel Donoso Pareja directed for several years in San Luis Potosí. For instance, Ignacio Betancourt's already classic short story "De cómo Guadalupe bajó a La Montaña y todo lo demás" ("About How Guadalupe Descended to The Mountain and All the Rest") is an irreverent, humorous, and highly inventive exploration, from a working-class perspective, of the poor and their ideological manipulation by the government and the Catholic Church.

As a genre integrally linked to the development of the urban bourgeoisie and petit-bourgeoisie, the novel is not likely to be the creative vehicle of choice for *campesino* or lumpen intellectuals. Of the above writers, Ramírez and Pérez Cruz are unusual because of their lumpen backgrounds. Ramírez is from the inner-city slum Tepito and has not had the benefit of a post–elementary school education (his published texts preserve spelling and punctuation errors), while Pérez Cruz, in spite of his education, continues to live in Ciudad Nezahualcóyotl, the largest shantytown in the Western Hemisphere. They are therefore potential examples of what Gramsci called "organic intellectuals," since they come from a social class that is emerging as a historical agent. Unfortunately, some of these writers (like the middle-class writers of La Onda, which will be discussed below) uncritically incorporate the sexism of their environment into their discourse. For instance, the works of Armando Ramírez, an author of mass-market best-sellers who has the distinction of being Mexico's first lumpen novelist, tend to be sensationalistic in their presentation of sex and violence, including violence against women. (For instance, see *Violación en Polanco* [*Rape in Polanco*].)

On the other hand, Cristina Pacheco, like Elena Poniatowska, focuses on the problems of poor women and children, including rape, physical and sexual abuse, and sexual blackmail by men controlling basic necessities such as water. Pacheco, a prize-winning journalist, grew up in a peasant family that immigrated to Mexico City from the provinces. This background, together with her regular contact with the urban poor through her profession, has moved her to serve as their advocate in short stories published in the weekly column "Mar de Historias" ("Sea of Stories") in the newspaper *La Jornada* (many of which have subsequently been collected into several books). Pacheco also interviews poor people on her weekly television program, "Aquí Nos Tocó Vivir" ("It Was Our Lot to Live Here"), on her radio show, and sometimes in her weekly column in the magazine *¡Siempre!*

New Subjectivities: Women and Gays

As an intellectual feminist movement developed in Mexico City during the 1970s, a substantial number of serious women narrators and poets began publishing, a much greater number than had existed at any other point in Mexican history. Peggy Job estimates that more than fifty women have published novels or short-story collections since 1970.[11] Rosario Castellanos (1925–1974) and Elena Poniatowska had pried open the door that these new generations of writers streamed through. These two were not, of course, the only women publishing in Mexico before 1968; however, they were by far the most prolific and renowned, in addition to being the writers—female or male—who most consistently and directly addressed the intersection of class, race, and ethnicity with gender and power.

The first wave of these new women authors, most of whom are currently in their forties and early fifties, tends to portray middle-class female subjectivity, generally within a realist framework and from a first-person point of view. They include Aline Pettersson (b. 1938), *Círculos (Circles,* 1977), *Proyectos de muerte (Projects of Death,* 1983), *Sombra ella misma (Herself a Shadow,* 1986), *Los colores ocultos (The Hidden Colors,* 1986), *Piedra que rueda (Rolling Stone,* 1990), and *Querida familia (Dear Family,* 1991); María Luisa Puga (b. 1944), *Cuando el aire es azul (When the Air Is Blue,* 1980), *Accidentes (Accidents,* 1981), *Pánico o peligro (Panic or Danger,* 1983), *La forma del silencio (The Form of Silence,* 1987), *Intentos (Attempts,* 1987), and *Antonia* (1989); Esther Seligson (b. 1941), *Tras la ventana un árbol (Behind the Window a Tree,* 1969), *Otros son los sueños (Others Are the Dreams,* 1973), *Luz de dos (Light of Two,* 1978), and *La morada en el tiempo (Dwelling in Time,* 1981); Silvia Molina (b. 1946), *La mañana debe seguir gris (The Morning Should Stay Gray,* 1977), *La familia vino del norte (The Family Came from the North,* 1987), *Dicen que me casé yo (I Got Married, They Say,* 1989), and *Imagen de Héctor (Image of Héctor,* 1990); Bárbara Jácobs (b. 1947), *Doce cuentos en contra (Twelve Stories Against,* 1982) and *Las hojas muertas (The Dead Leaves,* Premio Xavier Villaurrutia, 1987); and Angeles Mastretta (b. 1949), *Arráncame la vida (Mexican Bolero,* 1985) and *Mujeres de ojos grandes (Big-Eyed Women,* 1990). Margo Glantz (b. 1930), a leading literary critic, also began publishing fiction during this period; her autobiographical novel *Las gen-*

ealogías (*Genealogies*, 1981), which will soon appear in English, is especially inventive in its approach to narrating the experience of Jewish intellectual immigrants in Mexico.

In the area of popular music, the singers who are most closely allied with these writers are the "new song" performers Amparo Ochoa, Betsy Pecanins, and Tania Libertad, who draw extensively on folk music, political poetry, jazz, and the blues and who increasingly represent women's subjectivity in their works. (See their joint album *Mujeres* [*Women*, 1989], with music and lyrics by Federico Alvarez del Toro.)

In conjunction with the organization of the women's movement, a gay and lesbian rights movement also appeared, and, along with it, the gay male novel. The best of these works to date is still the first one, *Las aventuras, desventuras y sueños de Adonis García, el vampiro de la Colonia Roma* (1979; translated as *Adonis García*, 1981), by Luis Zapata (b. 1951). It is presented as the transcription of an oral monologue by a gay male prostitute who, as the title indicates, is likened to the protagonist of a picaresque novel. While this novel, like those of heterosexual Onda authors, celebrates a male sexuality centered obsessively on the phallus, it does not objectify women in the process; rather, female characters are quite marginal, outside the orbit of desire, without being stereotyped. Nor is there an unproblematic presentation of the protagonist's male sexual partners and clients in a way that might tend to objectify them; rather, in its unflinching treatment of sexuality and prostitution, the novel explores the economic and psychosexual dynamics of a wide range of homoerotic relationships in the alienated context of contemporary urban society. Other noteworthy gay novels include *Las púberes canéforas* (*The Prepubescent Nymphs*, 1983), by José Joaquín Blanco (b. 1951), which sets a story of crime and erotic obsession against the inner-city cabaret culture of poor homosexuals; and *Utopía gay* (*Gay Utopia*, 1983), by José Rafael Calva (b. 1953), which explores the effects on a male academic couple when one of them becomes pregnant. As chapter 6 will show, lesbian literature did not begin to be published until the very end of the 1980s, even as the gay male novel subsided.

No One Knows Anything: The Political and Historical Novel

In addition to the testimonial writers discussed above, there are a few other novelists of the past two decades whose work might be considered committed in the classic sense, since it expresses an integral project for political and social change. The ultimate model for such writing is José Revueltas (1914–1976), the independent Marx-

ist writer and activist who served as mentor to the student movement and attempted to assume sole responsibility for it when it was
repressed. While he was a political prisoner, Revueltas wrote *El
apando* (*Solitary,* 1969), his last, and arguably his best, novel, in
which the violence and degradation of the prison serve as an allegory
for contemporary Mexican society.

During the 1980s María Luisa Puga (b. 1944) and, especially,
Agustín Ramos (b. 1952) have attempted to follow Revueltas' model.
Puga, who is one of the few Mexican women authors to devote her
life entirely to writing, has published several books of narrative, notably the novels *Las posibilidades del odio* (*The Possibilities of Hatred,* 1978) and *Pánico o peligro* (*Panic or Danger,* 1983), and her second collection of short stories, *Intentos* (*Attempts,* 1987). Her works,
which address a wide range of social and psychological issues, examine colonialism and other conflicts associated with racial, class, and
gender divisions to a greater extent than any woman writer since
Poniatowska. Yet these works, while ambitious and interesting,
often give the impression of being unpolished, drafts rather than
finished works. Agustín Ramos' three novels are ambitious and inventive, especially the latest one; they are *El cielo por asalto* (*Heaven
by Assault,* 1979), *La vida no vale nada* (*Life Is Worth Nothing,*
1983), and *Ahora que me acuerdo* (*Now that I Remember,* 1985).
Ramos demonstrates considerable narrative skill in addressing political issues from a Marxist perspective: urban guerrilla movements, student activism, militancy in opposition parties, the massacre of June 10, 1971, and various historical instances of class
struggle and colonialism, ranging from prehispanic Mayan culture
to the Paris Commune. He places these issues in the context of
changing gender roles and the crisis of the couple, although the narrative attitude toward women vacillates between empathy and objectification. On the one hand, his female characters are frequently
agents, the ones who make crucial decisions about their own lives
and their intimate relationships; yet, on the other hand, their motives tend to be portrayed, in traditional terms, as inscrutable.

A number of interesting works from this period address the themes
of political corruption and censorship. The novels and plays of
Vicente Leñero (b. 1933) and Jorge Ibargüengoitia (1928–1983) have
eloquently and persistently reminded the Mexican reading public of
actual cases of murder, corruption, and censorship in post-1968
Mexico. Leñero's novel *Los periodistas* (*The Journalists,* 1978) documents government repression of Mexico City's major daily newspaper, *Excélsior,* for daring to criticize the president. (In 1988 Leñero

was himself a victim of censorship when his play, felicitously entitled *Nadie sabe nada* [*No One Knows Anything*], was closed down by the government because it incorporates part of the national anthem for satiric purposes and portrays the bribing of a journalist by a high public official. Following a public protest by the intellectual community and acts of resistance by the theater troupe, the play was reinstated.) *Pretexto* (*Pretext*, 1979), by Federico Campbell (b. 1941), depicts the censorship and repression of journalists in Tijuana. The best-selling *Arráncame la vida* (1985; translated as *Mexican Bolero*, 1990), by Angeles Mastretta (b. 1949), recreates the political corruption of the 1940s from the perspective of a provincial governor's wife; and *Morir en el golfo* (*To Die on the Gulf*, 1985), by Héctor Aguilar Camín (b. 1946), centers on the corrupt leader of the oil workers' union who was subsequently toppled by the Salinas government. A masterpiece of the post-1968 political novel is *Las batallas en el desierto* (*Battles in the Desert*, 1981), by José Emilio Pacheco (b. 1939), which explores relations between Mexico's class structure and economic and cultural colonization by the United States as these were institutionalized during the late 1940s, and the disintegration of values in contemporary Mexico. (This novella will be analyzed in detail in chapter 4.)

The historical novel has also achieved new prominence during the 1970s and 1980s. Fernando del Paso, whose works tend to depart dramatically from the Mexican narrative tradition, has brought new prestige to the historical novel with his third monumental book, *Noticias del imperio* (*News of the Empire*, 1987). Each of his novels addresses a key episode in Mexican history: *José Trigo* (1966), the railroad workers' movement of 1958; *Palinuro de México* (1977), the Revolution and the student movement of 1968; and *Noticias del imperio*, the French intervention and empire (1864–1867). In his extensive use of humor and play, del Paso breaks with the solemnity of the historical novel and the Mexican literary tradition in general while challenging official history. (Chapter 3 will examine *Palinuro de México*, as well as sections of *Noticias del imperio*.) Another writer who satirizes history is Jorge Ibargüengoitia, who wrote skillful parodies of both the Mexican Revolution and the novelistic genre it inspired in *Los relámpagos de agosto* (*The Lightning of August*, 1965), and of the Wars of Independence in *Los pasos de López* (*The Steps of López*, 1982).

While there has been no resurgence of the *indigenista* novel as a genre, this period has seen the publication of a few historical novels that adopt perspectives sympathetic to the vanquished.[12] Noteworthy among these are *Ascensión Tun* (1981), by Silvia Molina (b. 1946), and *Gonzalo Guerrero* (1980), by Eugenio Aguirre (b. 1944). The former portrays two marginal subjectivities set against the Caste Wars of Yucatán: that of an orphaned Indian boy and that of a mad *ladina* (non-Indian) woman. Aguirre's novel turns the Conquest on its head, presenting the point of view of one of Cortés' soldiers who was taken captive and assimilated into Mayan culture and then chose not to be "rescued" by the Spaniards. More recently, Homero Aridjis (b. 1940) has published a two-novel sequence retelling the "discovery" and conquest of Mesoamerica from the Spanish perspective: *1492, vida y tiempos de Juan Cabezón de Castilla* (*1492, Life and Times of Juan Cabezón of Castile*, 1985) and *Memorias del Nuevo Mundo* (*Memories of the New World*, 1988). The quinquecentennial will undoubtedly inspire more works along these lines.

La Onda Reaches Middle Age

Although testimonial, political, and historical novels have figured prominently in Mexican narrative since 1968, it is exaggerated to consider, as Sara Sefchovich does in her recent book, that most novels of this period have been highly politicized.[13] Just as participants in the student movement became polarized in the wake of their defeat, with the vast majority withdrawing from political activism, so writers have tended to become polarized into a minority interested in engaging social and historical issues and a majority preferring to focus on existential and psychological questions, generally divorced from their larger social context.

As Juan Villoro (b. 1956), a leading younger writer, has noted, at the end of the 1970s and beginning of the 1980s the economic prosperity brought about by the oil boom presented fledgling writers with "un país lleno de becas, premios, editoriales, revistas, tarjetas de crédito Plan Joven, talleres literarios . . . y nos formamos ante las ventanillas para pedir empleo" (a country full of fellowships, prizes, publishers, journals, Youth Plan credit cards, literary workshops . . . and we lined up in front of the windows to ask for jobs).[14] As a result of this easy incorporation into the literary milieu, Villoro believes that the early texts by members of his generation "rehuyen la diferencia, la confrontación con los mayores" (shun difference, confrontation with their elders).[15]

One fictional mode which engages in a limited degree of social critique and has been extremely influential during the 1970s and 1980s, especially among younger male writers, is La Onda. This is a trend which José Agustín (b. 1944) and Gustavo Sáinz (b. 1940) inaugurated in the mid-1960s and which Agustín has continued to cultivate, with considerable popular success, ever since. In his works Agustín has eloquently portrayed the shallowness, hypocrisy, and existential emptiness of middle-class society in its preoccupation with conformity and consumerism. These themes, together with the hip conversational style of La Onda (which will be discussed in chapter 5), have been adopted by numerous younger authors, both novelists and short-story writers, including Armando Ramírez, Ethel Krause (b. 1954), Carlos Chimal (b. 1954), and, to some extent, Villoro. Adriana Malvido quotes Ramírez as recently arguing that "más del 80 por ciento de los escritores nacidos en México después de los cincuenta, escribimos bajo la influencia de José Agustín, de un lenguaje que nos removía, nos inquietaba, nos provocaba, y quien lo niegue miente" (more than 80 percent of the writers born in Mexico after the fifties write under the influence of José Agustín, of a language that moved us, disturbed us, provoked us, and whoever denies it is lying).[16] Krause's first book, *Intermedio para mujeres* (*Intermission for Women*, 1982), is especially interesting for its appropriation of Onda language to critique bourgeois female culture, the mother-daughter relation, and "liberated" young women's alienated experience of sexual relationships.

Over the years Agustín's works have given literary expression to the Mexican youth culture that blossomed during the late 1960s and early 1970s. La Onda tended to emphasize the countercultural rebellion and search for more authentic values and experiences through rock music, sex, psychedelics, and a sense of group identity, but usually to the exclusion of a more profound social critique or a sense of political or social responsibility. As we shall see in chapter 5, Agustín's latest novel, *Cerca del fuego* (*Near the Fire*, 1986), and his most recent short-story collection, *No hay censura* (*There Is No Censorship*, 1988), attempt to politicize La Onda but with mixed results, since the Jungian master scheme tends to dehistoricize the political critique and women continue to be portrayed as mere vehicles, whether for evil or for its transcendence through self-knowledge and a return to the family.

Throughout the 1980s the tendency toward relatively apolitical writing has continued to enjoy more prestige in many intellectual circles. Consequently, some leftist writers who have felt cubbyholed by critics as social realist writers have, at least temporarily, depoliticized their work in the process of taking up experimental or fantastic fiction.[17] Moreover, many novels and short-story collections that do overtly engage political themes fail to address the multiple dimensions of these questions, such as the highly problematic constitution of gender roles and sexual preference in contemporary Mexican society.

Cartographies of Desire

If the collective protagonist of novels of the 1940s and 1950s, as exemplified by *Pedro Páramo* (1955), by Juan Rulfo (1918–1986), is the rural community, that of the novel of the following three decades is the city, which in this highly centralized nation means the Federal District, Mexico City. Moreover, the conception of the capital established by Carlos Fuentes (b. 1928) in *La región más transparente* (*Where the Air Is Clear*, 1958) changed during the 1970s and 1980s; the city as social mosaic or mural became the city as map and body. The misguided modernization and corruption that Fuentes had addressed in his first novel (the title of which is, in retrospect, darkly ironic) have produced two overlapping tendencies in the urban novel: the apocalyptic text and the novel of nostalgia.

The apocalyptic novel shares the dark vision of destruction that has been expressed most eloquently over the past thirty years in the prose and poetry of José Emilio Pacheco. This view reached its peak in the late 1970s and the 1980s, the years of the oil boom followed by the economic crisis. For instance, in *Si muero lejos de ti* (*If I Die Far from You*, 1979), by Jorge Aguilar Mora (b. 1946), an expatriate returns to a city that has sunk into its subterranean lake, only to witness a major earthquake. The protagonist urinates over the putrid debris of his home town:

> . . . puertas derribadas, orina, letreros caídos, orina, periódicos, restos de comida, colchones desgastados, orina, ollas, platos sucios, tenedores, latas de cerveza, vestidos, zapatos, macetas rotas, aparadores, orina, orina, orina, orina, orina, revista, calcetines, asientos de coches, árboles desarraigados, sillas de restorán, discos, carteles, toallas, orina, ventanas, orina, libros deshojados, canastas de mimbre, carpetas bordadas, orina, orina, cuadros sin cristal, orina, muñecas, orina, orina . . . (522)

> (. . . torn-down doors, urine, fallen signs, urine, newspapers, leftover food, ripped mattresses, urine, pots, dirty plates, forks, beer cans, dresses, shoes, broken flowerpots, store windows, urine, urine, urine, urine, urine, magazine, socks, car seats, trees pulled up by their roots, restaurant chairs, records, posters, towels,

urine, windows, urine, books with their pages torn out, wicker baskets, embroidered carpets, urine, urine, picture frames with no glass, urine, dolls, urine, urine . . .)

Fuentes himself has contributed extensively to this developing view of urban apocalypse, which was latent in *Aura* (1962), became explicit in "Estos fueron los palacios" ("Those Were the Palaces," from *Agua quemada* [1981]), and is foregrounded in his latest book, *Constancia y otras novelas para vírgenes* (*Constancia and Other Novels for Virgins*, 1990). In all five short novels of this collection, a virginal woman becomes the focus of male erotic obsession; her elusiveness symbolizes a national innocence that can no longer be recovered. In "Gente de razón" ("People of Reason"), a group of male architecture students plans to combat urban blight by constructing a garden in downtown Mexico City, which is compared to a combat zone; at the same time, they are all obsessed with their professor's daughter and the "interior garden" of her eroticism. In "La desdichada" ("Our Lady of Misfortune"), two male students' resistance to urban deterioration and social change leads to their obsession with the statue of a virgin by that name, a symbol of art in the classical sense. Fuentes' most complete exposition of this view occurs in *Cristóbal nonato* (*Christopher Unborn*, 1987). Here the City of Palaces has become Makesicko City, the diseased capital of a nation ruled by the right wing and so thoroughly colonized by the United States that its street signs feature phonetic English spellings of Spanish and Náhuatl words, like "Whatamock" for "Cuauhtémoc." Mexico in 1992, five centuries after the Europeans "discovered" the New World, is portrayed as

una angosta nación esquelética y decapitada, el pecho en los desiertos del norte, el corazón infartado en la salida del Golfo en Tampico, el vientre en la ciudad de México, el ano supurante y venéreo en Acapulco, las rodillas recortadas en Guerrero y Oaxaca. . . . Esto quedaba. Esto administraba el gobierno federal, su presidente panista, su aparato priista, su burguesía financiera ahora totalmente adicta al sector público, . . . su policía impuesta a un ejército desbandado por descontento y desmoralización. (27)

(a narrow, skeletal, decapitated nation, her chest in the northern deserts, her heart stopped in the outlet to the Gulf in Tampico, her womb in Mexico City, her festering and syphilitic anus in Acapulco, her cut-off knees in Guerrero and Oaxaca. . . . This is what was left. This is what the federal government administered, with its president from the PAN, its bureaucracy from the PRI, its financial bourgeoisie now totally addicted to the public sector, . . . its police put in charge of an army that has disbanded out of discontent and demoralization.)

Against these visions of the decayed social body, recent novelists have attempted to anchor their identity in specific neighborhoods associated with a less alienated past. Therefore, the novels of the last two decades obsessively tick off names of streets, which their protagonists roam with a despair tempered by affection. Again, it is José Emilio Pacheco who provides the model for this kind of text, in *Las batallas en el desierto*.[18] As we shall see in chapter 4, while Pacheco portrays the city as a symbol of the economic and political "disaster" of the 1980s, he also describes it as the repository of what humane values still remain in Mexican society.

This affection for "my concrete," as Guillermo Samperio (b. 1948) calls it, and for constructing "a verbal museum" to counter the city's self-destruction,[19] is apparent in the titles of several recent literary works: *Calles como incendios* (*Streets Like Fires*), *De la calle* (*From the Street*), *La calle que todos olvidan* (*The Street that Everyone Forgets*), *Gente de la ciudad* (*People of the City*), *Cuentos de tierra y asfalto* (*Tales of Earth and Asphalt*), *El vampiro de la colonia Roma* (*The Vampire of the Colonia Roma*), *Las reinas de Polanco* (*The Queens of Polanco*), *La Plaza, Plaza de Santo Domingo, Violeta-Perú* (the name of a city bus line). José Emilio Pacheco's latest book of poetry is entitled *Ciudad de la memoria* (*City of Memory*). The title of José Agustín's fifth novel, *Ciudades desiertas* (*Deserted Cities*, 1982), alludes to the alienation of everyday life in the United States. By implicit contrast, he suggests that Mexican cities are "inhabited," that they continue to harbor a community, a sense of collective identity.

Many recent books have also taken their titles from *boleros*, popular love songs from the 1940s and 1950s: *Si muero lejos de ti, Arráncame la vida, La vida no vale nada, Amor de mis amores* (*My Love of Loves*), *Amor perdido* (*Lost Love*). To some extent these titles reflect the wave of nostalgia which is currently apparent in both literature and popular culture, with the revival of music and cinema from the so-called Golden Age of the 1940s. (There is a radio program called "The New Nostalgia.") The use of *bolero* titles represents an ironic appropriation of *lo cursi*, of melodramatic, excessively romantic aspects of national culture, resulting in a postmodernist celebration and ironization of exaggerated sentimentality. However, the novelty of this device wore off rather quickly; by the late 1980s the use of such clichéd titles had itself become a cliché of new Mexican narrative.

John Brushwood has detected a conservative impulse in the recent narrative marked by nostalgia, including both historical novels, like Eugenio Aguirre's *Gonzalo Guerrero* and Fernando del Paso's *Noticias del imperio,* and "novels that offer nostalgic views of the authors' generational experiences."[20] Along with these thematic considerations, Brushwood notes the return to traditional narrativity or storytelling as an indicator of the writers' conservatism. While both tendencies are undoubtedly present in much post-1968 Mexican narrative, it is not clear that either nostalgia for a less alienated past or reappropriation of realism is itself an indicator of political conservatism. We will have occasion to examine specific examples in the chapters on del Paso and Pacheco.

The sort of ambivalence that U.S. intellectuals tend to feel toward New York City at the end of the century is not unlike Mexican writers' attitude toward their own metropolis. Since the naturalist novel of the prerevolutionary period, as perfected by Federico Gamboa and Mariano Azuela, the notion of the city as whore has held sway over the male literary imagination. Novelists of the last two generations tend to link this dissection of the dying city with male journeys over what is described as prostrate female terrain. In Luis Arturo Ramos' best novel to date, *Violeta-Perú,* this comparison is present in the text and even more explicit on the book cover. The lumpen protagonist spends his time drinking and hallucinating about tests of masculine valor as he travels all over the capital by bus. Mexico City is portrayed on the cover as a voluptuous woman that a man's hand holds up by her hair, which is bright red and resembles the arms of an octopus; the length of her nude body is traversed by tire tracks. In José Agustín's *Cerca del fuego* (which we will examine in chapter 5), this feminization of the metropolis takes the form of "la Reina del Metro" ("Queen of the Subway"), a lumpen sex goddess who emerges from the city's entrails—from the ruins of pre-Hispanic civilization, embodied by the earth goddess Coatlicue—to serve the male protagonist as a vehicle for transcendence.

Younger male writers have appropriated these symbols and modified them somewhat to incorporate a political dimension. For instance, in Agustín Ramos' novel *Ahora que me acuerdo,* the city is compared to the male body or the self and the horizon to the open body of a woman. This image later shifts from sexual to military terrain: to the city as strategic map, to be reclaimed by the popular movements that grew out of the railroad workers' movement of 1958 and the student movement of 1968. During the late 1980s a new generation of women writers would begin to subvert the paradigm altogether.

The Novel as Monument and Miniature

The first epigraph that opens this chapter is taken from an essay in which Pacheco contrasts the works of two male writers of the Generation of 1910, Alfonso Reyes and Julio Torri. Elsewhere he has applied the same comparison, of pyramids and fleas, monuments and miniatures, to the novels of his contemporary, Fernando del Paso. Throughout his career, argues Pacheco, del Paso has set about to construct masterpieces, in the realm of pyramids, rather than in that of *pulgas vestidas,* or "dressed fleas"—that quintessential miniature of Mexican folk art in which the artist decorates a pair of actual fleas so that, when viewed through a magnifying glass, they resemble a bride and groom.[21] As we shall see, del Paso's first novel, *José Trigo* (1967), has a pyramidal structure; both this work and the climactic chapter of his second novel, *Palinuro de México* (1977), center on Tlatelolco, the site of an Aztec pyramid. In fact, all three of his novels, published at ten-year intervals, are monumental works, enormously long and complex, ambitious versions of the "total novel." A key trait of del Paso's narrative is the use of enumeration, taken to excess. At the same time, many of the fragments or building stones that make up his second and third books are self-contained, capable of standing alone as short stories, coherent gems within the fragmentary whole. On the other hand, the three novels that Pacheco has published to date are characterized by a painstakingly precise, simple style and (with the exception of *Morirás lejos*) a realist narrative structure; they are dressed fleas of a sort. Poniatowska, like del Paso, tends toward excess; she has noted in interviews that she has pared down several of her books from between one and three thousand pages of manuscript to the two or three hundred pages of the published texts. Similarly, José Agustín has noted his tendency toward dispersion, his constant need to constrict his narrative impulses, to pull in the reins.[22] Perhaps Carlos Fuentes is the clearest example of the novelist who works within both tendencies; with the exception of *La cabeza de la hidra* (*The Hydra Head,* 1978), all his recent works are either total novels or novellas: on the one hand, the monumental *Terra nostra* (1975) and *Cristóbal nonato* (1987); on the other, the spare *Agua quemada* (*Burnt Water,* 1981), *Una fa-*

milia lejana (*Distant Relations*, 1980), *Gringo viejo* (*Old Gringo*, 1985), and *Constancia y otras novelas para vírgenes* (1990). Nevertheless, in his ambitious attempt to write the Human Comedy of Mexico in twenty-two volumes, as outlined opposite the title page of *Cristóbal nonato*, Fuentes provides the quintessential example of the writer as monument builder.

These two contradictory tendencies, toward the total novel, on the one hand, and the novella and short story, on the other, have pulled Mexican narrative of the past twenty years in opposite directions. Writers born in the 1950s and 1960s, in particular, have gravitated toward the shorter forms, in keeping with the sentiment expressed by Juan Villoro's character in the second epigraph above. The story it is taken from is set in Monte Albán, Oaxaca, amid the ruins of the Zapotec-Mixtec pyramids. In the course of the "navigable night," interpersonal relationships and a "monumental" conception of the world, as expressed through language, are also shown to be in ruins.

Taken together, the formal and thematic characteristics discussed above might be seen as constituting four major tendencies in the post-1968 Mexican novel, as exemplified by the authors studied in the following chapters: testimonial and documentary narrative (Elena Poniatowska), the total novel (Fernando del Paso), neorealism (José Emilio Pacheco), and Onda narrative (José Agustín). In each case, the novelist began to publish before 1968 but has produced the bulk of her/his works and established her/himself as a major author during the seventies and eighties. All four texts studied were written before 1985, which initiated a new phase in the restructuring of Mexican society (which we will examine in chapter 6).

Hasta no verte Jesús mío (1969), Poniatowska's first novel, is a model for testimonial fiction and other literature that strives to represent nonhegemonic subjectivities, including those of poor women, female artists, and political dissidents. It reproduces popular Mexican dialects and ideology, just as Fernando del Paso and José Emilio Pacheco incorporate the language and liberal humanism of the intellectual, urban middle class that came of age during the 1940s, and José Agustín textualizes the irreverent countercultural perspective of sixties youth culture. Poniatowska's works constitute the novel as collaborative process or dialogue.

Fernando del Paso is probably the author closest to Carlos Fuentes (the Fuentes of *Terra nostra* and *Cristóbal nonato*) in his affinity for complex, linguistically experimental, total novels, the novel as high modernist monument or pyramid. In the case of del Paso, this project has led to the production of one lengthy "masterpiece" per decade. In fact, he is probably a better novelist than the Fuentes of the 1970s and 1980s. The disproportionate attention afforded Fuentes' works in U.S. universities over the past twenty-five years has promoted an image of this author as *the* Mexican novelist after Rulfo, in contrast to the general critical evaluation of his later works (following *La muerte de Artemio Cruz*) in Mexico. Del Paso's second novel, *Palinuro de México*, adopts a high modernist, Joycean model, borrowing extensively from the European and U.S. traditions, ranging from the commedia dell'arte to Rabelais, Sterne, Swift, Lewis Carroll, and Ambrose Bierce, in order to address two turning points in modern Mexican history, the Revolution and the student movement. Even as Poniatowska's book *La noche de Tlatelolco* is the definitive testimonial account of 1968, *Palinuro de México* contains the most eloquent fictional treatment of the massacre at Tlatelolco, a grotesque rendering in the style of the commedia.

José Emilio Pacheco is perhaps the most versatile of the four authors treated. In addition to being the leading Mexican poet of his generation, Pacheco is a master of literary journalism and the short story, and his three novels to date demonstrate a command of both experimental, metafictional narrative, in the case of *Morirás lejos* (*You Will Die Far Away*, 1967), and neorealism, in the case of *El principio del placer* (*The Pleasure Principle*, 1972) and *Las batallas en el desierto*. The latter, Pacheco's third novel, is an outstanding example of the novel of the city and of the return to realism during the 1980s. Like many novelists and short-story writers of this period, Pacheco has adapted traditional storytelling and realist genres— in this case, the *Bildungsroman*—in order to trace the roots of contemporary political and social problems. The result is a somewhat postmodernist documentation and ironization of the commodification of national culture, the novel as shopping list.

Finally, José Agustín's *Cerca del fuego* is the novel as *I Ching*, visionary pastiche and puzzle. It represents an ambitious but flawed attempt to politicize the so-called Onda narrative of the 1960s in the context of the political and economic crisis of the 1980s. However, this attempt to address the interrelation of psychological, interpersonal, and political issues ultimately is undermined by the Jungian and patriarchal models underlying the text.

A patriarchal model, in fact, permeates much contemporary Mexican narrative, constituting a subtext that tends to be rendered invisible by virtue of its very ubiquity. One object of my analysis, then, will be to explore narrative contradictions between political and social critique, on the one hand, and conceptions of gender roles and relations, on the other. My theoretical models are necessarily eclectic but are united by an interest in the textualization and critique of power relations. At various points I draw, for instance, on Foucault's study of institutions, Bakhtin's essay on the *Bildungsroman*, García Canclini's ideas regarding Latin American popular culture, Monsiváis' and Jameson's analyses of the counterculture, and contemporary U.S. feminist film theory. In my close examination of each of these pivotal Mexican novels, I am interested in how each author imagines the constellation of social factors which work to shape subjectivity in contemporary Mexican society, and how this subjectivity is shaped by and affects one's affiliations on various levels, with family, social class, the neighborhood or community, political and social movements, the nation, and that anachronistic institution: the authoritarian, patriarchal, dependent capitalist state.

The foundations of this ultimate pyramid, weakened throughout the period which began with the student movement of 1968, have been further shaken by the popular movements which arose in the wake of the major earthquake of September 19, 1985. After examining the four post-1968 novels, in chapters 2 through 5, we will look in chapter 6 at the shock waves which have spread through Mexican narrative since the 1985 disaster.

2. Gender, Genre, and Authority: *Hasta no verte Jesús mío* (1969), by Elena Poniatowska

I live to the rhythm of my country and I cannot remain on the sidelines. I want to be here. I want to be part of it. I want to be a witness. I want to walk arm in arm with it. I want to hear it more and more, to cradle it, to carry it like a medal on my chest.

In 1963 I had what I believe was the fundamental encounter of my life, with Jesusa Palancares. . . . I think about her with reverence. I love her. I talk to her inside my heart. Inside my head. My breasts love her: because of her I also love being a woman.

—ELENA PONIATOWSKA, "A QUESTION MARK ENGRAVED ON MY EYELIDS," 124, 116—117

The publication in close succession of *Hasta no verte Jesús mío* (*Here's Looking at You, Jesus,* 1969) and *La noche de Tlatelolco* (1971; translated as *Massacre in Mexico,* 1975)[1] established Elena Poniatowska (b. 1932) as Mexico's leading practitioner of documentary fiction and preeminent committed writer. Beyond their acclaim with literary critics, both books are among the most widely read in the history of Mexican letters; the former novel is currently in its twenty-fifth edition in Ediciones Era (published in 1987), while the latter is in its forty-fifth edition.[2] Moreover, in 1986 the Ministry of Public Education published forty thousand low-priced copies of *Hasta no verte.* The popularity of these works with both critics and the Mexican reading public undoubtedly owes much to their engagement with pressing social and political problems that had been brought to the forefront of national consciousness by the student movement of 1968.

More than any other treatment, documentary or fictional, of 1968, *La noche de Tlatelolco* captures the contagious enthusiasm of the

Josefina Bórquez and Elena Poniatowska, 1963. Photograph by Héctor García.

students and their sympathizers, along with the horror elicited by the brutality with which they were repressed by the Mexican government. Poniatowska achieves this powerful effect through a collage technique that juxtaposes the voices of numerous participants in and observers of the movement, thus enhancing the dialogic dimension of the novel and focusing on the community—Mexico City—as literary and political protagonist. In doing so Poniatowska is working in the highest tradition of Mexican fiction; one might say that she has replaced the apathetic, defeated peasant community which is the collective protagonist (the very literal ghost town) of Juan Rulfo's *Pedro Páramo* (1955) with an assertive, forcibly subdued, yet not defeated urban community. Here the villain is no longer an immoral local cacique, product of Mexico's nineteenth-century civil wars, but the postrevolutionary inheritor of this institution on the federal level: the president. In fact, on October 2, 1968, two presidents were responsible for the assault on the peaceful meeting at Tlatelolco, the Plaza of the Three Cultures: Gustavo Díaz Ordaz and Luis Echeverría (who, as minister of the interior at the time, gave the order to fire, and who was then chosen by Díaz Ordaz and the PRI to be the next president).

From the beginning of her career Poniatowska has simultaneously pursued two narrative lines: testimonial and other documentary narrative addressing political issues, and works in a more lyrical, "literary" style that treat personal, often autobiographical situations and events. Her earliest works of this type are the novel *Lilus Kikus* (1954), about the adventures of a precocious, imaginative little girl; and *Melés y Teleo (apuntes para una comedia)* (*Youreadme and Ireadyou* [*Notes for a Comedy*], 1956), her sole excursion into drama, which lampoons the leading Mexican intellectuals of the 1950s. *De noche vienes* (*You Come at Night*, 1979), a collection of short stories written over two decades, critiques her own class, the Mexican aristocracy, particularly the mistress-servant relationship. *Querido Diego, te abraza Quiela* (1978; translated as *Dear Diego*, 1986) is an epistolary novel based on actual love letters from the Russian ex-patriate painter Angelina Beloff to the husband who had abandoned her, Diego Rivera. *La "Flor de Lis"* (*The "Fleur-de-lis,"* 1988), a novel with strong autobiographical overtones, deals with a young girl's immigration from France to Mexico City, the dynamics of her aristocratic, female household, and her pivotal encounter with a French priest-worker that leads her to reflect on social injustice and responsibility, but also on *machismo* and the mother-daughter bond.

The other, documentary vein includes *Hasta no verte Jesús mío* and *La noche de Tlatelolco*, as well as *Todo empezó en domingo* (*It All Began on Sunday*, 1963), a series of vignettes of popular urban culture, illustrated by Alberto Beltrán; and *Gaby Brimmer* (1979), a collaborative autobiography of a woman who became a writer and mother in spite of suffering from severe cerebral palsy. *Fuerte es el silencio* (*Strong Is the Silence*, 1980) documents contemporary social and political problems and popular movements, while *¡Ay vida, no me mereces!* (*Oh Life, You Don't Deserve Me!*, 1985) is a collection of biographical-literary essays about three leading contemporary Mexican writers (Castellanos, Rulfo, and Fuentes) and the literature of La Onda. *Nada, nadie: Las voces del temblor* (*Nothing, No One: The Voices of the Earthquake*, 1988), her latest work of testimonial literature, is about the disaster of September 19, 1985, the revelations of government incompetence and corruption, and the grassroots mobilizations that sprang out of it. Poniatowska also has three collections of interviews with artists, writers, and politicians, *Palabras cruzadas* (*Words Exchanged*, 1961), *Domingo siete* (*Sun-*

day's Seven, 1982), and *Todo México* (vol. 1, 1990), and she is currently preparing several more volumes of collected interviews for publication.

Along with *La noche de Tlatelolco, Hasta no verte Jesús mío* is Poniatowska's masterpiece to date. It fulfilled the same function of advocacy for the urban poor that *La noche* did for the politicized middle class. This work is based on the oral history of Josefina Bórquez (1900–1987), alias Jesusa Palancares,[3] whom Poniatowska overheard shouting angrily in the laundry room of an apartment house she was visiting. Attracted by the washerwoman's spunk, Poniatowska arranged to interview the elderly Bórquez at her shantytown home on the outskirts of Mexico City every Wednesday for a year, during 1963–64. The close but difficult dynamics that developed between interviewer and informant during the early stages of their relationship is described in two essays by Poniatowska, published in 1979 and 1984 ("Hasta" and "Testimonios"). Subsequently, the two women remained friends for two decades, until Bórquez's death in May 1987.[4]

Jesusa Palancares has understandably inspired the same sort of admiration in the novel's readers as Josefina Bórquez did in Elena Poniatowska. She is an outspoken, assertive women who has managed to fend for herself for half a century against overwhelming odds and who holds all political and social institutions, including patriarchy, in healthy contempt. Her personal experience has corroborated the emptiness of all commitments made to the Mexican people by the Revolutionary bureaucracies, and she is not about to be taken in by more false promises. Moreover, her use of the Spanish language is not only entertaining and disarmingly beautiful, but also constitutes an implicit challenge to predominant assumptions about the poverty of poor people's intellectual resources and imagination.

Nevertheless, the tendency of extant criticism to focus on these admirable qualities has obscured other elements in Jesusa's ideology that contradict the portrait of her as a self-sufficient protofeminist. Various patterns of behavior point to Jesusa's profound internalization of certain male values and her longstanding deference to patriarchal authority, in spite of her protestations of independence from and contempt for men. These include her close bond with her brother and nearly incestuous relationship with her father, while viewing her mother and sisters with some condescension; her adoption of racist and misogynist attitudes and of violent behavior; and her nearly total deference to religious authority, as embodied by various male figures, particularly her Spiritist guides.

In the life of Jesusa's real-life prototype, Josefina Bórquez, the exception to this male orientation was her relationship with Elena Poniatowska. As interviewer/editor/writer and as a member of the upper classes, Poniatowska enjoyed the sort of prestige and power, in Bórquez's eyes, that is associated with patriarchal privilege. Consequently, Josefina sought to ascribe to Poniatowska the role of confidante/confessor/guide that she previously had reserved for a series of male authority figures. Nevertheless, all evidence suggests that in her personal interaction with Bórquez, Poniatowska resisted adopting an authoritative role and in fact looked to her informant (who was thirty-two years her senior) for wisdom and guidance. We might say that just as Bórquez, on some level, wanted Poniatowska to replace her father, Poniatowska wanted Bórquez to replace her own mother. This double transference, as well as the unequal distribution of power endemic to the oral history relationship, helps to explain the complex pattern of approach-avoidance, of trust and respect alternating with rebellion, that Poniatowska describes in the older woman's behavior toward her.

The Author as Seamstress and Assassin

In the 1979 essay, the author writes of her close identification with her informant, whose strength and vitality she admired and learned from and whose Mexicanness she learned to acknowledge as her own. This sense of recognition is also apparent in her choice of a pseudonym for the purpose of protecting Bórquez's privacy while she still lived. In the first place, "Jesusa Palancares" is an unmistakably popular name, one that recalls the various peasant and lower-class urban dialects that Poniatowska incorporated into her character's speech.[5] The author has said that she named her character after Norberto Aguirre Palancares, the chief of the Agrarian Department during the presidency of Gustavo Díaz Ordaz (1964–1968), "whom I liked and who looked like a Mixtec god."[6] The selection of an unequivocally religious first name emphasizes the profound spiritual dimension of the character's life. Moreover, it is a feminized version of a male—indeed, a prototypically patriarchal—name, which is consistent with Jesusa's male identification, as we shall see. However, the character's last name, Palancares, bears the same sort of resemblance not to Bórquez but rather to Poniatowska. It is as if, in protecting her informant, the author baptized their joint fictional creation with elements of both their names and, perhaps, both their identities.

Poniatowska summarizes the nature of their collaboration as follows: "Ella y yo teníamos una relación personal muy amorosa, pero

un poco conflictiva" (She and I had a very loving personal relationship, though a bit conflictive).[7] To some extent the conflict may
have been sparked by the two women's different agendas in constructing the oral history and by the aggressive editorial stance that
Poniatowska adopted. She describes the editorial process in terms
that combine metaphors of "female" domesticity and "male" violence: "Utilicé las anécdotas, las ideas y muchos de los modismos de
Jesusa Palancares pero no podría afirmar que el relato es una trans-
cripción directa de su vida porque ella misma lo rechazaría. Maté a
los personajes que me sobraban, eliminé cuanta sesión espiritualista
pude, elaboré donde me pareció necesario, podé, cocí, remendé, in-
venté" (I used the anecdotes, ideas, and many of the idioms of Jesusa
Palancares, but I couldn't say that the story is a direct transcription
of her life because she herself would reject the idea. I killed the characters that I didn't need, I eliminated as many spiritualist sessions as
I could, I elaborated where it seemed necessary to me, I pruned,
sewed, mended, invented).[8] She goes on to explain that her interest
in the subject's life centered on the qualities of combativeness and
independence, precisely what differentiated her from the stereotypical model of the passive, resigned Mexican woman; she found a
focus for these characteristics in Bórquez's role as a *soldadera* in the
Mexican Revolution. For Bórquez, however, the exemplary character of her own life apparently lay in its illustration of religious pre-
cepts; she also talked insistently about her suffering, both physical
and economic.[9] Moreover, Poniatowska took liberties in recreating
Bórquez's language, combining it with the dialects of domestic workers from different parts of Mexico that she had known over the years
and thus creating a sort of idiosyncratic composite of popular female
speech. It is, then, not surprising that, when confronted with the
finished manuscript, Bórquez reportedly denied its authenticity:
"Usted inventa todo, son puras mentiras, no entendió nada, las cosas
no son así" (You invent everything, they're all lies, you didn't understand anything, that isn't the way things are).[10] However, when she
saw her patron saint, the Niño de Atocha, on the cover of the published book, she asked for copies to give to her colleagues at work so
they could read about her life. In other words, Bórquez was willing
to accept the veracity of the text once it was associated with a symbol of religious authority. As we shall see, this authority is essentially patriarchal, an extension of her father's and husband's considerable power over her at earlier periods of her life.

In these two articles, as elsewhere, our only access to information
about Bórquez/Palancares is through texts written by Poniatowska
because of the older woman's insistence on preserving her privacy.

How are we, as readers, to integrate into our understanding of the text the impossibility of determining how it deviates from Bórquez's sense of her own life, particularly in view of her initial rejection of its authenticity? Poniatowska has remarked that "Jesusa inventaba una vida anterior e interior que le hacía tolerable su actual miseria" (Jesusa invented a former, interior life that made her current poverty tolerable).[11] I take for granted that the subject's view of her own life is necessarily a fiction, and the interviewer's vision of her life is another fiction. Any narrative is necessarily selective and partial, an invention of what was, interlaced with a chronicle of what might have been. How, then, does the testimonial genre in general, and this particular *testimonio*, reconcile these two competing stories and the ideologies underlying them?

One increasingly popular solution for the critic's dilemma in approaching *Hasta no verte Jesús mío* is to ignore its biographical dimension and treat it strictly as a novel. However, this solution begs the question of editorial mediation and collapses the specificity of human lives and identities into the relative safety of abstractions. As a growing body of theory and criticism is seeking to demonstrate, the *testimonio* is a narrative genre unto itself, neither biography nor autobiography, fiction nor journalism.

New Sources: The Interviews

During September 1988 and April and May 1989 Elena Poniatowska gave me access to transcriptions of some of her interviews with Bórquez, the first of which is dated March 4, 1964, as well as several early and late drafts of the novel. The first one is from 1963, judging from Bórquez's statement that she was born in 1900 and was now sixty-three, and the last one is marked "penultimate version" and is dated December 1967.

What these materials reveal is that, in the novel, Poniatowska was remarkably faithful to her informant's story and language. It was not infrequent for the author to pose the same question on two or three occasions in order to seek clarification or to verify that she had understood. At times Bórquez would reiterate an earlier, contradictory statement and then become angry with Poniatowska for finding it contradictory. Also, much of the friction between the two women seems to have derived from their different value systems and understandings of human psychology, rooted in their upbringing and experience as members of different social classes. Where Poniatowska sought complex motivations for behavior, Bórquez found simple and, to her eyes, obvious explanations. For instance, when she spoke of her husband's desire to kill her, Poniatowska apparently interrupted to ask why; she replied, "¿Que por qué me quería matar? Porque no quería que yo me quedara viva" (Why did he want to kill me? Because he didn't want me to stay alive). To a similar question about why her sister's common-law husband had tried to kill her, Bórquez replied, "Pus porque son locos los hombres" (Why, because men are crazy). Elsewhere she stated that men are innately unfaithful: "Lo train de herencia" (They've inherited it). Josefina also maintained that she had not been upset when her husband was killed in the Revolution: "Yo no sentí feo. No. ¡Pa' qué? ¡Pa' qué sentía yo feo si yo quería que él se muriera?" (I didn't feel bad. No. What for? Why would I feel bad if I wanted him to die?).

Elsewhere in the conversation it became clear that there was a fundamental disagreement between the two women about the importance, and even the existence, of romantic love. Poniatowska insisted that Bórquez must have been in love at some point in her life, and Bórquez was equally insistent that, while she had been fond of male friends (she used the words *aprecio* and *estimación*), such as the taxi driver (Antonio Pérez), she had never been in love with anyone, not even her husband. On the other hand, she admitted to feeling great jealousy and anger toward her women friends who would leave her to go off with men. Her husband had loved her, she explains, but she had not loved him: "Yo no lo quise. . . . Porque, no, no, no. Era un hombre de muchas mujeres, muy mujerero, y muy parrandero, y muy celoso" (I didn't love him. . . . Because I didn't, no, no. He was a man who had many women, a real womanizer, and a real partier, and very jealous). She explained that she did not believe in the concept of romantic love, that the love stories she would hear on the radio were lies. When Poniatowska suggested that it was not normal not to love, Bórquez either responded in kind, suggesting that it was her interviewer who was abnormal for believing in love, or she would point out that beliefs and emotions are relative: "Pues no será normal, pero para mí sí es normal porque yo no los sé querer, pues . . ." (Well, it may not be normal, but for me it is normal, because I just don't know how to love them . . .).

An interview dated May 11, 1964, contains an eloquent speech by Bórquez regarding the disadvantages of marriage for (poor) women compared to the independence and happiness that comes with being single:

Es muy bonito vivir sólo sin que nadie le reclame a uno. La vida es más bonita así solito uno, sin quién le pegue a uno un grito. Va uno por la calle muy felíz sín que haya ningún reclamo. Pero vaya usted por ése que tiene su mujer y sus hijos, y luego muy felices andan paseándose ellos, sin saber que sus hijos tienen hambre, sus mujeres están careciendo de lomás indispensable, y éso no es de justicia. Por éso no tiene uno que meterse en danzas. Por eso mismo vivir sólo sín buscarse compromisos ajenos [sic].

(It's really nice to live alone, without anyone blaming you. Life is nicer this way, all by yourself, without anyone to holler at you. One goes down the street, very happy, without being blamed for it. But you take that guy who has his wife and kids, and pretty soon the men are out having the time of their lives, without realizing that their children are hungry, their wives are going without the basics, and that isn't right. That's why you shouldn't get tangled up with anyone. That's exactly why it's better to live alone, without making any commitments except to yourself.)

In the same conversation Poniatowska probed Josefina's relationship with Pedro Aguilar, suggesting that he had not always behaved badly toward her, since he had tended her legs when they were frostbitten, and he had bought her pets. Bórquez responded that men are *convenencieros* (self-serving), that Pedro had taken care of her so people wouldn't talk, and that he had not bought her animals; they had been his pets, gifts to him. She shrewdly described her role as wife as follows: "Pos era su gata del, su criada, su gata sin sueldo. La mujer no es más que la gata sín sueldo. Limpia el suelo, vete al mandado, lava los trastes, haz la comida, y dale de comer a tu marido, lávalo, plánchalo, y sín ningun centavo que uno gane. Eso es la gata de balde. ¡Mejor no ¡Pus qué [sic]" ('Cause I was a maid to him, his maid, his unpaid servant. Women are nothing but maids without salaries. Clean the floor, run errands, wash the dishes, make the food, and feed your husband, wash for him, iron for him, and without earning a cent. That's the maid you don't have to pay. It's better not to! What for!).

While these interviews and rough drafts contain no information that fundamentally changes our understanding of the literary text or of the informant on whom Jesusa is based, they do state more emphatically certain traits and beliefs, as well as revealing new information about the dynamics of the interview relationship, and the two conflicting ideologies out of which the text was fashioned. In what follows, I will use the informant's real name, Josefina Bórquez, to refer to the actual person on whose life the novel is based, as she is portrayed in Poniatowska's essays and interviews (with the understanding that this, like all portraits, is also mediated, although less extensively than in the novel). When referring to the somewhat more fictional character in the novel, I will use the pseudonym that Poniatowska has given her, the name that, for readers of Latin American literature, has come to embody popular female strength against overwhelming material and psychological odds—Jesusa Palancares. My assumption throughout is that there are more similarities than differences between the character and the person and that, even with all the difficulties inherent in distinguishing the raw material of a life from its fictional elaboration,[12] the story can teach us some important things about the functioning of gender constructs and religious ideology in the context of rural and urban poverty and can simultaneously illuminate the intersection of feminist and social concerns in contemporary Mexican narrative.

Peasant Migration and the Picaresque Novel

Following an introductory chapter that situates the narrative within the ideological framework of spiritualism,[13] the novel traces the feisty woman's life from her troubled childhood in rural Oaxaca (chapters 2–6), through her participation as a *soldadera* in the Mexican Revolution, her abusive marriage and premature widowhood (chapters 7–12), to her lonely travails in the slums and shantytowns of Mexico City during the period 1917 to 1969 (chapters 13–29, roughly the second half of the book). As Edward H. Friedman has observed in a particularly insightful study of the novel, the narrative follows a circular movement of incident, response, commentary, followed by a new incident, and so on. Typically, "the pattern begins with an event in which someone abuses Jesusa, followed by a feeling of mistrust on her part and a vow to detach herself from others, continued service to those in need, continued abuse, disillusionment, and so on."[14]

Hasta no verte Jesús mío conforms to many of the characteristics that Claudio Guillén has identified with the picaresque novel, including the first-person autobiographical perspective, with a heavily philosophical, reflective dimension; the protagonist's orphanhood, occasioning his abandonment of his hometown and series of ordeals, including service to many masters; his emphasis on subsistence; and his scathing critique of various social classes and professions. If the classic picaresque hero's odyssey takes him "horizontally through space and vertically through society,"[15] Palancares' class movement is only slightly vertical (from servant to independent vendor and washerwoman), emphasizing the radical absence of opportunities for social mobility in postrevolutionary Mexico. (Significantly, the protagonist closely identifies freedom with geographical mobility.) Like the picaresque hero, Palancares maintains the position of a "half-outsider" vis-à-vis subproletarian society; her material and psychological needs prevent her from remaining entirely outside of that society, in spite of her condemnation of it.[16] Finally, the episodic structure that Guillén has identified in the picaresque narrative is eminently present in Poniatowska's novel. The following passage of the novel, which Poniatowska has acknowledged that she invented in its entirety,[17] synthesizes the "freight-train" pattern, involving "endless stories within the story," of the *pícaro*'s life:[18]

Y desde entonces todo fueron fábricas y fábricas y talleres y changarros y piqueras y pulquerías y cantinas y salones de baile y más fábricas y talleres y lavaderos y señoras fregonas y tortillas duras y dale y dale con la bebedera del pulque, tequila y hojas en la madrugada para las crudas. Y amigas y amigos que no servían para nada, y perros que me dejaban sola por andar siguiendo a sus perras. Y hombres peores que perros del mal y policías ladrones y pelados abusivos. Y yo siempre sola, y el muchacho que recogí de chiquito y que se fue y me dejó más sola y me saludas y nunca vuelvas y no es por ai María voltéate y yo como lazarina, encerrada en mi cazuela, y en la calle cada vez menos brava y menos peleonera porque me hice vieja . . . cada vez más desmadejada en esta chingadera de vida. (147–148)

(And since then it's all been factories and factories and workshops and shops and holes-in-the-wall and pulque bars and cantinas and dancehalls and more factories and workshops and laundries and mistresses who were a pain in the ass and hard tortillas and more and more pulque, tequila, and herbs first thing in the morning for the hangovers. And women and men friends who were good for nothing, and dogs that would leave me all alone to go chasing after their bitches. And men worse than lousy dogs and thieving cops and mean bums. And me always alone, and the boy I took in when he was little and that went off and left me more alone than ever and say hello and never come back and that isn't the way, María, turn around, and me like a beggar, shut up in my shack, and less and less of a fighter out in the streets, because I got old . . . weaker and weaker in this fucking life.)

This is, of course, not the first contemporary Mexican testimonial narrative characterized by these features of the picaresque; Ricardo

Pozas' *Juan Pérez Jolote* (1949), the life history of a Chamula Indian man which covered a similar time span, is an important precursor, and probable literary model, in this and other respects. In view of large similarities in the socioeconomic circumstances of sixteenth-century Spain and twentieth-century Mexico, it should not entirely surprise us to find this literary coincidence. John Beverley has traced the development of capitalism in Golden Age Spain, resulting in a "'relative surplus population'—what contemporary sociologists call marginalized social groups—that has been expelled from its traditional forms of life in the countryside but not yet absorbed by the developing capitalist labor market."[19] He interprets Lazarillo de Tormes as

> the product of that still familiar disintegration of the family unit as it passes from an agrarian milieu, where its functions and forms are consecrated by centuries of tradition, into the city life as a marginal subproletariat. His predicament presupposes a separation from agrarian community life and mutual aid systems like the *compadrazgo*; he is, from puberty onwards, "on his own." As such he constitutes a new form of freedom and mobility, but also of degradation, made possible by market society: the individual.[20]

Certainly these observations are equally applicable to Juan Pérez Jolote and Jesusa Palancares, peasant migrants in the evolving market system of twentieth-century Mexico. It would be an over-simplification, however, to interpret their situation as strictly one of alienation; as we shall see, social scientists such as Larissa Lomnitz have identified extensive systems of mutual assistance, based on compound and extended family structures, in the shantytowns of Mexico City. Moreover, Beverley seems to take for granted that traditional village society is necessarily healthy and supportive, an assumption that Poniatowska's novel—and much recent social research—eloquently contradicts. Indeed, what Poniatowska's novel documents is the survival of the human spirit in highly conflictive and alienating rural and urban milieus.

As is highlighted in the above excerpts from *Hasta no verte Jesús mío*, Palancares' style of self-presentation, as mediated by Poniatowska, is tough, strong-willed, implacable, and yet characterized by (unconscious) appeals for sympathy disguised as macho bravado. For instance, the narration is interspersed with expressions of a death wish; she portrays death as preferable to the considerable suffering she has endured throughout her life. Her weapons for defending herself from her own need for human companionship and emotional support are denial and an exacerbated sense of individualism, both of which are apparent in her relationship with Elena Poniatowska, as illustrated by the novel's epigraph:

> Algún día que venga ya no me va a encontrar; se topará nomás con el puro viento. Llegará ese día y cuando llegue, no habrá ni quien le dé una razón. Y pensará que todo ha sido mentira. Es verdad, estamos aquí de a mentiras; lo que cuentan en el radio son mentiras, mentiras las que dicen los vecinos y mentira que me va a sentir. Si ya no le sirvo para nada, ¿qué carajos va a extrañar? Y en el taller tampoco. ¿Quién quiere usted que me extrañe si ni adioses voy a mandar? (8)

> (Someday when you come you won't find me anymore; you'll just run up against the wind. That day will come and when it does, there will be no one to tell you what happened. And you'll think it's all been a lie. It's true, it's a lie that we're here; what they tell on the radio are lies, lies are what the neighbors say and it's a lie that you're going to miss me. If I'm no longer of any use to you, what the hell are you going to miss? And they won't miss me in the shop either. Who do you think is going to miss me if I'm not even going to say good-bye?)

Much of Jesusa Palancares' appeal lies in the persistent strain of optimism underlying this vociferous pessimism born of decades of disappointments and betrayals. Her life story, as she tells it, is punctuated by her acts of generosity, which more than counterbalance the harsh judgments she makes of herself and others.[21]

The Life History as Confession

While Bórquez's skepticism regarding the veracity of the text probably reflects, to some extent, her combative personality, it probably also derives from the problematic nature, rooted in issues of class and power, of the ethnographic relationship between interviewer and informant. Recent critics of the oral history genre, including Langness and Frank,[22] have identified transference, countertransference, and identification as common phenomena in this situation. Moreover, Poniatowska's remarks indicate that Bórquez became emotionally dependent on her while rebelling against this dependency. This dynamic, together with Bórquez's profound religiosity, suggests a therapeutic or confessional situation. As Michel Foucault has persuasively argued, since the Middle Ages at least, Western societies have established the confession as one of the main rituals we rely on for the production of truth. . . . we have passed from a pleasure to be recounted and heard, centering on the heroic or marvelous narration of "trials" of bravery or sainthood, to a literature ordered according to the infinite task of extracting from the depths of oneself, in between the words, a truth which the very form of the confession holds out like a shimmering mirage.[23]

As Foucault notes, the Christian confession, as well as the Freudian "talking cure," have taken sex as their privileged theme; the obligation to hide sex in daily life has been complemented by the duty to reveal it in private confession.[24] If we view *Hasta no verte Jesús mío* as a confession, then it is one that makes violence, rather than sex, its narrative core. Indeed, sexuality might be seen as the empty center of Jesusa Palancares' life, the silence emanating from self-censorship or self-denial. While the narrator does discuss other characters' sex lives, she does so primarily for the purpose of condemning their immorality and selfishness and establishing an implicit contrast with her own chaste behavior. She steadfastly denies having had sexual feelings or having engaged in sexual activities since being widowed at age seventeen (having married at thirteen, when Pedro was twelve, according to the interviews). The unskeptical reader is therefore startled when she describes suffering from an advanced case of syphilis, an episode that she narrates in a characteristically matter-of-fact tone. It is possible that she contracted the disease from her husband and that it was dormant for years; but the episode raises a doubt in the reader's mind regarding the narrator's reliability. In this and many other passages of the novel, Palancares' disingenuousness and disenchantment seem to coexist with a stubbornly maintained innocence.

The Typicality of an Extraordinary Woman

Although critics such as Tatum, Hancock, and Friedman have unanimously viewed Palancares as a "typical" character, representing either Mexican women in general or, more specifically, poor Mexican women, Poniatowska maintains that Jesusa is far from typical. As evidence the author cites the protagonist's single status (for the last seventy years of her life), her failure to have children, and her fierce independence, in sharp contrast to the stereotype of female passivity and resignation.[25] It seems clear that such a broad generalization ("poor Mexican women"), which fails to take into account such factors as ethnicity, geographical and class situation, and historical period, cannot be very useful. However, if we further narrow the field to include only mestiza women immigrants to Mexico City from the countryside during the first decades of the twentieth century, how typical is Jesusa Palancares of this group? A partial answer to this question is suggested by comparison of her personality and behavior with findings from recent psychological and anthropological studies of Mexican peasants and shantytown dwellers.

In their study of mestizo villagers from central Mexico during the 1960s, Erich Fromm and Michael Maccoby found a predominant strong maternal (as opposed to paternal) identification among both men and women which they believed was reinforced ideologically by the Mexican Catholic emphasis on the Virgin of Guadalupe and the Christ child, as opposed to God the Father and the adult Christ.[26] (111–114). To the extent that these psychologists' findings are reliable and can be generalized to mestizo peasants from Oaxaca, they would suggest that Palancares is exceptional from a very early age in being father-centered. This psychological tendency was exaggerated by the early death of Jesusa's mother.

As for Palancares' independence, Larissa Lomnitz's study of Mexico City shantytown dwellers during the 1970s found that 70 percent of residents moved to the city in family groups and lived with relatives upon arrival in Mexico City. The survival of shantytown dwellers depended on these family networks, which developed into systems of reciprocal exchange of assistance. While these networks typically consisted of members of an extended or compound family, they sometimes incorporated unrelated neighbors. Palancares, then, would be categorized among this minority contingent of the shantytown population which, in the absence of blood relatives in the city, tends to form fictive kinship ties. Lomnitz's study moreover found that single people living with nuclear families were usually older relatives, and that it was rare for people of any age to live alone.[27] This suggests that, as Poniatowska has observed, Palancares was unusual in her steadfast refusal, following widowhood at the age of seventeen, to remarry or form a marriage-like union and in her solitary life-style late in life. Her atypicality or difference, then, may hinge on these two pivotal issues of gender identification and independence. Yet, as we shall see, while her male identification leads to a fierce refusal to be dominated or "governed," it is a style of independence which can by no means be seen as entirely admirable; rather, it combines self-sufficiency and rebelliousness with manipulation and contains elements of misanthropy and authoritarianism, which find partial expression in violence, racism, and self-hatred.

Toward the Authoritarian Personality:
Male Identification, Racial Self-Hatred, and Violence

In his acute study of *Hasta no verte Jesús mío,* Edward H. Friedman convincingly argues that the protagonist admires men for their privileged status rather than their morality. However, I take exception to his statement that "Jesusa does not like men and, in fact, does everything within her power to avoid them."[28] On the contrary, Palancares' life is marked by competition and conflict with women, beginning with her mother and sister, an attitude which is complemented by her strong identification with and idealization of men, beginning with her father and her brother Emiliano and culminating in her male spiritual advisors. This gender preference carries over into Jesusa's attitudes toward homosexuality; her tolerance of gay males even extends to "Manuel el Robachicos," while her condemnation of lesbianism is categorical.[29]

Following the first chapter, which places the narrative within the framework of spiritualism, Palancares' life history begins with the premature end of her childhood as a result of her mother's early death in a context of extreme poverty. She describes how she leaped into the grave in a futile attempt to protect her mother's face from the shovelfuls of dirt and as an expression of her own bereavement and death wish: "Quería que me taparan allí con mi mamá" (I wanted them to cover me up there with Momma) (17). The poignance and emphatic positioning of this episode draw the reader's attention to the loss of Palancares' mother and to the tragedy of her truncated childhood: "Mi mamá no me regañó ni me pegó nunca. Era morena igual a mí, chaparrita, gorda y cuando se murió nunca volví a jugar" (My mother never scolded me or hit me. She was dark just like me, short and fat, and when she died I never played again) (20). However, there are few subsequent mentions of her mother in what follows, and these emphasize her preference of her father over her; the central figure in Palancares' psychic economy is unambiguously her father, Felipe Palancares. Nevertheless, although Jesusa's death wish would surface again after Emiliano's death, she is impassive before her father's death (allegedly because she didn't witness it). However, years later, the extremity of her grief over the death of a pet suggests that it was a delayed reaction to the earlier, much greater emotional loss.

Jesusa Palancares' identification with her mother is, in many respects, pivotal to her self-image and ideology. After her mother's death, her older sister Petra returned to live with the family and act as surrogate mother, but Jesusa rejected her. Jesusa offers two explanations. In the first place, she hadn't been raised with Petra so didn't love her: "Ya estaba acostumbrada a mano de hombre, a la mano de mi padre" (I was used to a man's hand, to my father's hand). Furthermore, her sister, unlike her father, was dark-complexioned (here, and throughout the novel, she contradicts herself regarding her own skin color): "Petra era trigueña, más prieta que yo. Yo tengo la cara quemada del sol pero no soy prieta, pero ella sí era oscura de cuerpo y cara. Salió más india que yo. Dos sacamos el color de mi papá y los otros dos fueron prietitos. Efrén y Petra, Emiliano y yo, mitad y mitad" (Petra was brown, darker than me. My face is sunburned but I'm not dark, but she was dark, both her body and her face. She came out more Indian than me. Two of us got my dad's color and the other two were dark. Efrén and Petra, Emiliano and I, half and half) (31).[30] Thus, she associates dark skin color (i.e., Indian characteristics) with her mother and European descent with her father; in keeping with dominant Mexican ideology, she valorizes her European ancestry over her Indian heritage. Perhaps not coincidentally, after all members of her immediate family have died and she is converted to Spiritualism, it is only the light-complexioned sibling, Emiliano, that Jesusa recalls with affection and that she describes as repeatedly returning from the dead to save her from her excessive drinking: "Emiliano . . . siempre fue bueno conmigo. Durante años me cuidó cuando anduve de borracha en las cantinas. Se materializaba, se servía de otros cerebros y me sacaba de las juergas. Se me presentaba en otro señor y me decía: 'Vámonos.' Y yo me le quedaba mirando. 'Pues vámonos,' le decía yo muy dócil" (Emiliano . . . was always good to me. For years he took care of me when I was a barfly in the cantinas. He would turn up, take over other people's minds, and get me out of my drinking sprees. He'd appear in another man and say to me, "Let's go." And I'd stand there looking at him. "OK, let's go," I'd say obediently) (15–16). As for her older brother, Efrén, Jesusa seems to associate his dark complexion with his alcoholism and immorality: "Era muy prieto, muy borracho y muy perdido" (He was very dark, a drunkard, and a lost soul) (27). The racial self-hatred that is implicit in her characterization of her familial relations becomes even more explicit when she describes advising her philandering husband that if he was going to cheat on her, he should at least choose lovers who were "less Indian" than she: "Siquiera cuando se meta a hacerme guaje, búsquese una cosa buena, que no sea igual a mí de india . . . Una cosa que costiée" (When you fool around behind my back, at least look for something good, not as Indian as me . . . something that's worth a lot) (104).

Palancares recognized and manipulated the power that she had

over her father throughout her childhood: "Mi papá hacía lo que yo
quería" (My dad did what I wanted) (21). She claims that he, like her
mother, was permissive but not affectionate. Yet her narrative reveals ways in which he indirectly expressed affection for her. While
her mother still lived, Jesusa wouldn't let her brush her hair; she
only conceded that privilege to her father: "El tenía la mano suave-
cita. . . . Sólo de él me dejaba peinar" (He had a very gentle hand. . . .
He was the only one I would let brush my hair) (21). Moreover, it was
her father who painstakingly fashioned Jesusa's few rudimentary
toys, most of which were typically masculine (stone marbles, an arrow, a slingshot, a stuffed squirrel doll). This father-daughter bond to
play and pleasure was, to a large extent, broken by the mother's
death: "Después nunca me volvió a hacer nada. Nunca más. Se hizo
el sordo o todas las cosas le pasaron como chiflonazos" (Afterward
he didn't make me anything else. He pretended he didn't hear me or
else everything just went in one ear and out the other) (18).

After her mother's death, the primary emotional link that father
and daughter maintained appears to be their spiritual bond with nature; Felipe Palancares would take his children to hunt for turtle
eggs on the beach of Salina Cruz at night, and later, during the Revolution, he took Jesusa to bathe in the river. At the time of Palancares'
narration, when she hasn't returned to the coast in many decades,
the sea continues to symbolize sensuality and freedom for her: "El
chiste es . . . resistir el golpe del agua en el cuerpo, vestido o en-
cuerado, para sentir el agua viva. . . . Yo era chaparrita y fuerte y
sabía esperar las olas. . . . Es muy sabroso el golpe del agua del mar"
(The trick is . . . to stand up to the waves breaking against your body,
naked or clothed, to feel the living water. . . . I was small and strong
and I knew how to wait for the waves. . . . The feel of the ocean
water breaking is wonderful) (25–26). As for the river, she associates
it with paternal companionship, a sense of belonging and of privacy
without solitude: "Iba al río con mi papá, siempre con mi papá. . . .
¡Es bonito meterse donde cabe uno bien y ni quien lo vea a uno! . . .
Jamás volví a ir al río, ya no tenía papá, ¿quién me llevaba?" (I would
go to the river with my dad, always with my dad. . . . It's nice to go
into the water where you fit right in and where no one can see you!
. . . I never went back to the river, I no longer had a dad, who would
take me?) (70). The feeling of well-being and freedom that the protagonist associates with the ocean is generalized to include the countryside in general, in contrast to the city: "Como desde chiquilla no
me hallé sino con la libertad, todo mi gusto era andar sola en el
campo o arriba de un cerro" (Since I was a little girl I wasn't happy
unless I was free, so my only pleasure was to walk alone in the coun-

tryside or on the hilltops) (28). Beyond this shared pleasure in nature, Jesusa suggests that she and her father shared certain characteristics: cleverness, the ability to fend for themselves, and the inability to cook (which she identifies as innately female) (22, 26, 28).

The protagonist's strong Oedipal attachment to her father is expressed most vividly by her possessiveness toward him, which is especially apparent in her description of incidents in which, after her mother's death, he began to bring women home to care for his children and share his bed. Jesusa would not tolerate her father's maintaining sexual relations with a woman other than her mother; moreover, she herself was quite literally being replaced, since she and her father customarily slept together. Palancares' narration of the sequence of events reveals a disingenuousness that is characteristic of her narrative voice: "Yo dormía con mi papá, pero como es tierra caliente, nos tendíamos en una hamaca, y nunca dejé que se fuera a acostar con la mujer ésa. Entonces ella empezó a emborracharse con lo del mandado, váyase a saber por qué" (I slept with my dad, but since it's hot country, we lay in a hammock, and I never let him go sleep with that woman. So she began to get drunk with the grocery money, who knows why) (21). The day after the woman, in effect, accused Jesusa of incest (a charge that would be repeated more explicitly by Felipe's later sexual partners), Jesusa stoned her until she left, using the woman's alcoholism as a pretext. (Certainly, in conditions of such poverty, the squandering of money on drink was a real matter of concern; yet, in a classic example of the double standard, Jesusa was willing to tolerate the alcoholism of male members of her family.)

To a large extent Jesusa adopted the role of matriarchal protector and avenger to Felipe Palancares' roles of irresponsible father and innocent victim of opportunistic, scheming women. These are gender roles which Fromm and Maccoby found to be prevalent among the residents of the mestizo village that they studied; the psychologists suggest that the male ineffectuality is a symptom of the disintegration of the traditional patriarchal system, in the context of the rural pauperization brought about by the Díaz dictatorship.[31] In its extreme form this syndrome alternates with "sadistic machismo" (leading to the sort of domestic violence which we find in the Palancares household).[32] In keeping with this model, Jesusa tells us that her father acknowledged her right, indeed her obligation, to beat up his sexual partners:

Siempre tuvo sus mujeres y eso sí, yo siempre les pegué porque eran abusivas, porque eran glotonas, porque se quedaban botados

de borrachas, porque se gastaban el dinero de mi papá. . . . Eso
era lo que a mí me daba más coraje, que se acabaran el dinero de
mi papá, eso sí que no, por eso le golpié a sus queridas. . . . El
sabía que yo tenía que pegarle a todas sus mujeres, menos a mi
madrastra. (67–69)

(He always had his women and, yes, I always beat them because
they took advantage, because they were gluttons, because they
would be falling down drunk, because they would spend all my
dad's money. I couldn't put up with that; that's why I beat up
his lovers. . . . He knew I had to hit all his women, except my
stepmother.)

A key contradiction in Palancares' narrative of her early life
emerges from its presentation of false male saviors. On the surface
the narrator seems to embrace a chivalric view of men (probably
learned from popular ideology and romance novels) as rescuers of
damsels in distress; yet time and again her story reveals the "savior"
to be a wolf in sheep's clothing. For instance, after he returned to his
father's house, Jesusa's alcoholic brother Efrén regularly beat his
wife, Ignacia. Jesusa (who attacked her father's first lover and regularly beat her sister Petra) came to her sister-in-law's defense, even
though Ignacia systematically beat her. After Efrén's violence had
caused his wife to miscarry, his father, in turn, beat him and ran the
couple out of the house. In doing so he claimed to be protecting the
woman, but in effect he merely assuaged his conscience by removing
the abusive relationship from his sight and his potential intervention. After Efrén fell into a ditch in a drunken stupor and drowned,
Felipe took Ignacia back into the Palancares household, once again
appearing to rescue his daughter-in-law. However, when he subsequently impregnated her, it became apparent that his intervention
was not disinterested; rather, he had exchanged "protection" for sexual access. It is interesting that this is one of the few incidents in her
tale about which Jesusa casts some small doubt, prefacing the last
part of the story with the phrase "según cuentan" (so they say); she
apparently finds it difficult to accept that her father has taken sexual
advantage of her sister-in-law. Jesusa's greatest concern with regard
to this liaison, however, is not for Ignacia's welfare; rather, she re-
grets that the relationship produced a relative who is unaware of his
kinship with her. For her the significance of this episode lies not in
its exemplification of sexual abuse but in its contribution to the disintegration of the Palancares line and the dispersal of the family.
　Similarly, Petra, her other dark sibling, was kidnapped at age fifteen by a virtual stranger and forcibly kept in an abusive relation-

ship for three years. (Through a strange twist of logic, Jesusa blames her sister's disgrace on her mother's excessive cleanliness; it was their mother's fault that Petra was outside the house, fetching Jesusa's freshly washed blanket, when she was kidnapped: "Por eso de la recochina limpieza le birlaron a su hija" [Because of her filthy cleanliness they snatched her daughter away from her] [32]. On the other hand, it doesn't occur to Jesusa to blame either parent for not attempting to locate and save their missing daughter.) It was left up to another stranger, Cayetano, to rescue Petra from her kidnapper; he then saved up his wages for a year in order to return her to her family. After he did so, he asked for her hand in (common-law) marriage. Thus, his chivalry proved to be as deceptive as his father-in-law's toward Ignacia; it was a means of incurring a debt that would be repaid through sexual possession of the victim. Moreover, Cayetano proved to be no less dangerous than his predecessor; three or four months after they began living together, he inexplicably tried to murder Petra in her sleep. As with Ignacia, it was a sibling (Emiliano), rather than the father, who saved the woman's life; but Petra, like her (and Jesusa's) mother, eventually died of fright.

Similarly, Jesusa's apparent power over her father's life, including his sexual relationships and money, masks his complete control over her person and his authority to choose her husband and thus determine her future. It is a power that he arbitrarily relinquishes and resumes at will, to Jesusa's anguish. (On a psychological level, she interpreted his intervention as a sign of affection; moreover, as a female, she herself was not allowed to fill the power vacuum left by his paternal negligence.) In part Felipe Palancares' irresponsible behavior seems to be motivated by (or, at least, the narrator would have us believe it is motivated by) jealousy of his favorite daughter's potential suitors. As noted above, his behavior is apparently not atypical and may correspond to a breakdown in traditional patterns of patriarchal authority.

Whether or not her father fulfilled his paternal obligations, there is no doubt that his duty was defined by a patriarchal system and that Jesusa was subject to the traffic in women.[33] In the narration of her early life she repeatedly portrays her interactions with men in terms of ownership and exchange. For instance, on more than one occasion during her childhood, her father was punished for not protecting her from abuse. During the Revolution, when enemy troops captured her and four other *carrancista* women, Zapata kept them in his camp for two weeks, then personally delivered them, unharmed, to Felipe Palancares. In doing so he proved his military superiority over the *carrancistas* and, at the same time, demonstrated his respect for their male honor by refraining from taking sexual advantage of his female war booty. Moreover, Zapata appealed to Felipe Palancares' own sense of chivalry by entrusting him with the responsibility of defending the women from possible punishment by their jealous husbands. Since the men's honor had been called into question by the incident, they exacted the women's promise never to reveal the story of their imprisonment by males of the enemy camp. By keeping the secret for over fifty years before finally divulging it to Poniatowska and idealizing the figure of Emiliano Zapata, Bórquez expresses implicit approval of this chivalric code of female exchange.

The traffic in women also functioned, to Jesusa's great detriment, in the case of her marriage to Pedro Aguilar. Her father had relinquished his paternal authority in anger over her speaking Zapotec to the soldiers from Tehuantepec (indicating his racism, jealousy, and compulsion to control his female "property") and her subsequent defiance of his attempts at corporal punishment. Jesusa sought protection from paternal abuse from a more powerful male, her father's military superior. (Earlier, a female friend of her mother's had not had sufficient social power to defend Jesusa successfully from her stepmother's violence.) When Pedro Aguilar, whose attempts to control Jesusa had also been frustrated, then proposed marriage to her and she declined and asked to be sent home to Oaxaca, it was up to the general, as her surrogate father, to determine her future. He based his decision on neither Jesusa's wishes nor those of her family but rather on a generalized distrust of male sexual aggression toward women. Rather than place her at the mercy of the entire male crew of the merchant ship that would have taken her back to Tehuantepec, the general reasoned, he preferred to place her fate in the hands of one man.

Previously, Aguilar's insistence on prepaying for Jesusa's merchandise at the local store, against her strenuous objections, was at once a display of macho bravado and an overt attempt to buy Jesusa by quite literally indebting her to him. Once he finally had achieved possession of her through the general's patriarchal disposition, he exacted revenge for her disdain, keeping her under lock and key, beating her, and "using" her sexually ("me ocupaba") without concern for her own sexual desire and satisfaction. In turn, throughout her narrative Palancares steadfastly refuses to acknowledge having such desire. Whether or not her father and husband managed to make her renounce sexual behavior (a question which the novel answers ambiguously) they, along with the general social climate, certainly convinced her to repress sexual discourse. However, as we shall see, these desires were to resurface later in the form of spiritualist revelations. Initially Jesusa adopted the obedient and submissive role that was expected of her. When she finally rebelled against Pedro's abuse in his absence by engaging in precisely the sort of behavior that he feared (managing a bar and buying herself a sumptuous wardrobe, i.e., drinking, flirting, and experiencing pleasure in his absence and therefore beyond his control), he punished her by forcing her to dress like a man and prohibiting her from bathing. In other words, he responded to her assertive, stereotypically masculine actions by forcing her symbolically to renounce her female sexuality, by making her appearance match her "dirty," "male" behavior.[34] Her second, direct act of rebellion came when she defended herself against his physical abuse; however, she continued to serve her husband from a position of inferiority (as marked by her continued use of the formal verb form *usted* when addressing Pedro, although he addressed her as *tú*).[35]

The only positive memories that Palancares preserves of the man who was briefly her husband are the nights when he lovingly cared for her frostbitten legs and the evenings when he would read novels to her. The narrative pleasure that she clearly takes in storytelling and in recounting spiritual revelations and dreams apparently had its inception in this early savoring of romance. However, even in this context Pedro insists on exerting his absolute control over his wife, contradicting Jesusa's imaginative interpretations and commanding her to accept his interpretations as authoritative. Not surprisingly, he does not teach her to read for herself. In a sense he is like a religious adviser, preaching dogma to the uninformed; as we shall see, in the Spiritist Church Jesusa will eventually find another source of patriarchal authority, if a somewhat more flexible one.

Aguilar is spared being portrayed as a two-dimensional villain by these episodes and by another incident that reveals the psychological (and, implicitly, the sociological) roots of his cruelty. Jesusa describes going home with Pedro to visit his grandmother and observing his tender reunion with the goat that had nursed him and acted as his surrogate mother during his childhood. (She tells us that the goat died, presumably of grief, the day after their visit ended.) It is characteristic of their uncommunicative relationship that she never learned what had become of her husband's parents. This pathetic portrait of emotional deprivation is in keeping with psychological profiles of abusive men; the classic wife-beater is a man who has suffered extreme abuse or neglect as a child and attempts to exert total control over his wife in compensation. Since achieving such control over another human being is not possible, his frustration may find an outlet in violence.[36] This dynamic may be exacerbated when the object of the man's oppression responds by rebelling (i.e., by asserting her subjectivity), as Jesusa did. Beyond this, family violence can result from repressed feelings of anger and frustration in other dimensions of a man's adult life, such as an alienating work environment or unemployment and the consequent inability to support himself and his family. As David Gil has argued, in contemporary capitalist societies

> submission to structural violence is a "normal" aspect of adult everyday life. . . . Hierarchical structures, male dominance, and irrational, arbitrary authority are frequent attributes of home life in such societies, all of which are relevant to the task of preparing children for adjustment to a lifetime of structural violence. Male dominance and hierarchy are, of course, particular forms of socially structured inequalities, rooted in and maintained by coercion and violence and tending, in turn, to induce counterviolence.[37]

Through years of witnessing and experiencing emotional deprivation and abuse, Jesusa in turn adopted her culture's male propensity toward violence, especially the physical and emotional abuse of women and children.[38] Researchers have noted the prevalence of an extremely authoritarian structure in Mexican mestizo peasant families, involving the use of severe corporal punishment to inculcate in children the qualities of obedience and submission.[39] As a girl she enjoyed stoning lizards and iguanas to death, an activity that she identifies as typically masculine (19–20). After Jesusa literally had run her father's first lover out of the house, he left her and her brother tied and locked up when he went to work. Furthermore, he, unlike her mother, customarily beat his children, especially his eldest son, Efrén (27). It is significant that, rather than blame him for doing so, Jesusa views his abuse of her older brother as justified by the latter's wickedness. She even observes that she followed his example when she later had problems with her adopted son, Perico, beating him and locking him up. What she fails to acknowledge in this context is that, ironically, her abuse of her own son achieved the same negative results as her father's brutal punishment of her brother.[40] Indeed, she recognizes no cause-and-effect relationship between child abuse and rebelliousness; rather, she fatalistically attributes the problem to predestination: "Mi papá quiso evitarle las malas compañías, como yo a Perico, pero con todo y eso, él siempre las agarró. Así es que ya el que nace de mala cabeza, ni quien se lo quite" (My dad wanted to keep him from hanging out with the wrong crowd, like I did with Perico, but even so, he always kept bad company. So if someone's born bad, no one can change him) (27).

In commenting on her own behavior and that of other characters, Palancares frequently resorts to a dual system of logic. On the one hand, she mouths Christian beliefs regarding good and evil: Docility and obedience are good and will be rewarded, while aggressiveness and stubbornness (which in some situations might more accurately be interpreted as assertiveness and strength of character) are bad and will be punished by God. Yet such statements are almost invariably followed by a contradictory expression of the folk wisdom that she has learned and that has been reaffirmed by her experiences: If one doesn't defend oneself from the many forces of evil and aggression in the world, one is stupid and, in effect, deserves the suffering that inevitably follows on submission and resignation. One example of this is her discussion of her brother Emiliano's docility. According to Jesusa, he was the best-tempered of her siblings: "Era un hermano tan manso ese Emiliano; un pedazo de azúcar no empalagaba tanto" (That Emiliano was such a gentle brother; a lump of sugar wasn't as sweet) (53). Yet she goes on to recognize that his exaggerated deference to patriarchal authority, in contrast to her own headstrong assertiveness, led to his death: "Pero de nada le sirvió ser el único que nunca le contradijo a mi papá. . . . Con razón dicen: caballo manso tira a malo y hombre bueno tira a pendejo" (But being the only one who never contradicted my dad did him no good. . . . That's why they say: A gentle horse turns bad and a good man turns into a stupid ass) (53).

This ambivalence is also apparent in Palancares' self-portrait as an outspoken and headstrong rebel; she describes herself and her relatives as ultimately accepting these qualities as God-given, unchangeable traits, a conviction which allows her to feel a certain pride in qualities that are not socially acceptable in women. While Palancares was not physically abused by her biological parents (having thwarted her father's one attempt to beat her), she was regularly beaten and, on one occasion, stabbed by her stepmother, Evarista, and she witnessed and sometimes participated in the abuse of family members, usually women. Jesusa resigned herself to being mistreated because she wanted to stay near her father and she had nowhere else to go. In this respect, hers was a standard reaction to psychological and economic dependence. Moreover, she accepted Evarista's rationalization that she beat the child for her own good; she even expresses gratitude for this extreme form of discipline, to which she attributed having learned domestic skills that later proved necessary to her survival (52). Of perhaps equal importance, these skills allowed her to maintain her economic independence, which protected her from further abuse. When her stepmother got carried away and inflicted potentially lethal harm, stabbing her with a knife in a fit of anger, Jesusa first repressed the incident, "forgetting" that she was wounded until someone noticed the blood, and then attempted to protect her attacker from punishment. (Similarly, she repeatedly attempted to protect her father from knowledge of her abusive relationships, allegedly because his absences made him powerless to protect her, but probably also because experience had taught her that he wouldn't attempt to intervene.) According to Palancares' logic, then (which is the rationalization characteristic of child abusers), severe corporal punishment is justified by children's disobedience and is necessary to reform their behavior: Spare the rod and spoil the child.

Critics have tended to focus on Jesusa's spirited self-defense, beginning with the moment that she fights back against the aggressive taunts of Pedro's lover, then against Pedro's increasingly brutal beatings, followed by other incidents in which she strikes out first rather than subject herself to abuse, especially by men. While this assertiveness is clearly one of the qualities that makes Palancares appealing to readers, especially feminists, one should not lose sight of her continued, often gratuitous use of violence throughout much of her life, which suggests that her survival strategy involved adopting *machista* ideology and behavior. "Yo era rete fina para pegar," she boasts at one point, ". . . antes, hasta comezón sentía en las manos" (I was real good at beating people up . . . those days, my hands would even begin to itch) (150–151). In view of the extensive wife and child abuse that Jesusa witnessed and of which she herself was a victim, it is not surprising that she herself should have abused her own adopted child.[41] Nor can we view her participation in the Revolution, and later in the Cristero Wars, as a neutral element in shaping her character; not surprisingly, sociologists have documented that military environments encourage violent domestic behavior.[42] Although she comments on more than one occasion that she has lived a "bad" life, drinking and fighting too much, it seems that her conversion to Spiritism has mitigated these tendencies. Catholic (and Spiritist) dogma proscribes these and other activities that she found enjoyable (for instance, dancing), and she has been robbed of contact with nature, another of the few pleasures of her life, by the urban environment. By the time she narrates her story, she has been left with only three sources of enjoyment: food, spiritual revelations, and talking. It should come as no surprise, then, that two focal points of her narrative should be eating[43] and Spiritist ecstasies (a focus that Poniatowska admits to altering in the novel),[44] or that these descriptions should be characterized by the sensuality and eroticism that are absent or repressed in other areas of her narrative and her life.

Toward the Authoritarian Personality: The Prison as Home and Chapel

Much of the fourth chapter of the novel is devoted to Palancares' description of working in the Tehuantepec women's prison at age ten, an episode in her life that illustrates the power relations articulated by various social institutions in rural Mexico at the beginning of the century. The scene concerns an anonymous woman who has been imprisoned following her conviction for seven murders. The construction of the prison antedates that of the Panopticon, as Foucault describes it; it more closely approximates the model of the dungeon. The living quarters of Jesusa, her stepmother, Evarista, and her mother, Fortunata, stood between the street (the public sphere) and the long row of mostly empty cells. Palancares interprets this arrangement as serving the needs of security, of confinement and exclusion from the larger society, and implicitly of surveillance: "Así es de que no había por donde fugarse" (So there was nowhere to escape) (34). Moreover, there was a hierarchy of female prisoners. Although drunks spent the night in the cells closest to the street and were occasionally allowed access to the light and relative openness of the prison yard, the sole murderer was relegated to the uninterrupted darkness, heat, and enclosure of the farthest cell.

Thus banned from social contact by virtue of her larger "debt" to society ("debía siete muertes" [she owed seven deaths]), this high-security prisoner asked that Jesusa be allowed to sleep in the cell with her because she was afraid (Palancares does not specify of what: the supernatural? loneliness?). Even more interestingly, Evarista, the prison rector's daughter, allowed Jesusa to do so. This suggests, first of all, that her stepmother was relatively unconcerned with Jesusa's welfare. To a certain extent this may derive from a generalized attitude toward children as servants; it probably also reflects the absence of a blood tie between Evarista and Jesusa, which would probably have entailed a greater sense of responsibility. In any case, unless we view the action as sadistic (and Jesusa's adult assessment does not seem to support this interpretation), the jailer's acquiescence implies a greater degree of trust in the prisoner than one would expect. This trust, in turn, suggests that the power arrangement in the prison is not strictly hierarchical. Rather, to some extent it conforms to Gilles Deleuze's description of "primitive" societies, in which "the network of alliances . . . cannot be reduced to a hierarchical structure or to relations of exchange between filial groups. Alliances take place between small local groups, which constitute relations between forces (gift and countergift) and direct power. . . . the alliances weave a supple and transversal network that is perpendicular to vertical structure . . . and form an unstable physical system that is in perpetual disequilibrium instead of a closed, exchangist cycle."[45] Jesusa's description of the prison's vastness and of their sleeping arrangement ("La cárcel era inmensa de grande. Dormíamos pegadas a la reja" [The prison was immense. We would sleep right up against the bars]) suggests that she, too, was afraid, but not of the convicted mass murderer. Rather, it was from her that Palancares first learned the pleasure of narrative, as the prisoner recounted her life: "Le gustaba hablar en voz alta y me contaba su vida y yo le fui tomando el gusto" (She liked to talk out loud and she would tell me her life story and I began to take a liking to it) (38). This is a pleasure which, when later meted out by her husband/jailer, was to allow Jesusa temporary escapes from the prison of her marriage; by the time she is old and has moved from the position of listener to that of speaker, it becomes a vehicle of self-disclosure, of intimacy, even of immortality, through the novel.

Ultimately the convicted murderer and Jesusa were both prisoners, trapped by social institutions that allowed no mobility and isolated from the rest of the prison community, even as they were alone in the larger society. (The prisoner had no family; Jesusa's father had left her with an abusive stepmother.) When a severe earthquake took place and the roof of the prison caved in, the jailers evacuated the building but forgot about their two charges trapped in the far cell. Thus, what might have been a metaphor for the collapse of anachronistic social structures instead serves to underline the *desamparo*, or forsaken condition, of the victims. Moreover, Palancares' extremely understated narration of the events—she describes having an objective, matter-of-fact conversation with her stepmother after the disaster—masks her anger and fear. Afterward all the drunks were freed, but the murderer was left in prison, where she now felt even less secure. In an ironic reversal of the Panopticon, in which the jailers create the impression of watching the prisoners without themselves being seen, she asked to be moved to the cell nearest the street so she could keep an eye on her jailers and thus diminish her loneliness and fear: "Se pasaba todo el día cerca de la reja para mirar a la gente" (She would spend all day near the bars so she could watch

people) (39). Throughout the narration Palancares poses the opposi-
tions of darkness versus light and of heat and enclosure versus openness and movement; but heat is also the paltry human warmth to
which the prisoner is drawn, as to a flame, as she flees the oppressive
darkness of her cell.

Just as Jesusa learned the pleasures of storytelling from this
woman, she also learned the utopian dimension of miracles from
her. The Niño de Atocha—later to become Palancares' patron saint
(and to watch/preside over the novel, from his cover throne)—an-
swered her prayers, which were communicated through prayer
candles financed by small loans from her jailer (another example of
light symbolism). These loans constitute further evidence that the
relationship between jailer and inmate was characterized not only
by hierarchy and oppression but also by an implicit alliance based on
shared poverty and faith.

First, the saint appeared to the prison community in the form of a
mysterious child who brought the murderer baskets of food. While
the importance of food in a situation of poverty might seem obvious,
if we accept Palancares' descriptions of sumptuous prison meals,
both jailers and inmates ate very well indeed: "Era media res la que
se cocinaba a diario. Un día se hacía guisado en verde con pepita de
calabaza y hierba santa, otro día en jitomate y chiles colorados. Les
dábamos también *gina do shuba* que en otras partes le dicen
cuachala, un mole de maíz tostado" (We would cook a side of beef
every day. One day we would make beef stewed in green sauce with
pumpkin seeds and herbs, another day in tomato and red chile sauce.
We also would give them *gina do shuba*, which they call *cuachala*
in other places, a *mole* sauce made out of toasted corn) (35). (It was
only later, when Palancares became a servant in Mexico City, that
she experienced severe deprivation of food.) These shared meals suggest another sense in which prison life was not strictly hierarchical
and punitive. However, eating also has a psychological significance
that the narrator acknowledges in another context: "Dicen que el
huérfano no tiene llenadero porque le falta la mano de la madre que
le dé de comer y a mí siempre me dio guzguería. Comía desde las
cinco de la mañana hasta las ocho de la noche" (They say the orphan
can never get his fill because he doesn't have a mother's hand to feed
him, and it always made me crave more. I would eat from five in the
morning until eight at night) (42). Thus, the saint's gifts of food, like
the jail's elaborate meals, negated the fact of poverty while simultaneously consoling the murder emotionally or spiritually.

Next, reappearing in the form of a young lawyer, the Niño de
Atocha mysteriously arranged for the woman to be pardoned and he

miraculously transported her to the state of Zacatecas to give thanks at his altar. (Palancares' spiritual revelations also imagine her savior to appear to her in the form of a Christ child or a handsome young man; she describes the latter as a representation of Christ or the devil; in the latter case, he is highly eroticized.) The saint's final gift to the prisoner, then, is of freedom and mobility (the two are closely linked in Jesusa's imagination), but in this case, ironically, the recipient of the miracle perceives mobility as another form of confinement, as exclusion from the only community she knows, that of the prison in Tehuantepec.

This episode closely resembles the first miracle allegedly performed by the Niño de Atocha, as described in literature sold near Catholic churches in Mexico in 1988 (which is presumably similar to the literature that would have been available earlier in this century). According to the "Novena y Triduo dedicados al milagrosísimo Niño de Atocha" ("Novena and Triduum Dedicated to the Most Miraculous Child of Atocha"), the faithful can gain the favor of this saint by carrying out charitable works, especially by caring for the ill and for poor, abandoned children (advice that Jesusa Palancares took very much to heart throughout her life). The saint allegedly performed his first miracle in the city of Durango in February 1829, when he appeared, in the form of a handsome young man, mysteriously to free a woman prisoner who had languished for long periods of time in several jails with no means of defense. Although the Niño told the prisoner to follow him, she lost sight of her savior, only to find his effigy in the sanctuary dedicated to him in Fresnillo, Zacatecas.[46] The close similarity of this legend to Jesusa Palancares' tale of the prisoner in Tehuantepec raises interesting questions about the relationship between religious doctrine, memory, and storytelling. It seems likely that either Josefina Bórquez at least partially invented her tale, consciously or not, based on her knowledge of Church literature, or her informant, the prisoner, had done so in relating her own adventures. (The third possiblity, that Poniatowska had added the legend to her novel, was discounted by the author.)[47]

After realizing that she had been liberated by a saint (more specifically, an incarnation of Christ), the prisoner's story continues, she struggled to save enough money to return home—a theme that recurs several times in Palancares' narrative—and, when she finally reached the isthmus, the first people she looked up were her former jailers, Evarista and Fortunata. The scene is described more like a reunion of former neighbors than of former antagonists. It seems clear that, in spite of their neglect of the prisoner and her profound loneliness, she felt that she belonged, in a perverse way, to the prison

community, a society of poor women that has reproduced, in micro-
cosm, the power structure of the larger society, yet with important
differences. As Foucault has pointed out, the prison is only one
manifestation of a structure that permeates contemporary society in
forms as diverse as the school, the factory, the hospital, and the bar-
racks (with all of which Palancares' life will intersect, except the
school). Given her radical solitude, then, why shouldn't the convict
feel nostalgia for the dark, hot cell where she had nevertheless eaten
well and where her existential fear had been mitigated by the company of a child who hung on her every word? And, in the anonymity
and alienation of the metropolis many years later, devoid of kin like
the murderess, why wouldn't Jesusa Palancares remember her former cellmate on some level and fight her way back into jail time and
again, ready to resume telling her own tale to her fellow prisoners—
of the penal system and of female poverty—as well as to that emis-
sary from privileged society who must have seemed like Jesusa's
own Niño de Atocha, Elena Poniatowska?

The Appropriation of Patriarchal Power through Religion

The sort of thinking that Palancares applies to justify child abuse—
the theory that severe punishment and atonement purify sinners,
saving them from future sins—is reinforced by the teachings of the
Spiritist Church, "la Obra Espiritual" ("Spiritual Work"). For example, when Jesusa felt betrayed by the one man (besides her father)
that she ever loved, Antonio Pérez, and he subsequently developed
an advanced case of syphilis, she interpreted this as an instance of
divine retribution. Just as, during the Revolution, a *curandero* had
elicited Jesusa's advice in deciding whether and how Pedro should be
cured from witchcraft, her spiritual guide involved her in deciding
the extent of punishment that Antonio would receive for his mis-
behavior; she was able to negotiate, in several stages, a progressively
briefer period of suffering for her errant lover. It is significant, however, that she did not argue that God spare Pérez altogether and that
she apparently derived a certain voyeuristic pleasure, mixed with
pity, from observing his difficulty in walking and from imagining
the painful deterioration of his penis or "animal." What's more, Palancares says that she had suspected from the beginning that the
other woman had syphilis, the devastating effects of which she had
had ample opportunity to observe in her work at a women's hospital.
(Characteristically, she had reserved her compassion for the men
with whom the female patients came into contact; in this situation,
as others, she followed the fundamentalist Christian dogma that

woman is the perpetrator, and man the victim, of sin.) Nevertheless, she didn't attempt to warn Antonio that he would be exposing himself to a serious disease. She explains her failure to intervene with the conviction that he wouldn't have believed her, that he would have attributed her warning to jealousy. While, on the one hand, this perception bespeaks a knowledge of human psychology, it is also consistent with her pessimism regarding the human capacity to effect positive change. When Antonio miraculously recovered from the illness, with no apparent medical intervention, her faith was reaffirmed; God had punished him for his callousness toward Jesusa and had at the same time demonstrated mercy toward both Antonio and her by not taking him from this world, and her company, altogether. When Palancares describes later coming down with an advanced case of syphilis herself, she expresses (feigns?) surprise and innocence, offering neither a physiological nor a religious explanation. The attractiveness of Spiritism for Jesusa Palancares, then, lies in the illusion of supernatural control that it gives her. What she cannot accomplish directly can be achieved—and frequently with more dramatic effect—through her spiritual guides. The infliction of suffering on others provides perverse consolation for her own unhappiness. At the same time, with the manipulation of divine power comes a compensation for her own profound sense of powerlessness (a sense that is, of course, grounded in her severe social limitations as a poor, older woman).

Spiritism was introduced to the Latin American elites during the nineteenth century, eventually finding its way to the urban and rural lower classes, where it became syncretized with folk Catholicism. This occultic religion, which is based on the theories of Allan Kardec (a pen name for Leon Denizarth Hippolyte Rivail, France, 1804–1869), is similar in most respects to orthodox Christianity, particularly in its concept of the dual (material and spiritual) nature of humanity and in its ethical emphasis on good conduct as a basis for reward. The major difference lies in its belief in possession (in some cases, through mediums and assistant mediums, or *mediunidades*) as a means of communication between incarnate spirits and incorporeal beings. It differs from Spiritualism in subscribing to the idea of multiple incarnations. According to Alan Harwood, "the metaphysics of psychiatry . . . derives from Protestantism; the metaphysics of spiritism stems from folk-Catholicism. . . . Like Catholicism, it attributes ultimate responsibility to the powers of the supernatural world."[48] In his study of Spiritism among a Puerto Rican community in New York City, Harwood found that the spirit world is hierarchical in two senses. The moral hierarchy consists of five levels: untranquil spirits; the spirits of ordinary people; the spirits of respected leaders; the morally perfect spirits, such as saints, angels, and seraphim; and God. Moreover, there is an additional, vertical hierarchy within each level or cadre (*cuadro*) of spirits. A guardian angel is assigned to each embodied spirit at birth; he is assisted by incorporeal spirits of lower rank, called protectors and guides. According to the teachings of Kardec, "spirits pass through a series of reincarnations, each of which allows the spirit to enhance its moral purity by overcoming the suffering and ethical dilemmas entailed in life on earth. Life is thus seen as a test (*prueba*) of the spirit which, if passed satisfactorily, entitles it to ascend the celestial hierarchy. Failing the test entails no demotion in rank but may occasion a stiffer *prueba* in the next reincarnation."[49] This spiritual hierarchy, however, is complemented by a certain egalitarianism, since all spirits are believed to pass through all ranks. Thus, an incarnate spirit's situation on a particular moral (and material) plane in the hierarchy does not preclude his/her occupation of a superior plane in another incarnation. Hence Palancares' belief that she was a queen in an earlier life and that the poverty and suffering of this life are punishment for previous misconduct; hence also her implicit hope that her future incarnations may be happier.

In his study of the Puerto Rican Spiritist community, Harwood found a disproportionate number of women, particularly women over forty. He and other researchers have found that Spiritist and Spiritualist churches tend to appeal especially to individuals and communities that are undergoing periods of transition and social readjustment. The church provides a sense of community, in effect a therapy group, for isolated individuals and a means of reestablishing contact with deceased kin and thus symbolically transcending death. By providing concrete diagnoses of and cures for illnesses and social problems, Spiritism provides the believer with a sense of certainty and control in uncertain situations. The phenomenon of possession also constitutes an enhancement of status for people like Jesusa who otherwise have low social standing. At the same time, possession provides a context for acting out behavior that is unacceptable to society or the individual; in Palancares' case, it provides a locus of fantasy and erotic desire.

Moreover, Spiritism allows Palancares to depend emotionally on a new set of patriarchal figures, her protector (Manuel Antonio Mesmer, 1734–1815, the German physician who devised the theory of animal magnetism or mesmerism) and her guides, all of whom the religion posits as morally purer and therefore more authoritative and powerful than herself. Raymond Prince has explained how spiritualist religion operates as what he calls "primitive psychotherapy":

> [It] makes no attempt to provide the patient with insight into his own personality or to render him independent. On the contrary, the common technique is to place him within a cone of authority as it were—he is assigned to the care and control of a benevolent spirit. . . . In exchange for protection and succor, the patient must provide the spirit with food or other offerings, must behave in certain prescribed ways and follow certain taboos. There is an exchange of freedom for protection. . . . insight is the prerogative of the healer and not of the patient.[50]

Prince goes on to characterize the "cone of authority" (which brings to mind the pyramidal structure of Mexican society):

> Consider a cone of light at the vertex of which is an omniscient spirit who is the source of light. All men within the cone of light are healthy, fertile, and prosperous; in the darkness beyond men are dying, or sick and prey to all manner of anxieties. To enter the cone of light requires purification, and to remain requires obedience. Halfway to the base of the cone is the circle of healer-priests who because of their proximity can communicate directly with the spirit, but the common man who rests at the base of the cone can communicate only with the healer. Under special circumstances, the spirit may descend from the apex and mount or enter the healer and speak of spiritual things to the men below; or the spirit may mount the laity directly, generating within them and their companions-in-light salubrious actions.[51]

In his study of Pentecostal and other religious sects in predominantly Catholic Guatemala, Bryan Roberts has observed their important social function for low-income urban dwellers without kin in the city, especially women who were separated from their husbands or were wives of alcoholics.[52] In his estimation, Peter Fry has gone one step further in his analysis of Pentecostalism and Umbanda (an African-based variant of Spiritism) in urban Brazil by arguing that the function of such sects is not merely social but ideological as well; they provide "a framework for interpreting daily events in ways that are broadly congruent with an individual's social and economic position and prospects." As Roberts explains, Fry contrasts the Puritan ethic preached by the Pentecostals, and its consistency with the values of the Brazilian middle class and skilled working class, with the autocratic hierarchy of Umbanda, which tends to appeal to people from the small-scale sector of the economy:

> Umbanda is organized around cult centres which are controlled autocratically by cult leaders; it has an eclectic and variable cosmology in which both good and evil are necessary parts of ritual efficacy and by which individuals develop particularistic relations with their spirits. The devotees demand help against malevolent forces that have been inflicted on them undeservedly, such as ill-health, unemployment, frustrations in love or other basic problems of urban living. Umbanda, then, is organized by clientage and specializes in short-term ritual solutions to the difficulties and insecurities of life in the cities and rural areas.[53]

Fry goes on to argue that the authoritarianism and particularism of Umbanda constitute "the other face of industrial capitalism in underdeveloped countries"; this religion "is plausible because the particularistic relations which are established with the spirits in the hopes of the granting of favors are homologous with the real relationships established for the benefit of men in society." Even the language used by followers of Umbanda is borrowed from capitalist business relations.[54]

Alone in the city, without kin and abandoned by a succession of ungrateful adopted children and pets (except for Perico, who has finally returned but, she says, out of self-interest rather than love), betrayed by a series of "revolutionary" social institutions, old and confronted with a future of illness and death, Palancares turns to Spiritism for a sense of companionship, power, and hope. The promise of reincarnation offers a concrete reward for her good deeds that have gone unacknowledged: a new life, the chance to start again on more favorable terms. Moreover, her religion offers her the illusion of participating in divine retribution over those who have hurt or disappointed her and the fantasy of a rich erotic life: "Yo tengo tres [protectores] . . . al final de la curación, llega mi protector Luz de Oriente que es el más guapo de los tres. Pero yo los quiero igual a todos. Nomás que Luz de Oriente me mira con mucha hambre. Tiene hambrosía en los ojos a todas horas. Y me deja pensando" (I have three [protectors] . . . at the end of the cure, my protector Light of the East arrives, the handsomest of the three. But I love all three of them equally. He has hunger in his eyes at all hours. And he sets me to thinking) (14).

This erotic dimension of religion is not without ambiguity, even in Jesusa's imagination. In the opening dream sequence of the novel, the same handsome spirit turns into her abusive husband, Pedro, determined to exert the ultimate control by taking her with him into death: "Cuando yo la vea perdida, te mando a ti por delante y acabo contigo," Pedro had told her (When I see that all is lost, I'll send you ahead of me and finish you off) (11). In her dream, as in her waking life, Jesusa recognizes that it is her fear (and, implicitly, her own valor and assertiveness) that has saved her from both her worldly and her spiritual "protectors." Yet on other occasions, she relegates complete control to her spiritual guides: "Mi protector Mesmer . . . me tiene dominada ahora. Me levanta, me hinca, hace lo que quiere conmigo. . . . No me mando yo. Así es de que todo lo que el protector quiere, pues que lo haga en mi envoltura. Yo no puedo oponerme" (My protector Mesmer . . . has me dominated now. He lifts me up, makes me kneel, does with me what he likes. . . . I don't control myself. So whatever the protector wants, let him do it with my form. I can't oppose him) (302). When the Spiritist congregation begins to look down on and slight Jesusa, she develops the ability to communicate with Mesmer's spirit without the intervention of a medium; the circle closes, as she withdraws from the Spiritist community that had afforded her companionship, to possession in solitude. This allows her to reclaim the power that she had relinquished to the medium intermediaries, yet to continue attributing responsibility for her life to the spiritual realm, even as she derives a vicarious sense of control from it.

In this context of solitude, the conclusion of the novel synthesizes Palancares' peculiar mixture of feisty individualism and implicit neediness, as directed to the interviewer, whom she apparently resents for having succeeded (with her cooperation) in penetrating her intimacy. It also captures the pessimism and misanthropy which characterize Palancares' appraisal of human nature and interpersonal relations but which are contradicted by her continuing actions on behalf of others: "Yo no creo que la gente sea buena, la mera verdad, no. Sólo Jesucristo y no lo conocí. Y mi padre, que nunca supe si me quiso o no. Pero de aquí sobre la tierra, ¿quién quiere usted que sea bueno? Ahora ya no chingue. Váyase. Déjeme dormir" (I don't think people are good, to tell the truth, no. Only Jesus Christ, and I never met him. And my father, and I never knew if he loved me or not. But here on Earth, who can you expect to be good? Now stop bugging me. Go away. Let me sleep) (316). By ending the novel with this defiant statement of self-sufficiency, Poniatowska turns her subject's implicit accusation on the reader. One is left with a sense of guilt at having listened to Palancares' confession, at having thus intruded into a life of despair that has become less private in the telling; yet it has also become less anonymous and solitary. A statement of defiance and an implicit challenge, the ending in effect embraces the collectivity that Jesusa Palancares, like her real-life counterpart Josefina Bórquez, categorically rejected during the span of twentieth-century Mexican history that was her life.

The publication in the same year of both *La "Flor de Lis"* and *Nada, nadie: Las voces del temblor* demonstrates that Elena Poniatowska is continuing to mine both veins of her narrative trajectory: the lyrical/autobiographical and the documentary/biographical. Two current book projects extend her commitment to popularizing the life stories of exemplary individuals (perhaps following in the Catholic hagiographic tradition that she learned at the Convent of the Holy Cross near Philadelphia). In this case her subjects are Tina Modotti, the Italian-American photographer and activist who served in the Spanish Civil War and adopted Mexico as her home; and Demetrio Vallejo, leader of the railroad workers' movement and a political prisoner for over a decade. Thus, Poniatowska continues to explore the development of political commitment in two types of activists that have long fascinated her: the woman artist and the working-class labor organizer.

In addition, she has moved increasingly away from her initial focus on male political and artistic leaders and toward questions of female subjectivity, from various class and ethnic perspectives.[55] In recent years Poniatowska has been an outspoken supporter of popular political and social movements, including the feminist wing of *cardenismo,* and the urban housing movement, led by Super Barrio Gómez; she also played a key role in organizing the female garment workers' union (el Sindicato 19 de septiembre), in collaboration with Evangelina Corona and other seamstresses, following the 1985 earthquake, in which so many sweatshop workers died. At the same time, she has written numerous essays and prologues for books by Mexican women photographers, who have become custodians of the documentary tradition initiated by Tina Modotti and who, like Poniatowska, tend to emphasize female subjects. These include Mariana Yampolsky, Graciela Iturbide, and the collective authors of *Compañeras de México: Women Photograph Women.*

In addition to the biographies of Modotti and Vallejo, Poniatowska is currently finishing a collection of essays about Mexican women entitled *Luz y luna, las lunitas (Moonlight, Starlight).* This book addresses such diverse groups as the conservative Catholic devotees of Tlaxcala, who weave carpets of flowers and dress the statue of the

Virgin for religious holidays; and the economically and sexually independent Zapotec women of the combative village of Juchitán, on the Isthmus of Tehuantepec. The former are not so distant from the author's pious upbringing and, possibly, from a certain continuing attraction to a nonreligious spirituality. The latter embody her aspirations for female autonomy and assertiveness, in the political, economic, interpersonal, sexual, and creative spheres, within the panoply of cultures still coexisting in the homeland she has adopted with such passion.

Elena Poniatowska. Photograph © 1991 by Nancy Crampton.

3. The Novel as Pyramid: *Palinuro de México* (1977), by Fernando del Paso

Sus novelas son obras compulsivas que resumen en alardes nemónicos caudales torrenciales de datos e ideas para redundar en una visión monumental.

(His novels are compulsive works that summarize, in mnemonic fireworks, torrential outpourings of facts and ideas, resulting in a monumental vision.)

—FELIPE EHRENBERG ON FERNANDO DEL PASO

COLOMBINA SACA OTRO CARTEL (con letras Futura Bold mayúsculas): "¡Abajo el PRI monolítico, abajo el poder piramidal!"

(COLOMBINE TAKES OUT ANOTHER POSTER (with Futura Bold capital letters): "Down with the monolithic PRI, down with pyramidal power!")

—FERNANDO DEL PASO, *PALINURO DE MÉXICO*

Fernando del Paso (b. 1935) is currently Mexico's most prominent exemplar of the Latin American tradition of combining a literary vocation with a diplomatic career. (Renowned Mexican authors who combined these professions during the 1960s and 1970s include Rosario Castellanos, Octavio Paz, and Carlos Fuentes.) Del Paso had studied medicine in Mexico during the 1950s. Later, he lived in London for fourteen years and worked first in advertising, then as a broadcaster for the BBC and Radio Francia Internacional. In 1986 he was named cultural attaché to France, where he presently serves as Mexico's consul general.

Del Paso's first novel, *José Trigo* (1966), earned him a certain degree of respect among Mexican critics, albeit not universal; and his second, *Palinuro de México* (*Palinurus of Mexico*, 1977), brought

Fernando del Paso. Photograph courtesy of Editorial Diana.

him international recognition and two major literary prizes, the Premio de Novela México and the Premio Rómulo Gallegos in Venezuela. It established him solidly as a writer's or a critic's writer, the highly intellectual architect of monumental, complex, and difficult novels. However, with the publication of *Noticias del imperio* (*News of the Empire*, 1987), del Paso crossed over to a broader reading public and has enjoyed even greater critical acclaim; his work has been compared favorably to that of Carlos Fuentes and he has even been mentioned, along with Fuentes and Octavio Paz, as a possible candidate for the Nobel Prize. (The possibilities of this happening are, of course, significantly diminished since Paz won the 1990 prize.) The reasons for this change in the reception of del Paso's works are not altogether clear, since this third book is not a more significant novel then *Palinuro*. Nevertheless, it is somewhat more "readerly" in its proliferation of absurd and amusing stories-within-stories and its constant allusions to Mexican history, rather than to other literary texts. Moreover, historical novels were enjoying a newfound popularity during the 1980s, and the climate was ripe for a sweeping saga based on that curious episode in Mexican history, the French intervention. Finally, the author's prominent diplomatic role cannot be discounted as a factor in his newfound prestige as a writer as well as an artist. The point is not that his literary reputation is unwarranted but rather that it has been undeservedly delayed. At the same time, however, at present del Paso seems to be enjoying the sort of uncritical, universally enthusiastic reception that has been enjoyed at various points by Rulfo, Fuentes, and Paz.

More than any other author in this study, del Paso conceives his novels as monuments or edifices. His leading critic, Robbin William Fiddian, recently has referred to them as "monumentos barrocos o frisos de complicado relieve" (baroque monuments or friezes with complicado relief). Del Paso himself has acknowledged that he and Carlos Fuentes "tendemos a la epopeya, al gran fresco, al mural" (tend toward the epic, the great fresco, the mural).[1]

Del Paso's first novel, *José Trigo* (1966), takes as its subject Mexico City's urban working class and the railroad workers' strike of 1958–59. The protagonist, Luciano, is a fictional representation of the principal leader of that movement, Demetrio Vallejo, also the subject of one of Poniatowska's current book projects. Much of the action of *José Trigo* is set in the Nonoalco-Tlatelolco neighborhood, where the student massacre of 1968 was to occur.

Several critics have noted that this novel has the structure of a pyramid. Its two sections consist of nine chapters each, the first having an ascending movement and the second descending. The sections are divided by a segment entitled "El puente" (The Bridge), so the effect on the reader is of climbing up the narrative pyramid, resting on the platform, and climbing back down. This analogy is reinforced by the extensive use of Aztec mythology in the novel, most obviously in "El puente," which is written in the form of a Náhuatl chronicle and compares the protagonist, Buenaventura, to Nanantzin or Nonocihuatzin.[2] As noted earlier, José Emilio Pacheco has taken this metaphor one step further in referring to all of del Paso's works as pyramids, novels conceived as monuments.

The human body, rather than a building in the strict sense, is the organizing principle of his second novel, *Palinuro de México*. However, important secondary images include the family home, a Porfirian mansion converted into a boardinghouse after the Revolution; and the Colonial apartment building across from the Plaza de Santo Domingo in which the protagonists, Palinuro and Estefanía, live. The stairway of this building is the setting for Palinuro's absurd death in the climactic chapter, after he has been shot accidentally by the Mexican army bent on repressing the student movement. Both buildings embody Paradise Lost, unproblematic earlier phases in the development of the individual (the childhood and adolescence of the somewhat autobiographical protagonist, Palinuro) and his society (*cardenismo* in the 1930s and the "Modernization" of the 1950s). In each case the beauty and elegance of prerevolutionary societies has been preserved in a less elitist, postrevolutionary context, which contrasts with the unspoken present of urban decay.

Chapultepec Castle is the center of del Paso's third monumental novel, *Noticias del imperio* (*News of the Empire,* 1987). The author also drew a series of sketches entitled "Castles in the Air" in 1980, when he was beginning work on this novel about the French intervention, which briefly succeeded in installing the Hapsburg monarchy of Maximilian and Carlota in Mexico (1864 to 1867). These ephemeral emperors built the castle for their residence at the site of Moctezuma's summer palace in Chapultepec Park.

The complexity, fragmentary structure, and sheer size of Fernando del Paso's novels, which were written at ten-year intervals and range from 536 to 668 pages in length, present the critic with a formidable task. In their aspiration to be "total novels," these works are comparable to Carlos Fuentes' *Terra nostra* and *Cristóbal nonato* (*Christopher Unborn,* 1986), as well as, to a certain extent, to Jorge Aguilar Mora's two novels, *Cadáver lleno de mundo* (*Cadaver Full of the World,* 1971) and *Si muero lejos de ti* (*If I Die Far from You,* 1979). The title of the final chapter of *Palinuro* makes its all-encompassing design explicit: "All the Roses, All the Animals, All the Plazas, All the Planets, All the Characters in the World."

Del Paso's closest literary model is Joyce, although he draws extensively on the French and Spanish and, especially, the English literary traditions. His novels are cerebral, self-conscious, and playful, indulging—sometimes to excess[3]—in linguistic games and minute listings of objects and attributes, which are intended to communicate the infinite variety of human experience. These lists often bring to mind ceremonial rituals or sequences, solemn processions that take on a darkly comical aspect when viewed through a distorting lens.

In *Palinuro de México* these lists focus on the human body in all its forms and mutations: the body as love object and source of pleasure, as medical cadaver and irreverent source of knowledge, as corpse and symbol of social martyrdom and rebirth. Reproduction, birth, physiological functions, disease, death, resurrection: All these material manifestations of life are explored obsessively. The body as at once miraculously complex and alarmingly fragile, as intricately interrelated with all other objects in the universe. The hidden beauty of putrefaction: the rainbow of colors created by farts, watermelons that grow out of dung. Excrement as our daily bread (decay as a wellspring of renewal), the prostitute's cadaver that transforms into the body of the loved one (pollution and death as a source of purification and resurrection). The death of a person as the death of an individual, while rebirth entails the renovation of the universe.

The other obsession, here as in all of del Paso's work, is language as a vehicle of celebration and of parody. Among the discourses that the novel lampoons are those of commercial advertising, pornography, romantic discourse, and psychoanalysis. Within the narrative tradition, it at once pays homage to and gently mimics *Tristram Shandy, Gulliver's Travels, Alice in Wonderland,* and the Mexican novel of the Revolution. Del Paso, like Fuentes, works within a high modernist framework, particularly the British-U.S. tradition. In 1981, when asked about the novelists that have most influenced his writing, he cited William Faulkner, James Joyce, Joseph Conrad, Erskine Caldwell, Thomas Wolfe, and Virginia Woolf; the dramatists he most admired were William Saroyan, Arthur Miller, Elmer Rice, and Tennessee Williams.[4] In a 1980 interview with Jorge Ruffinelli, he explained that prior to the publication of *José Trigo* he had been influenced almost exclusively by English-language literature; however, while writing *Palinuro,* he also studied French and Spanish authors. (He read both English- and French-language texts in Spanish translation.) Del Paso situated himself among the "boom" generation in Latin America, particularly Ernesto Sábato, José Lezama Lima, Julio Cortázar, Mario Vargas Llosa, and Gabriel García Márquez.[5]

The Palinuro of del Paso's second novel is a Mexican medical student (who, also like the author, works in advertising for a time). His name alludes to the essay "Who Was Palinurus?" in Cyril Connolly's *The Unquiet Grave* (1945):

> allí conocí por primera vez el mito de Palinuro, el piloto de la nave de Eneas. Aunque yo había leído antes *La Eneida,* realmente no me había fijado en Palinuro. Palinuro se queda dormido al timón de la nave, cae al mar, dormido lo arrastran las aguas hasta el Cabo Espartivento o Cabo Palinuro, como se llama hasta la fecha, y ahí los habitantes, por un motivo baladí, por robarle las ropas, lo matan. A través de Cyril Connolly aprendí que el mito de Palinuro era el símbolo del hombre—en el caso de mi novela, de un muchacho—que se deja arrastrar por sus sueños, y a causa de ellos muere.[6]

(There I found out, for the first time, about the myth of Palinurus, the pilot of Aeneas' ship. Although I had read *The Aeneid* before, I had never really noticed Palinurus. Palinurus falls asleep at the wheel of the ship, falls into the sea, the water carries him, sleeping, up to Cape Espartivento or Cape Palinurus, as it's called to this day, and there the inhabitants, for a petty reason, in order to steal his clothes, kill him. Through Cyril Connolly I learned that the myth of Palinurus was the symbol of the man—in the case of my novel, of a boy—who lets himself be swept away by his dreams, and because of them he dies.)

Del Paso's novel is narrated in first person, alternately by Palinuro and his alter ego, *yo*. The protagonist's family history, as related to him by his grandfather, intersects with World War I and the Mexican Revolution; and his life history coincides with the Vietnam War and the student movement, in which he is involved just long enough to be killed by the Mexican army. The other main narrative line centers on Palinuro's relationship with his cousin/lover, a nurse named Estefanía. The novel seems to address a dual purpose: to recreate certain episodes and stories from the author's life (including his family history, medical studies, forays into the art world and advertising, and residence in London) and to interpret the significance of a key year in that life, 1968, for the nation as a whole. In what follows I will examine the presentation of the student movement and the Revolution in this novel, as well as three incidents from del Paso's third book, *Noticias del imperio*, which shed light on certain key concepts portrayed in the earlier novel.

Tlatelolco, Stairway to the Pyramid: The Student Movement as Tragic Farce

The vast majority of novels and short stories that interpret the student movement of 1968, many of which focus on the massacre at Tlatelolco, are realist. The danger in naturalistically representing events that are so highly charged, both politically and emotionally, is that the text may lapse into melodrama or into an oversimplified portrayal of heroes and villains. Fernando del Paso attempted to avoid these pitfalls by writing the penultimate chapter of *Palinuro de México*, entitled "Palinuro en la escalera" ("Palinuro on the Stairs"), in the style of the commedia dell'arte, the Italian popular theater form which developed during the Renaissance and which featured stock characters and improvisation from a plot outline. In a personal interview in 1981, the author explained his selection of this genre for narrating the climactic events of the novel:

El movimiento estudiantil en sí tuvo mucho de farsa. Pero no fueron los estudiantes los farsantes, sino numerosos grupos polí-

ticos, así como individuos, que trataron a toda costa, desespera-
damente, de capitalizar el movimiento. La farsa, la ironía, la
paradoja, se dieron también en las propias matanzas: los sol-
dados, que en el caso de México como en el de la mayoría de
los países latinoamericanos proceden de las clases bajas, son el
pueblo, se enfrentaron a estudiantes pequeñoburgueses que
trataban de reivindicar a ese pueblo, de combatir el hambre, la
injusticia social. La confusión y el pánico que rodearon ese frus-
trado intento de revolución que desembocó en la nada, le agre-
garon un tono melodramático y tragicómico a la situación. La
farsa, pues, era el único camino que yo podía tomar.

(The student movement itself had a great deal of farce about it.
But it wasn't the students that were the farceurs but rather many
political groups, as well as individuals, who tried in every way
possible, desperately, to capitalize on the movement. Farce,
irony, paradox also occurred in the massacres themselves: The
soldiers, who in the case of Mexico, as in most Latin American
countries, come from the lower classes—they are the people—
confronted petit bourgeois students who were trying to vindicate
that people, to combat hunger, social injustice. The confusion
and panic that surrounded that frustrated attempt at revolution
which led to nothing added a melodramatic and tragicomic tone
to the situation. Farce, then, was the only road that I could take.)

The author has acknowledged that in writing "Palinuro en la escalera," along with numerous other passages of the novel, he was
greatly influenced by surrealist literature and painting.[7] He cites
Elena Poniatowska's *La noche de Tlatelolco* as the book that most
influenced his understanding of the movement. Although he was
still living in Mexico City in 1968 (he left the country on October 3,
1969), he characterizes himself as an observer, rather than a participant, in the student movement.[8] Nevertheless, it was a pivotal event
in his life, as it was in the lives of many Mexicans:

El conflicto estudiantil en México a mí me conmovió de una
manera profunda, como jamás pensé que lo iba a hacer. De alguna manera yo cambié y fui otro a partir de ese conflicto, y
sobre todo cuando dejé México, un año después, y empecé a con-
templarlo en perspectiva. Nunca pensé que la novela iba a tratar
sobre ese asunto; yo pensaba escribir algo sobre el 68 pero no
en esa novela, y de pronto también ese asunto se apoderó de la
novela: desde el punto de vista del volumen no ocupa mucho

espacio, ya que la novela trata de muchas cosas, pero es sin embargo el asunto más importante y el clímax de *Palinuro.*[9]

(The Mexican student conflict moved me profoundly, as I never thought it would. Somehow I changed and was a different person after that conflict, and above all when I left Mexico, a year later, and began to contemplate it in perspective. I never thought that the novel was going to address that issue; I planned to write something about '68 but not in that novel, and suddenly that issue also took control of the novel. In terms of volume it doesn't take up much space, since the novel deals with many things, but even so, it is the most important issue and the climax of *Palinuro.*)

The chapter in question is set on the stairway to the apartment building where the protagonist lives with Estefanía. Palinuro, who was not active in the student movement, found himself caught up in the enthusiasm and joined the 400,000 people who marched on the *zócalo* on August 27. While the demonstrators "desecrated" this ultimate public space with their presence, two medical students rang the bells of the cathedral. After the demonstration, 3,000 students decided to pitch tents and spend the night on the *zócalo*, symbolically retaining the territory to which they had won access, but they were forcibly removed by soldiers with tanks. This was a turning point in the movement, since in the past only the police and riot police, or *granaderos*, had repressed demonstrators; now it became clear that the president was prepared to send the army out against Mexico's civilian population. In "Palinuro en la escalera," the protagonist has been wounded on the *zócalo* (he has been stabbed by a bayonet and dragged three meters by a tank), but there is an overlapping of time frames, so that the massacre at Tlatelolco has also occurred as well.

The stage directions define the play as an edifice: "Obra en cuatro pisos con un prólogo en la planta baja, un epílogo en un desván y varios intermedios sorpresivos" (Work in four stories, with a prologue on the ground floor, an epilogue in a loft, and several surprising intermissions).[10] There are two levels of action in the play: on the second level is "reality," which occurs in both time and space, although, in a playful strategy typical of del Paso's work, the narrator gives the date (Wednesday, August 28) but raises some (spurious) doubt as to the year ("Let's say . . . 1968"). This level is portrayed by Palinuro, his friends (Estefanía and his alter ego, *yo*), and his neighbors (the bureaucrat, the concierge, the drunk doctor, the mailman, and the policeman).

On the first level of the stage is "fantasy," which exists outside of time and is portrayed by the characters from the commedia dell'arte: Arlequín, Scaramouche, Pierrot, Colombina, Pantalone, Tartaglia, El Dottore, and El Capitano Maldito. These characters act out, in parodic form, the events of the student movement, not strictly in chronological order: the fight between high school gangs that was met with police violence, instigating the movement; the march of August 27; the general university strike; the army's tearing down the colonial door of San Ildefonso High School with a bazooka; the Silent Demonstration; the military occupation of the National University, followed by the rector's resignation; and the protest by government employees on the *zócalo*. Moreover, these characters, true to their comedy role, mimic the actions of the "real" characters. In fact, some of them are only slightly exaggerated versions of these characters, especially El Dottore and El Capitano Maldito, who correspond closely to the doctor and the policeman in Palinuro's apartment building. To a certain extent, Colombina is Estefanía, and Arlequín and Pierrot are Palinuro and his double, *yo*. While the commedia characters' buffoonery expresses irreverence toward both the government and the students, it is clear that they empathize with the latter. According to del Paso, he found them "muy adecuados para encarnar la picardía y el humor negro mexicanos, soeces y alambicados, ingeniosos, llenos de alusiones sexuales, albureros" (very appropriate for embodying Mexican picaresque and black humor, crude and pedantic, ingenious, full of sexual allusions, double entendres). At the same time, del Paso points out the paradox that, for all their bizarre behavior, these characters "turned out to be much more understandable" than the politicians and bureaucrats on the plane of "reality."[11] Their antics on the first level of the stage are especially grotesque when juxtaposed with the tragic events on this second level. By the time the play (and Palinuro) reaches the fourth floor, reality and fantasy will be confused, never to be the same again (681).

Throughout the play Palinuro, gravely wounded and bleeding profusely, laboriously drags himself up several flights of stairs toward his apartment on the Plaza Santo Domingo, while *yo*, Estefanía, and several neighbors look on and discuss his condition, the student movement, and various banal topics. Estefanía cries and brings bandages for the Doctor to apply to Palinuro's wounds, while *yo* is alarmed and offers to help him up the stairs, to no avail, and the neighbors adopt attitudes ranging from flippancy to mild concern. One of them assumes that Palinuro is drunk and makes him coffee;

another brings him food; another attempts to call the police when he finds out that the wounded man is a student.

In addition to the traditional commedia characters, del Paso has added another, quintessentially Mexican, character to the "fantasy" level of the play: La Muerte, who adopts twenty-four different disguises, including those of Death-the-Ragwoman (who sells dead students' shoes and clothing), Death-the-President (who, like Gustavo Díaz Ordaz, pompously assumes sole responsibility for the massacre), Death-the-Announcer (who prattles on to television viewers about the "Olympic" competitions between students and riot police), Death-the-Ladder-Vendor (for those social climbers who might be amenable to selling out to the government), Death-the-Motherland (crying, like La Llorona, over her dead children), and Death-the-Author. In drawing on the traditional (and, by now, stereotypical) Mexican motif of laughing at death, this character underlines the black humor of the farce.

Although in the first five hundred pages of the novel there has been scant reference to Palinuro's political beliefs, and his involvement in the student movement lasted no more than a day, we are meant to understand that his participation in the August 27 march profoundly moved him, with its sense of collective commitment to the goals of political honesty, democracy, and social justice. Also, he has himself become one of the government's victims. We are therefore asked to suspend our disbelief when the more or less apolitical, and mortally wounded, Palinuro eloquently assumes the role of spokesperson for the movement. In the dialogue with his callous and apathetic neighbors, his is the voice of morality and outrage, punctuating the other characters' platitudes and chatter with ironic commentary. He serves as the author's spokesperson in explaining the meaning of Tlatelolco: "¡Se trata de no olvidar, eso es todo! . . . Nada tiene remedio ya. Lo único que queda es empeorar las cosas. Tratar de mejorar algo, o creer que se puede mejorar, es seguirle el juego a esos cabrones" (It's a matter of not forgetting, that's all! . . . There is no solution for anything now. The only thing left is to make things worse. To try to improve something, or to believe it can be improved, is to play those bastards' game) (638–639). This sentiment parallels del Paso's opinion, as expressed in a personal interview in 1981, that the student movement was "a useless sacrifice," a "turning point in which history failed to turn."[12]

This chapter produces an overall effect of estrangement (in the Brechtian sense) and invitation to intellectual reflection. At the same time the incongruence between theme and style provokes a series of strong emotions, of shock, disgust, and sardonic humor, but without sustaining any emotional involvement in the action or identification with the characters, with the exception of Palinuro. His character is responsible for the tragic and pathetic dimension in what is fundamentally a satirical farce.

In fact, for many readers the tragedy of Palinuro's death is probably heightened by his lack of involvement in the movement, by virtue of his being nearly—but not quite—an innocent bystander, like the passersby who were killed at Tlatelolco. Through this characterization of the victim, the author in effect depoliticizes the reader's outrage. It is easier to elicit sympathy for an accidental victim than for one whose actions have provoked a violent response, particularly since some readers may not agree with all of those actions. Moreover, it is problematic in this novel, as in most novels about 1968, that the characters become martyrs; their heroism derives partially from their defeat.

Contrary to what one might expect, as the chapter progresses and the tone changes from farce to tragedy, the dramatic interest declines. The scenes in which Palinuro and the other characters brave the tanks as bullfighters are less affecting than they might be. Perhaps this is partially because it is here that del Paso extols the students' heroism, conceived in traditional terms of male valor that seem anachronistic to readers at the beginning of the 1990s but which, as we shall see, have continued to underlie del Paso's later work. For instance, this is the effect of Palinuro's statement that "el coraje . . . nos salvó del deshonor" (courage saved us from dishonor) and of his reverent speech about the "death" of a Che Guevara poster (682–684). On the other hand, the moment of Palinuro's death is poignant; eight students wearing white mime's masks run across the stage carrying torches, chanting, "Every dead student is a live torch!"

"A Bullet Very Near the Heart": Masculinist Oral History of the Revolution

"Una bala muy cerca del corazón ("A Bullet Very Near the Heart"), chapter 21 of *Palinuro de México,* presents the reader with various stories within stories, like Chinese boxes. As the "Nota Final" to the novel explains, this chapter "fue inspirado por una narración del escritor y periodista norteamericano Ambrose Bierce y por lo que pudo haberle sucedido a este escritor en las últimas horas de su vida" (was inspired by a narration by the North American writer and journalist Ambrose Bierce and by what might have happened to this writer during the last hours of his life). Ambrose Bierce (1842–1914?) was, of course, the free-thinking seventy-one-year-old satirist who went off to northern Mexico to join Pancho Villa's revolutionaries in 1913 and mysteriously disappeared; one legend has it that he was executed by Villa's army. (Carlos Fuentes was to retell the story a decade later in *Gringo viejo* [*Old Gringo*, 1985].) In del Paso's novel, the old gringo has been arrested by Villa's forces for allegedly spying on behalf of Gen. Pascual Orozco and is awaiting execution. Villa wants to extract information from the prisoner before he is killed, and he repeatedly sends the captain on horseback to interrogate him. The captain has gone without sleep for several days and goes about the task with great reluctance.

The story of the old gringo is told to Palinuro by his grandfather, who in turn claims to have heard it from the captain, from whose point of view the story is told. However, several slips of the tongue, inadvertent shifts from the third to the first person, make it clear that Palinuro's grandfather, at age twenty, was himself the captain. Moreover, he claims to have told the same story to Pancho Villa; since Villa is himself a character in the tale, this raises doubts as to the story's veracity.

The entire plot of this chapter is structured around male storytelling, the passing on of a male tradition of honor and creativity from one generation to another. The captain serves as a reluctant messenger between two storytellers, Pancho Villa and the old gringo. Villa also wants the captain to serve as an interpreter, although he speaks no English—Villa *orders* him to speak English; but the gringo solves the problem by speaking to the captain in Spanish. There is also a metafictional anachronism when the grandfather tells Palinuro that, when the captain first met him, the old gringo was reading the same book that "you" (Palinuro/the reader) are reading now, that is, *Palinuro de México*.

On several occasions, the messenger is nearly killed for bearing unsatisfactory news, as in a Greek tragedy, but on each occasion Villa pardons him out of a sense of paternal indulgence. They have the same first name, and the captain reminds Villa of the son that he never had. The captain's information is inadequate because, in the first place, the old gringo is probably innocent and, in the second place, the two Mexican soldiers have different conceptions of what the role of messenger consists of. Villa expects the captain to act as his agent and the gringo's enemy, while the captain thinks his responsibility is to relay information in an accurate, neutral fashion; he simply repeats what he is told by each of the antagonists. In fact, just as Villa identifies with him, the captain identifies to some extent with the old gringo. He, too, is a sensitive sort, as we know when he pauses to pick flowers for his wife or keeps the horse from stepping on partridges. Also, the captain has literary aspirations and dutifully records the gringo's words of wisdom in a notebook, and he has dreams or hallucinations, brought on by lack of sleep, which are a source of strange lyricism and humor in the story. Finally, when he meets the gringo he has a bullet lodged in his leg from an earlier skirmish, and over the years it will travel through his body. By the time he tells Palinuro the story, he is more or less the same age as the gringo was when he was presumably executed, and he also has a bullet "very near the heart." Thus, the bullet serves as a metaphor for old age and impending death.

Within the story itself, the old gringo is intent on rewriting a tale of his own, about the execution of another prisoner of war, Parker Adderson. This is an allusion to Bierce's Civil War story "Parker Adderson, Philosopher," from *Tales of Soldiers and Civilians* (1891). The story is a meditation on the nature of death and the appropriate way for a man to face his own impending end. Adderson, who admits to being a spy for the Federal army, confronts the Confederate general, who wishes to extract information from him prior to ordering his execution. The prisoner replies to the general's questions with witty and sarcastic remarks that make light of his impending death, arguing that he cannot dread something of which he will not be conscious once it occurs. The general is shocked by the condemned man's flippant attitude and admonishes him, "Death is horrible!" to which Adderson replies, "You can hang me, general, but there your power of evil ends; you cannot condemn me to heaven."[13] He assumes that he will be executed by hanging at dawn, as is customary in such cases. However, when the general suddenly orders the captain to take the prisoner out immediately and shoot him, Adderson the "philosopher" is caught off guard and loses both his composure and his reason, attacking the general with a knife. In the ensuing struggle both the general and the captain are mortally wounded. However, the general manages to reiterate the execution order for the deranged Adderson before facing his own death with unexpected serenity. The two men's attitudes toward death are thus reversed when theory becomes lived experience.

In *Palinuro de México*, the old gringo tells the captain an abbreviated version of this story; in del Paso's version, Adderson "cried and screamed like a woman" and killed the captain who was to execute him. Actually, it is del Paso, not Bierce, who has linked gender to cowardice; the original story says that the prisoner "leaped upon the general with the fury of a madman" and later "cowered upon the ground, and uttered unintelligible remonstrances." Del Paso's captain is dismayed by both the condemned man's exhibition of cowardice and the other captain's fate. (Del Paso does not mention that, in the original story, the condemned man also caused the death of the general who had ordered his execution, who was in a position comparable to that of Villa.)

Although it gives a first impression of satirizing Mexican history in its unromantic presentation of the two revolutionary soldiers, it actually conforms to the stereotypes of Pancho Villa as an unfeeling, self-interested, if somewhat comical killer and of Ambrose Bierce as a romantic hero, the writer as idealist and martyr. Each of the three characters has a different goal. Villa wants the captain to extract information from the gringo and then to execute him; in a less immediate sense, the story implies that, far from being moved by revolutionary ideals, he craves wealth and power. Villa passes time counting his money, and when the captain asks him to pardon the gringo, he responds by asking, "What's in it for me?" A leitmotif of the tale is Villa's watchfulness; his eyes take in, first, all of Mexico, then, via a map of the world, all of Europe. The captain is an antihero, a more or less humane fellow who tries halfheartedly to save the gringo's life but who is comically subservient to Villa and basically just wants to get it over with and go to sleep. As for the old gringo, he wants to rewrite his short story before he dies, possibly in a symbolic effort to save his own life, or, as the captain thinks, to have his character face death in a more dignified manner, thus increasing the likelihood that the writer will follow suit. In suggesting that the ending be rewritten, perhaps del Paso had in mind changing it to conform with another of Bierce's Civil War stories, "The Story of a Conscience," in which the roles are reversed: The prisoner of war behaves in an honorable fashion, while the captain who orders his execution twice behaves in a cowardly manner. He twice fails to pardon the prisoner, when gratitude and generosity dictate that he do so, because he places self-protection and duty over ethics. In the end this captain commits suicide.

As in this story, in del Paso's novel it is the prisoner of war, the old gringo, who is the tragic hero of the tale. What matters at this point in his life is not whether he dies, since in any case he has reached the end of his natural life, but how. Legend has it that Bierce went to Mexico seeking a more heroic death than what awaited him by natural causes, that he intended to join the forces of Villa in order to die in battle, defending a heroic cause. However, Carey McWilliams, Bierce's biographer, argues persuasively that there is no evidence that the writer intended to fight and die in battle; he wanted to cover the Revolution as a reporter, then continue on to the west coast of Mexico and South America. "I can see what's doing; perhaps write a few articles about the situation," he had written his daughter.[14] Moreover, Bierce was very conscious of being an outsider and a representative of an imperialist (his term was "expansionist") nation; he had written a friend, "To be a Gringo in Mexico—Ah, that is euthanasia!" McWilliams convincingly argues that, in all likelihood, Bierce was shot during the fighting that took place between the armies of Villa and Carranza at Torreón, very soon after he presumably joined up with Villa, and that he, like the Mexican soldiers he accompanied, was buried in an unmarked grave.[15] Yet del Paso, Fuentes, and other male writers who have been fascinated by Bierce's life have preferred to appropriate the more heroic legend. For them Bierce is the writer as iconoclastic hero and martyr.

This preoccupation with an honorable death also recalls Borges' short story "The South," in which gauchos embody the atavism represented by Villa, the peasant revolutionary, in del Paso's novel, and which provides the occasion for middle-class heroism. In both cases what is sacrificed is the imagination; the atavism and the banality (the gauchos and the city, Villa and the captain) survive. To some extent the old gringo anticipates the embodiment of imagination by the mad Empress Carlota in *Noticias del imperio* (*News of the Empire*, 1987).

Thus, in *Palinuro*, Villa, as the incarnation of brute violence and ignorance, kills Bierce, who represents the imagination. The worst revolutionary elements triumph over its nobler elements. By the same token, the peasantry wrests the Revolution away from the middle class; but this triumph is only temporary, since it is the captain, rather than Villa or Bierce, who will survive to wield political power in postrevolutionary Mexico. As an allegory for the Revolution, the story suggests that it was neither the best nor the worst elements that won out, but rather the banality of mediocrity.

Much of the story, then, hinges on traditional conceptions of male camaraderie and imagination, and there is only a partial questioning of conventional notions of male valor. In *The Devil's Dictionary* Ambrose Bierce defined valor as "a soldierly compound of vanity, duty and the gambler's hope" and a coward as "one who in a perilous emergency thinks with his legs." As for death, it is "the golden goal / Attained and found to be a hole!" In his journalism, Bierce reflected, "I fancy patriotism . . . is a glittering virtue. . . . Nevertheless, if I were a woman, denied military glory, I should try to cultivate a preference for righteousness. If, being a woman, I had girls I should try to bring them up with a less lively admiration for man-killers." [16] Thus, for Bierce, "righteousness" or morality is a higher value than valor, which is governed by self-interest, just like cowardice, and which entails needless and senseless destruction. Death, even what is conventionally considered to be heroic death, is meaningless, allowing no sense of purpose or transcendence.

"Una bala muy cerca del corazón" only partially subscribes to this interpretation. The title of the chapter may be taken to suggest that danger, and the valor it elicits, are very near the center of Mexican (male) national character. Palinuro, the grandson to whom the captain tells the story, will soon be tested by a literal bullet near his heart, placed there by the very regime that his grandfather fought to install and then served for many years.

The Writer as Scavenger: Rewriting News of the Empire

In del Paso's works, the ultimate test of manhood is a wartime execution, as it was for Ambrose Bierce. This situation constitutes a reckoning with death when there is no possible self-defense or salvation. An examination of two other examples, both occurring in del Paso's third novel, *Noticias del imperio*, can shed some light on the author's conception of heroism and its relation to gender. The title of the segment "Con el corazón atravesado por una flecha" ("With an arrow through the heart") even recalls the image of the bullet very near the heart. Both stories center on bravery in the face of torture and/or death. In the segment from *Noticias*, there are four images of male valor associated with punctured hearts/flesh: a message from Juárez's forces written in code and hidden in a chunk of meat; a fabulous diamond that a French soldier sews into his calf in order to smuggle it out of Russia; the *exvotos* (votive offerings) that the French general uses to torture a Mexican prisoner of war in an unsuccessful attempt to obtain information about the above message, including an image of a heart with an arrow through it; and the execution of the prisoner by an Indian, who will literally shoot an arrow through his heart. Of course, the religious imagery and the idea of bravery before great suffering suggest the figure of Christ; at the beginning of the chapter, del Paso makes this connection even more obvious, referring to the prisoner's arms, which are tied behind him, as "crucified" and naming him with the initials of Jesus Christ: Juan Carbajal.

The sadistic General Du Pin continually links the prisoner's torture to gender issues. The theme of cross-dressing is introduced in the initial description of the general himself, who wears a floor-length mosquito net pinned to his hat, like a bridal veil. (Or a nun's veil? In view of what follows, he could be seen as the would-be bride of Carbajal/Christ.) He tries to tempt Carbajal into coming over to his side by describing the cross-dressing of the French soldiers under his command:

> Nos encontramos un cajón lleno de pelucas de mujer y a veces mis hombres se emborrachan y se las ponen y bailan en la noche con antorchas encendidas y se divierten mucho. Dime . . . ¿no te gustaría a ti ponerte una peluca colorada y bailar una habanera con uno de mis hombres? Uno de ellos es un holandés muy grandote que con un solo brazo te podría romper la cintura.[17]

> (We found a chest full of women's wigs and sometimes my men get drunk and put them on and dance at night with torches lit and have a really good time. Tell me . . . wouldn't you like to put on a red wig and dance an *habanera* with one of my men? One of them is a great big Dutchman who could break your waist with just one arm.)

In an earlier segment of the novel, "Camarón, camarón," a Mexican spy had introduced this image of the imperial forces as androgynous but valiant, claiming that the French officers do not care if their soldiers "aren't very macho when they love each other, as long as they are very macho when they hate us" (219).

At the same time, the chapter attributes exaggerated machismo to the French general. The interrogation opens with macho boasts, with Du Pin claiming to have a bigger hat and a bigger moustache than Carbajal. This leads to chauvinistic bragging about Paris and Napoleon, which finally tempts the prisoner into responding and serves as a pretext for beginning the torture. Du Pin claims the prisoner's Texan hat (a gift from General Santa Anna) as a "hunting trophy." This comment and his earlier bragging suggest that the men's hats are phallic symbols. Therefore, when the general proceeds to remove Texan stars and Mexican *exvotos* from Carbajal's hat in order to use them as weapons, it seems coherent with his sadism that he should choose the prisoner's breast, lip, penis, testicles, buttocks, and nipple as the sites of torture. When Carbajal stubbornly refuses to divulge information, the general taunts him by calling him "macho," a term Mexicans use for their mules. Eventually he is moved to admit that the prisoner is "a stupid ass, but . . . very much a man" (274).

French cross-dressing and machismo are combined with punishment of presumed homosexuality and other violations of gender divisions. Du Pin claims that he is having silver stars pinned to Carbajal's buttocks so the prisoner, who has screamed in pain, will "seem even more like a queer." At another point General Du Pin rhetorically asks Carbajal's advice about what he should do if he captures La Barragana, a famous woman guerrilla who fights with Júarez's forces: "Pero tengo entendido que es muy valiente y no más por eso no sé qué voy a hacer con ella si la agarramos viva: si cortarle los pechos para que parezca más hombre, ya que eso es lo que le gusta, vivir y pelear como hombre, o si perdonarla en memoria de nuestra Santa Juana de Arco . . . ¿tú qué opinas?" (But I understand she is very brave and, just because of that, I don't know what I'm going to do with her if we capture her alive: if I should cut off her breasts so she will look more like a man, since that's what she enjoys, living and fighting as a man, or if I should pardon her in memory of our Saint Joan of Arc . . . what do you think?) (273) This argument is in keeping with Catholic patriarchal ideology, in which a woman can assume an active role only if she is a nun/saint, in which case her asexuality makes the sexual mutilation that Du Pin describes, a symbolic sex-change operation, unnecessary.

Subsequent chapters, regarding the execution of Maximilian, postulate that the French emperor and empress became Mexicanized during their occupation of the country, so thoroughly Mexicanized that one of them went mad and the other died: "Esa muerte y esa locura, por magníficas, merecen algo más de México" (That death and that madness, because they were magnificent, deserve something more from Mexico) (642). Moreover, while the emperors were mistaken, their motives were sincere; they were moved by a misguided desire to help their adopted land. Therefore, the narrator argues, Maximilian deserved to have a "more poetic, imperial execution" and to be buried in Mexican soil: "integrado[s] a esta tierra fertilizada al parejo con los restos de todos nuestros héroes y todos nuestros traidores" (integrated into this land fertilized equally by the remains of all our heroes and all our traitors) (643–644). In spite of del Paso's desire (as expressed by Carlota in the novel and by the author in interviews) to portray the emperor as neither simply traitor and usurper nor simply hero and martyr, Maximilian is portrayed fundamentally as a tragic figure, a martyr. If Maximilian was denied a noble death, the author portrays it as heroic and quintessentially Mexican:

Y a favor de Maximiliano está su muerte, están las gotas de sangre que se mezclaron con la tierra del Cerro de las Campanas y están sus últimas palabras, su *¡Viva México!*: al enfrentarse a su fin como lo hizo, lo transformó en una muerte noble y oportuna,

en una muerte valiente y, en resumidas cuentas, en una muerte
muy mexicana. (642–643)

(And in Maximilian's favor are his death, the drops of blood that
mingled with the earth on the Hill of the Bells, and his last
words, his *Long live Mexico!*: In confronting his end as he did,
his was transformed into a noble and opportune death, into a
valiant death, and, in short, into a very Mexican death.)

As for Carlota, she went heroically mad; as a primary narrator of the
novel, she is imagination as "la loca de la casa" (the madwoman of
the house) (in the royal "attic" that was Miramar Castle, where she
was ensconced for sixty years). The royal couple deserves to be re-
membered, then, for what the novel portrays as extreme versions of
paradigmatically male and female behavior: heroism and madness.

The motif of the *exvoto* in the shape of a heart recurs in these
chapters. The heart belongs to the Mexican soldier who ended up
giving the emperor the *tiro de gracia* during his execution with a
shot to the heart. The soldier had the *exvoto* fashioned out of a gold
coin that Maximilian had paid him, along with the other members
of the firing squad, in exchange for not aiming at his face. The soldier kept his end of the bargain, deferring to the emperor's vanity.
Yet later, according to this chapter and the *corrido* on which it is
based, stricken with guilt over having killed a hero and martyr (for
folklore compared Maximilian to Christ), he turned the gun on himself (577–584). Thus, the *exvoto* had not fulfilled its traditional purpose of mending the executioner's (or the emperor's) broken heart.
This episode associates three levels of loyalty: religious, political,
and interpersonal (Catholicism, patriotism, and romance). The Mexican soldier's allegiance is ultimately not to Juárez and his fledgling
republic nor to a Mexican sweetheart or family but to the French
Empire as object of unrequited love.

"Camarón, camarón," the segment cited above with regard to
French bisexuality, is narrated by a Mexican spy who "lives more off
the dead than off the living," supporting himself as a scavenger and a
storyteller. His description of himself shooing away dogs and rats
that were feeding on cadavers strewn about the battlefield is quintessentially Biercean; in fact, Bierce's depiction of the senselessness
of war is exaggerated in del Paso's story-within-a-story, in which not
only are there no heroes but everyone is a scavenger. Having scared
off the animals, the spy proceeds to desecrate the bodies himself, for
profit. When he finds that the Mexican soldiers have beaten him to
it, he attempts to sell the rat pelts. The spy's theft and marketing of

the coins, jewelry, and body parts of dead French soldiers introduce the symbol of the wounded heart as icon and currency and foreshadow Maximilian's posthumous fate; following his execution, the mortician would cut up the emperor's heart, along with his hair and beard, and sell the pieces.

This imagery parallels del Paso's efforts to piece together the fragments in order to restore a complete image of the emperor whose story has polarized Mexican readers for over a century into monarchists versus democrats, Francophiles versus nationalists. In this sense he is participating in the rewriting of national history by novelists of the 1980s. Yet, in his attempt to present a balanced portrait of an emperor, he ends up seeming to defend the French Empire.

If the narrator of "Camarón, camarón" is a scavenger of scavengers, he is also a forger of forgeries. He steals a French officer's wooden hand (a writing instrument, rendered useless) in order to sell it, then sells copies of the artificial hand (itself a simulacrum of life and creativity), and finally sells stories of the copies. Like the old gringo in *Palinuro de México*, he claims that he does not need a pen and paper in order to write; like Bierce, he is the male oral historian as demystifier of war. Even as the old gringo is the author as martyr, the spy is the author as scavenger and counterfeiter. He deals in stories about the impossibility of male valor in the face of death, just as his creator, Fernando del Paso, trades in the genealogy of male heroism: in the wars of the French Intervention, in the Revolution, and during the student movement.

A Portrait of the Artist as an Artist

Since 1973 del Paso has supplemented his literary activities with sketching and, during the past few years, painting. His drawings are complex, whimsical, or ironic representations, many of which began as doodles. Some of the early ones depict baroque structures, but the vast majority are of fantastic creatures who defy traditional categorization: Many are half-human and half-monster or beast, while others are androgynous. For instance, there is a sketch entitled "Catdevil" and a series entitled "Castles in the Air" (from the period when he was writing about Carlota in Chapultepec Castle), "Transvestites," "Bestiary," "Inoffensive Monsters," and "Nameless Monsters." Renowned artist José Luis Cuevas recently has compared del Paso's sketches to those of Miró, Paul Klee, and Roberto Matta. In the catalog from the novelist's second Mexican exhibition (1990), Cuevas muses on the relation between del Paso's literature and his art:

¿Existe alguna relación entre lo que escribe un escritor con lo que dibuja? En algunos casos sí. Pienso en Victor Hugo, William Blake y en Franz Kafka. En el caso de Fernando del Paso, hay dos formas de expresión nada emparentadas. Fernando del Paso está habitado por un pintor y un escritor que no se parecen entre sí. Quizá alguien pudiera refutarme, diciendo que hay algo que los une: el barroquismo. Pero aun así son dos barrocos distintos. Diría yo que el Del Paso escritor es diurno y el Del Paso pintor es nocturno. Me explico: el segundo pinta sus fantasmas que pueblan sus sueños. Las pesadillas que lo inquietan. El primero trabaja lo que el día, la luz, el sol, le permite recrear.[18]

(Is there any relationship between what a writer writes and what he draws? In some cases there is. I'm thinking of Victor Hugo, William Blake, and of Franz Kafka. In the case of Fernando del Paso, there are two forms of expression that bear no relation to each other. Fernando del Paso is inhabited by a painter and a writer who are nothing alike. Perhaps someone could refute me, saying there is something that unites them: their baroque character. But even so, they are two different baroques. I would say that del Paso the writer is diurnal and del Paso the painter is nocturnal. Let me explain: The latter paints the ghosts that inhabit his dreams. The nightmares that disturb him. The former works with what daytime, light, the sun allow him to recreate.)

Another well-known Mexican artist, Felipe Ehrenberg, describes this same tension as follows: "Sus novelas son obras compulsivas que resumen en alardes nemónicos caudales torrenciales de datos e ideas para redundar en una visión monumental. Sus dibujos en cambio surgen de lo impensado y son construidos hasta llenar la hoja con base en más y más irreflexiones espontáneas" (His novels are compulsive works that summarize, in mnemonic fireworks, torrential outpourings of facts and ideas, resulting in a monumental vision. His drawings, on the other hand, spring from the irrational and are built up until they fill the page, based on more and more spontaneous impulses).[19]

Interestingly, neither artist comments on del Paso's most recent series of paintings, a major focus of his 1990 exhibition in Mexico: his homage to the revered patriarch of Mexican painting, Rufino Tamayo. Del Paso mimics the vivid colors from Mexican folk culture and certain key themes associated with Tamayo's painting (watermelons, a smiling man drawn in "primitive" style). While the primary effect is one of respect and affection, the series has a parodic dimension, a sense of poking fun at an acknowledged master, of taunting a sacred cow. In this respect, the series recalls "Lo que el viento a Juárez" ("How the Wind Affected Juárez"), Francisco Toledo's brilliant ironic homage to another "untouchable" Oaxacan forefather, Benito Juárez (see chapter 6); however, Toledo's series is significantly better and therefore more successful in its demystifying project. As in his novels, Fernando del Paso the painter cannot resist undermining national monuments, even as he attempts to construct his own pyramids with stones from the ruins. However, as both Cuevas and Ehrenberg imply, it is del Paso's verbal edifices, rather than his pictorial ones, that constitute his legacy to Mexican culture.

4. Commodification and Desire in the Wasteland: *Las batallas en el desierto* (1981), by José Emilio Pacheco

México subterráneo . . . El poderoso virrey emperador sátrapa hizo construir para sí todo el desierto. Hemos creado el desierto . . .

(Subterranean Mexico . . . The powerful viceroy emperor satrap had the whole desert constructed for himself. We have created the desert . . .)

—JOSÉ EMILIO PACHECO, EL REPOSO DEL FUEGO (1966/1980)

José Emilio Pacheco (b. 1939) is perhaps the most versatile contemporary writer in Mexico, working as he does in every literary genre except theater. He is the major poet of his generation, as well as a leading novelist, short-story writer, and literary historian. Rather than aspiring to the hyperbolic "total novel" of Fernando del Paso or Carlos Fuentes, Pacheco works toward precision, conciseness, the elimination of excess, and understatement. Pacheco tends toward the neoclassical, with shades of the postmodern, rather than the baroque; his creations are dressed fleas or miniature portraits, rather than pyramids or murals.[1]

Pacheco is an extraordinarily erudite writer in the tradition of Alfonso Reyes. A perfectionist, he is continually revising even his published work, since his basic ontological position is the democratic, anti-elitist one that a literary piece never ceases to be a work in progress and that its author is inevitably collective, consisting of the writer and all of her/his readers. This has led Pacheco to invent heteronyms or apocryphal poetic masks (Julián Hernández and Fernando Tejada) and to include, along with original poems, translations or "versions" of works by poets from the United States, Europe, and Asia. In his newspaper and magazine columns over the years, it has led him to leave articles of criticism anonymous or to sign only his

José Emilio Pacheco. Photograph © 1991 by Nancy Crampton.

initials. (Paradoxically, the initials JEP have become an immediately recognizable substitute for his name by now, a sort of trademark.)

At the very foundation of Pacheco's poetics is this assumption of humility and anonymity, this affinity for merging with the collective, conceived in terms of civil society, embracing all social classes. His poetry departs from the primary referent, Mexico City, to encompass humanity, all of his contemporaries, those citizens of a murderous century that is now drawing to an apocalyptic close in "Los vigesémicos" ("Twentieth Centurians"). Beginning with *No me preguntes cómo pasa el tiempo* (*Don't Ask Me How the Time Goes By*, 1969), Pacheco has been at the forefront of Latin American "conversational poetry," along with Ernesto Cardenal, Nicanor Parra, and Antonio Cisneros. His poetic skills, which were already considerable in his first book of verse, *Los elementos de la noche* (*The Elements of the Night*, 1963), have matured steadily, culminating in the recent *Ciudad de la memoria* (*City of Memory*, 1989). Here, as in *Miro la tierra* (*I Watch the Earth*, 1986), regarding the 1985 earthquake, Pacheco adopts the Nerudian role of civic poet, of witness and critic of his epoch, of conscience for a society that has strayed far from the biblical city on the hill.

His narrative trajectory is as diverse as his overall literary production. Pacheco's first novel, *Morirás lejos* (*You Will Die Far Away*, 1967), was an experimental, metafictional meditation on the persecution of Jews throughout history, culminating, of course, in the Holocaust. His second novel, *El principio del placer* (*The Pleasure Principle*, 1972), has generally been considered a short story, since it was published in a collection together with several stories. However, its length and structure, as well as its underlying problematics, are very similar to those of *Las batallas en el desierto* (*Battles in the Desert*, 1981), which was published alone and is generally regarded as a short novel. Unlike *Morirás lejos*, both of these works are *Bildungsromane*, novels in the classic realist tradition narrating the coming of age of the protagonist and his generation in the context of an increasingly alienated society. Pacheco's short stories tend to fall into two categories as well: on the one hand, sober realist meditations on childhood as a training ground for alienation and corruption; and, on the other, fantastic stories commenting on the repetition of human suffering, largely due to destructive patterns of behavior (violence, tyranny, exploitation), throughout history. Both narrative modes utilize irony to achieve this social critique. Above all Pacheco is a writer concerned with the ethical dimension of human conduct and the striving for goodness in a society and a world that increasingly undermine morality.

The *Bildungsroman* of *Alemanismo*

More than any Mexican work of the two decades following the crisis of hegemony in 1968, Pacheco's novella *Las batallas en el desierto* conforms to Bakhtin's definition of the ideal *Bildungsroman*, in which the protagonist's "individual emergence is inseparably linked to historical emergence."[2] If at first glance Pacheco's work may be read as a story of first love and loss, a realist tale of coming-of-age, only a superficial reading would reduce it to this. Rather, the novel's success with Mexican readers and critics is largely due to its narrative sophistication on at least two levels that appeal to the post-1968 middle-class intelligentsia. On the one hand, it provides a revisionist account of an earlier juncture in contemporary Mexican history that helps to explain the current crisis of the economic and political system; on the other, it is permeated by a sense of tremendous collective loss that transcends the individual and psychological dimension. This loss is partially conveyed through Catholic imagery, which conveys an apocalyptic view of history. As we shall see, this attitude is consistent with the position that was formulated in Pacheco's early poetry, especially *El reposo del fuego* (1966, revised in 1980), and which has recently been restated in slightly modified terms in *Miro la tierra*.

Class Wars in the Wasteland

Because the plot of Pacheco's novella is essential in communicating his view of history, it will be useful to summarize briefly the story before proceeding with the analysis. The novel is narrated by the protagonist, Carlitos, some thirty years after the events that he is narrating have transpired. When it begins (in 1948, as we eventually surmise), Carlitos' family has recently moved from Guadalajara to Mexico City, where his father has bought a soap factory. While Carlitos' mother is the declassé heir of a conservative aristocratic family that lost its landholdings during the Revolution, his father is an "American success story," the son of a tailor who got a university education and, following several disastrous financial ventures, invested his in-laws' money in the factory. When U.S. multinational corporations invade the market, he is saved from ruin by selling out to them and becoming their employee. Subsequently, the factory prospers and the family becomes part of the new industrial bourgeoisie which looks to the United States for tastes and values. As the socioeconomic gap between the bourgeoisie and the lower classes widens under the developmentalist policies of Miguel Alemán (which will be followed in essence by future presidents), Carlitos' family becomes increasingly alienated from their fellow Mexicans.

Meanwhile, in the interpersonal sphere, before his family's change of fortune, the preadolescent Carlitos falls in love with Mariana, the mother of his best friend, Jim, and the mistress of a married cabinet minister. When Carlitos declares his love for Mariana, she gently discourages him, but a public scandal ensues. Carlitos' parents interpret his behavior as evidence of sin or madness; they attempt to "reform" him by sending him to confession and to be psychoanalyzed, and they try to quiet the scandal by transferring him to another elementary school. In other words, in their effort to make his behavior and ideology conform to convention, they have recourse to three of the main institutions of social control: the Church, psychiatry, and the educational system. Although at first Carlitos resists, his family and society eventually win, resulting in his adoption of hegemonic values and attitudes, including an exacerbation of his identification with U.S. commodity culture and a denial of his earlier sense of social responsibility to the vast majority of Mexicans who are poor.

Several months later, after this process is complete and his family has prospered under the Alemán regime, Carlitos runs into Rosales, a former classmate whose working-class family has become further impoverished due to the government's repressive labor policies. Carlitos buys the hungry Rosales a meal, and Rosales, in turn, tells Carlitos what became of Mariana, his first love object. According to Rosales, Mariana fought with her lover over his administration's misappropriation of funds intended for the poor, he publicly insulted her, and she committed suicide. Traumatized by this story, Carlitos tries in vain to find definitive corroboration of it; however, the little evidence he does find suggests that the account is probably true and that there has been a cover-up. Looking back on the incident some thirty years later, Carlos reflects wistfully on the impossibility of his ever knowing the truth of what happened to Mariana and, implicitly, on the irrevocable loss of his childhood innocence and ideals.

This tale of coming of age in Mexico City takes place at the end of the 1940s, during the presidency of Miguel Alemán and Mexico's full-scale entry into the structure of U.S. monopoly capitalism, which eventually resulted in an increased polarization of the class structure, the destruction (and, for the narrator, the vulgarization) of the environment through unregulated urbanization and industrialization, and a displacement of what the narrator considers to be "traditional" Mexican culture (a concept which, as we shall see, is very problematic) by U.S.-based mass culture and consumer commodities. Carlitos serves as the filter for perceiving and interpreting the changes that are being brought about in Mexican society and culture. On the one hand, the coalescence of the national and U.S. bourgeoisies begins to transform social institutions: notably the family, but also, to a lesser extent, education and the Church; on the other hand, it introduces new mechanisms for social control, including the mass media and psychiatry (which is portrayed in the text as vulgar Freudian analysis). Ideological hegemony by the new ruling class (the same hegemony which will be challenged in 1968) is achieved in a variety of ways. As we shall see in more detail later, one image that the novel insists upon is that of femininity, particularly as portrayed by the mass media during the 1940s, and the ways in which female images appealed to and shaped the aspirations and ideals—in short, the desires—of males, as their classes were being constituted and redefined by monopoly capitalism.

In spite of the narrator's alleged confusion about the year in which the story transpired, two historical allusions situate it in 1948, two years into Alemán's presidency. Recent scholarship of this period by historians and other social scientists concurs with Pacheco's fictional portrait: While Alemán was elected on a platform of accelerated economic growth based on private enterprise, coupled with political democratization, only the first of these goals was achieved, at the expense of both economic and political democracy. In fact, Alemán's policies of rapid industrial and agricultural development allowed for the growth of monopolies and the increasing dominance of multinational corporations to the detriment of national industry, land reform, and social services. The state played a dominant role in economic planning and became increasingly authoritarian, controlling trade-union activities and brutally repressing labor strikes. The government held wage increases in check while prices were rising more than 10 percent a year. As a result of these policies, income distribution became increasingly unequal. Meanwhile, government corruption was rampant. Alemán himself left office a millionaire, having enriched himself through graft and partnerships with U.S. investors, including the hotel magnate Conrad Hilton.[3]

Because it firmly situates the story of the preadolescent Carlitos in the chronotope of middle-class Mexico City neighborhoods under *alemanismo*, linking changes in the protagonist to changes in the social fabric of his time and place, *Las batallas en el desierto* corresponds closely to the particular type of *Bildungsroman* that Bakhtin has termed the "novel of emergence." In the standard *Bildungsroman*, "events change the hero's destiny, change his position in life and society, but he himself remains unchanged. . . . The hero is a *constant* in the novel's formula and all other quantities . . . can therefore be *variables*."[4] In the novel of emergence, on the other hand,

> changes in the hero himself acquire plot significance. . . . Time is introduced into man, . . . changing in a fundamental way the significance of all aspects of his destiny and life. . . . Man's individual emergence is inseparably linked to historical emergence. Man's emergence is accomplished in real historical time, with all of its necessity, its fullness, its future, and its profoundly chronotopic nature. . . . Human emergence . . . is no longer man's own private affair. He emerges along with the world and he reflects the historical emergence of the world itself. He is no longer within an epoch, but on the border between two epochs, at the transition point from one to the other. This transition is accomplished in him and through him. He is forced to become a new, unprecedented type of human being. It is as though the *very foundations* of the world are changing, and man must change along with them.[5]

Pacheco's novel presents precisely this "image of man growing in national-historical time."[6] The title refers to the battles being waged in the moral and spiritual wasteland of *alemanismo*. The war games of Carlitos and his schoolmates mimic the international wars of their parents' generation, as well as their domestic class antagonisms organized around the issues of race and sexual preference.[7] Moreover, Carlitos' family serves as a sort of allegory for the configuration of middle-class society and its gradual absorption into the structure of monopoly capitalism through collusion with the U.S. bourgeoisie. His mother is a descendant of the moribund landowning aristocracy, with its moralistic Catholicism and resistance to the social changes that accompany urbanization and industrialization. Carlitos' father, the son of a tailor whose education and marriage have allowed him to enter the urban professional class, is an entrepreneur who is first ruined, then made wealthy, by the invasion of the Mexican market by North American industries. His company's absorption by a U.S. corporation is foreshadowed by his adoption of the individualistic ethic of self-improvement and positive thinking, as well as his self-taught English classes. (The records teach him, significantly, defective English, a comment on his class' dual alienation, from the Mexican community and culture, on the one hand, and from the U.S. culture that they strive to emulate, on the other.)

Carlos' brother, Héctor, is a juvenile delinquent with openly fascist sympathies who will eventually attend the University of Chicago (an allusion to the conservative "Chicago School" of economics which the United States promoted in Latin America during the 1970s). Héctor's life then will synthesize his parents' disparate ideological legacies when he becomes an executive in a multinational corporation and at the same time a "caballero católico, padre de once hijos, gran señor de la extrema derecha mexicana" (a Catholic gentleman, the father of eleven children, an important member of the Mexican extreme right).[8] The smoothness of Héctor's transition from the roles of delinquent, right-wing militant and rapist to those of respectable family man and entrepreneur suggests that his apparent opposition to the establishment has no substance, that the sociopolitical and religious structure easily incorporates elements of fascism and tolerates violence against leftists, women, and the lower classes.

Thus, in attempting to make sense of an increasingly complex and confusing postwar world, Carlitos is exposed to a number of discourses representing different ideological positions. Those of the various members of his family are supplemented by several others. One such discourse is the nonviolent, humanitarian posture of his teacher, Mondragón, an ideological descendant of *cardenismo* at its most democratic; however, this dimension was quickly losing ground to the *desarrollismo* and dependency which were the less obvious legacy of Cárdenas' presidency. Moreover, Carlitos comes into contact with the extremes of Mexican society through two of his classmates: Harry Atherton, the personification of upper-class disdain; and Rosales, a boy from the slums who wavers between macho combativeness and defeatism.

Carlitos himself is initially depicted as an introspective outsider who instinctively rejects his brother's violence and his mother's authoritarianism and repression. His initial sense of alienation—of which Héctor's very different attitudes and behavior may be seen as a variation—is an indictment of the profoundly corrupt nature of his society; it would perhaps be more accurate to refer to Mexican society of the 1940s as an alienated society than to him as an alienated individual. As the adult Carlos reflects, "El amor es una enfermedad en un mundo en que lo único natural es el odio" (Love is a disease in a world where the only natural thing is hatred) (56). At the same time, he shares with most Mexicans, at least in theory, a yearning for the peaceful and just community predicted by the demagogic official rhetoric of the time: "Nuestros libros de texto afirmaban: visto en el mapa México tiene forma de cornucopia o cuerno de la abundancia. Para el impensable 1980 se auguraba—sin especificar cómo íbamos a lograrlo—un porvenir de plenitud y bienestar universales. Ciudades limpias, sin injusticia, sin pobres, sin violencia, sin congestiones, sin basura . . ." (Our textbooks confirmed this: Mexico, as can be seen on the map, is shaped like a cornucopia, a horn of plenty. For a still unimaginable 1980, a future of plenitude and universal well-being was predicted, without specifying just how it would be achieved. Clean cities without injustice, poor people, violence, congestion, or garbage . . .) (11).

The Utopia of *Maderismo*

For the adult Carlos, narrating from the vantage point of this "unimaginable" 1980 and from a perspective of profound disillusionment, positive values are associated with two utopias. On an explicit level, there is the future heralded by the media, a time of universal plenty which, given the nature of dependent capitalism, could never be attained. Armand Mattelart has described how the media appeals to the public's desire for a utopia of political freedom and participation, social harmony, and plenty. In reality, the public's role is reduced to passive participation, and history becomes an object to be consumed like any other. This is achieved largely through mystification of the relationship between the economic infrastructure and the ideological superstructure.[9] In the case of *alemanismo*, the Mexican public was led to believe that industrialization and development could be achieved merely by following the model of the United States, without taking into account the problematic nature of the unequal partnerships being established between U.S. and Mexican corporations, let alone the consequences of quelling all meaningful political participation and union organization and neglecting agrarian reform and social programs. From the present of the narration, postwar national optimism, like Carlitos' innocent trust regarding the future of Mexico as a middle-class, highly developed nation, can only be viewed with sad irony by a narrator whose naïveté has been revealed by history.

Somewhat less obvious but perhaps of equal significance is the presence in Carlos' narrative of a second utopia which is associated with the vanishing past of aristocratic elegance and liberal democratic ideals, linked to the immediate postrevolutionary period, and which is evoked in the narrator's memory by the figure of Francisco Madero's widow. At that time, we are to understand, an enlightened segment of the revolutionary elite still held forth the promise of achieving social justice while upholding democratic values. At the same time, it would preserve an aristocratic sensibility, as symbolized by the Porfirian architecture that is being demolished by bourgeois modernization. This recent past associated with the myth of Madero, the martyr (and perhaps, by extension, with the myth of Cárdenas) constitutes a sort of "Golden Age," or what Bakhtin refers to as historical inversion, an anachronistic ideal.[10] Recent historians argue that, with his repeated conciliatory gestures toward the conservatives, Madero prevented the revolution from following through to its ultimate consequences; in this sense, despite his democratic ideals, his policies can be seen as setting in motion a long process of betrayal of the revolutionary principles.[11]

Carlos' personal Golden Age contrasts in the novel with the prerevolutionary one mourned by his mother, consisting of a predominantly rural society dominated by an oligarchy with a highly stratified, Catholic world view that is above all antidemocratic. Her apocalyptic view of the present focuses on "la maldita ciudad de México. Lugar infame, Sodoma y Gomorra en espera de la lluvia de fuego, infierno donde sucedían monstruosidades nunca vistas en Guadalajara" (this accursed Mexico City. Infamous place, Sodom and Gomorrah awaiting the fire rain, a hell where horrors, the likes of which were never seen in Guadalajara, were daily occurrences) (50). If his mother's ideology posits urbanization as the principal source of moral corruption and social disintegration, for the narrator the city per se is not responsible. Rather, the decline in the quality of life is due largely to the invasion of Mexican society by the U.S.-controlled mass media and consumer culture.

Authentic and Commodified Culture

One major leitmotif of *Las batallas en el desierto* is the concomitant devaluation and gradual displacement of those elements of traditional Mexican culture which the novel posits as authentic. These include appropriated elements of colonial culture (such as the Spanish language, as against the neocolonialist English) and other elements of everyday life which have their roots in popular or precapitalist culture and may in this sense be seen as anachronistic (for instance, the extended family structure or traditional Mexican foods).[12] For preadolescent Carlitos these are material manifestations of underdevelopment and therefore of cultural deprivation; as such they are a source of embarrassment. The adult narrator, however, views his own childhood attitudes ironically. In the intervening decades, his scale of values has been inverted. In fact, one could argue that Carlos' current ideological position coincides in some respects with that of his mother during the 1940s. In both cases, remnants of precapitalist culture, because of their insertion in a less alienated social context, are validated as more "authentic" than elements of advanced capitalist, technological culture.

One could argue that this supposed "authenticity" is relative, since contemporary Mexican culture has been so heavily mediated under capitalism, even before the advent of the multinational corporations and the mass media, as Néstor García Canclini has amply demonstrated in *Las culturas populares en el capitalismo.*[13] Furthermore, in some cases the leftist critique of consumerism masks a class bias; in Susan Willis' words, "El 'consumidorismo' es la consecuencia natural de una orientación antimaterialista europea aristocrática, basada en el resentimiento de la clase superior contra el desarrollo del vulgar burgués. Los intelectuales radicales han sido atraídos a esta posición esencialmente reaccionaria . . . puesto que recurre tanto a su aversión por el capitalismo como a su sentimiento de superioridad respecto de la clase obrera" (Consumerism is the natural consequence of an antimaterialistic, European, aristocratic orientation, based on the resentment of the upper class against the development of the vulgar bourgeois. Radical intellectuals have been attracted to this essentially reactionary position . . . since it appeals both to their aversion to capitalism and to their feeling of superiority regarding the working class).[14] In fact, as Willis argues, many consumer goods serve real needs, reducing the time required for household labor; furthermore, even in the case of luxury consumption, as opposed to consumption for use, commodities' association with pleasure and fantasy appeals to human needs that are neither created nor wholly manipulated by the media.

Recent culture critics, including Hans Magnus Enzensberger, Fredric Jameson, and the Tabloid Collective, argue that the mass media, like all forms of culture, are not merely manipulators of consciousness but rather function through the expression of a utopian or collective impulse.[15] According to Enzensberger, who follows in the tradition of the Frankfurt School, "the attractive power of mass consumption is based not on the dictates of false needs, but on the falsification of quite real and legitimate ones."[16]

To a large extent, however, Pacheco's novel emphasizes the manipulative dimension over the utopian element in mass culture. The very language in which the adult Carlos relates his memories betrays a consciousness that has been shaped by consumer culture as propagated by the mass media. Rather than describing the sights, sounds, and smells of his childhood in rich detail, the narrator evokes it through relentless lists of products, brand names, and names of media personalities, suggesting the priority of quantity over quality, of mass production and interchangeability over originality, of novelty over endurance, of marketability over need (as Bakhtin would have it, of desire over historical necessity): "Vi la muerte en los refrescos: Mission Orange, Spur, Ferroquina. En los cigarros: Belmont, Gratos, Elegantes, Casinos" (I saw death in the soft drinks: Mission Orange, Spur, Ferroquina; in the cigarettes: Belmont, Gratos, Elegantes, Casinos) (64). Moreover, the media are depicted as catering to the public's wish for escapism and emotional release while encouraging them to divorce these individual psychological drives from collective social needs. Thus, at the movies Carlitos is emotionally devastated by the death of Bambi's mother but remains impassive before the death and suffering of millions of war victims as depicted in newsreels: "En el Cinelandia—junto a las caricaturas del Pato Donald, el Ratón Mickey, Popeye el Marino, el Pájaro Loco y Bugs Bunny—pasaban los noticieros: formación de bombas cayendo a plomo sobre las ciudades, cañones, batallas, incendios, ruinas, cadáveres" (In Movieland—along with Donald Duck, Mickey Mouse, Popeye the Sailorman, Woody Woodpecker, and Bugs Bunny cartoons—they showed the newsreels: bomb formations falling on cities, cannons, battles, fires, ruins, dead bodies) (21).

The Sensuality of Modernity

At the same time, the more complex intertwining of manipulative and utopian impulses is captured in the novel by the contradictory figure of Mariana. On the one hand, she represents modernity as that concept was understood by Mexicans during the late 1940s; that is, as Hollywood might have portrayed it. Above all, she is constituted as an image; as in the classical Hollywood cinema, "the figure of woman is aligned with spectacle, space, or the image, often in opposition to the linear flow of the plot. . . . There is something about the representation of woman which is resistant to narrative or narrativization."[17] Until the final scene of the novel, Mariana's image is static; it links sophistication, glamor, and unrepressed eroticism with access to commodity culture. In other words, she embodies the personal freedom provided by advanced technology and open sexuality outside the realm of the traditional extended family. When Carlos declares his love for her, she is nude beneath a silk kimono and holds a miniature razor, suggesting feminized luxury and technology, eroticism, and danger, and foreshadowing her subsequent rebellion and suicide. Even the baby picture of Mariana that Carlitos finds, in which she is lying nude on a tiger skin, captures this combination of Eros and Thanatos (35).

As in the Hollywood cinema of the 1940s, Mariana is deprived of a subjectivity, being reduced to the object of the desiring male gaze, portrayed as "the (impossible) place of purely passive desire."[18] Her positioning within consumer culture subjects her to its economics of desire; her passivity, or objectification, makes her susceptible to fetishization and display, situating her in a relation of resemblance to the commodity form.[19] For the male subject, Carlitos, she is woman as enigma; he—and by analogy the reader, who is also positioned in the narrator's male perspective—strives to know her from her image, rather than from her words and actions, which are for the most part negligible. (In designing the cover for the novel, Vicente Rojo has, perhaps unwittingly, reproduced this issue of Mariana's lack of subjectivity. The cover depicts a pin-up of Rita Hayworth, with a black bar covering her eyes, presumably to hinder identification of her image.)

Above all Mariana is an image of excessive female sexuality. Unlike the traditional Mexican housewife, Mariana has dared to violate the social codes by maintaining sexual relationships outside of marriage and having an illegitimate child. Convention posits the figure of Mother as outside of sexuality; yet Mariana combines maternity with a highly sexualized image that cannot be contained within the family and that is therefore threatening to the other children's mothers. Through her relationship with "el Señor," a married minister in the Alemán administration and a symbol of corrupt patriarchal power, Mariana has achieved a small degree of subjectivity that would otherwise not be available to a single woman, but, as in the case of the Hollywood femme fatale, this subjectivity is achieved "through manipulating the very position of erotic object conferred on her by patriarchy. Thus, the control is bounded by the terms of the system that defines the woman as 'loose,' and her existence continues in the service of men."[20]

As a mother her modernity is indicated by her permissiveness with her child, Jim, and her respectful interest in his friends. Unlike Carlos' mother and most other middle- and lower-class Mexican women, Mariana is not burdened with most traditional responsibilities of household labor and family. She has been "liberated" by the conveniences of the postwar North American middle-class home, which she has acquired in the form of an ultramodern *casa chica*. (Significantly, however, her apartment is located in the elegant but essentially middle-class Colonia Roma, rather than in the chic upper-class neighborhoods of Polanco or Las Lomas, suggesting that she may be one of a number of mistresses.) In exchange for the apartment and other amenities, she must devote her time to making herself sexually available to "el Señor" and desirable to his powerful friends. In one sense Mariana may be seen as symbolic not just of "modern" women but of the entire Mexican middle class of the 1940s in their willing subservience to a class that they acknowledged to be profoundly corrupt (the characters refer to the Alemán administration as "Alí Babá y los cuarenta ladrones," [Ali Baba and the Forty Thieves]) and in their slavish emulation of U.S. middle-class culture. Mariana is at once the ultimate consumer and the ultimate consumer product, endlessly acquiring furniture, kitchen gadgets, clothes, and cosmetics, yet producing only marketable images of herself as fetish for the male consumer.

Patriarchy, Dependency, and the State

On another level Mariana and Jim comprise a sort of Oedipal fantasy of a privileged life alone with mother without the interference of father or siblings. It is a family structure that benefits from the privatization of space in capitalist society and which is liberated from the repressive and authoritarian impulses of the traditional Catholic family like Carlitos'. Yet in fact Jim has two "fathers." His biological father is allegedly a U.S. reporter whose nationality and ties with the media reinforce the theme of the selling out of the Mexican middle class, of *malinchismo* as propagated by advertising. Jim himself promotes the story that his father is "el Señor," the government official known to be his mother's keeper and whose physical absence in Jim's life is compensated for by omnipresent photographs of "el Señor" presiding over public ceremonies. These images, commemorating state sponsorship of public works as a cornerstone of Mexican modernization, convey an oppressive power and suggest the intrusion of the patriarchal, technocratic state into the personal sphere.

In other words, both of Mariana's romantic ties, both of the alliances she forms in an attempt to achieve some degree of autonomy, are with representatives of the forces that were pulling Mexico away from the dream of a good society and toward a future of corruption, authoritarianism, consumerism, and both economic and cultural dependency. The problem implicit in Mariana's character, then, is how a society located on the periphery of the world socioeconomic system can acquire the material comfort of the metropolis without relinquishing authenticity and autonomy; that is, how it can achieve development without dependency. Carlitos' attraction to Mariana raises the same issue from yet another perspective; to fall in love with Mariana is to become infatuated with Hollywood's image of beauty, desirability, and modernity and implicitly to reject an identity which is either nationalistic or anti-imperialist, as well as any sense of solidarity with the lower classes of either country. In this sense Carlitos is mimicking his family's preference for North American movie stars over Pedro Infante, with his "cara de chofer" (chauffeur's face). In his embarrassment with his traditional home life, Carlitos personifies the self-hatred of his generation, the Mexican generation that made the uneasy transition into modernity. (Only half a generation away, we should remember, La Onda would appear, with its disdain for politics and its embrace of the anarchistic, libidinous dimension of the youth culture emanating from the United States and Europe, with its preference for rock-and-roll over *música ranchera*, psychedelic drugs over tequila, gringas over Mexican women. Yet this next generation would also be the protagonists of the student movement of 1968 and the organizers of the leftist political parties of the 1970s and early 1980s, which helped to prepare the way for the popular front led by Cuauhtémoc Cárdenas in the late 1980s.)

If Mariana seems to have stepped from a 1940s Hollywood screen to be a Mexican counterpart to Rita Hayworth, the love object of Carlos' sister Isabel is similarly mediated by images from U.S. mass culture. The narrator tells us that Isabel fell in love with Esteban, a has-been child actor, because he was the next best thing to a Hollywood movie star. Like Mariana, he is a Third World imitation of a First World cultural icon; unlike her, his imitation is a poor one that can't stand the test of time. Furthermore, his alcoholism and chronic unemployment suggest the futility and moral bankruptcy of cultural dependency. Both characters are driven to suicide; Esteban in despair over his resounding failure, in both his professional and personal life, and Mariana in belated recognition of her own inauthenticity and collusion with the forces of corruption.

In Mariana's case, the alleged suicide occurs after she publicly challenges her lover about his administration's undermining of social programs through corruption, and he, in turn, publicly humiliates her. It is significant that her attempt at autonomy is posited as a defense of the poor, whose betrayal she recognizes as the most flagrant violation of the Revolution's aims. Given her context, it would have been anachronistic to have had her speak on behalf of her sex, to have portrayed her as an incipient feminist. Up until this point, the excessive quality of Mariana's sexuality is acceptable, indeed is attractive, to patriarchy, as long as it remains contained within the boundaries of the *casa chica*, reproducing the marriage contract. However, when the subversive potential of her nonconformity is translated into an incipient subjectivity in the form of political criticism, patriarchy silences her through a discourse that converts the political into a moral category. Rather than accusing Mariana of being a subversive, "el Señor" accuses her of being a whore. She accepts his judgment—in fact probably acknowledges the extent to which it is true, in the metaphorical sense of her collusion with corrupt and repressive forces—and in destroying herself she renounces her objectification, having failed in her belated attempt to claim subjectivity. Her explosion in the face of patriarchy, then, is actually an implosion, turned inward, against herself. Even in death Mariana continues to be treated as an object of male fantasy; in Rosales' sensationalistic account, even the final, possibly apocryphal image of her being carried away on a blood-soaked stretcher suggests a voyeuristic male fascination, particularly since he is uncertain whether she shot herself, slashed her wrists, or merely took an overdose.

There is an implicit parallel between Mariana's defeat and that of Rosales' working-class family in their attempts at labor organization. When Rosales' mother loses her job because of her union activism, the boy is forced to drop out of school and make a meager contribution to his family's support by selling chewing gum on buses. The change is emblematic of the increasing control of the Mexican work force by the official labor union, the Confederation of Mexican Workers (Confederación de Trabajadores de México, CTM), as well as the lumpenization of certain sectors of the proletariat. The novel thus establishes a parallel between women and the working class as victims (and occasional co-conspirators) of the new coalescence of social forces in Mexico and as potential agents of change whose subjectivity is effectively beaten down by the system.

Memory and Desire

Both Carlos' and Isabel's love objects, then, can be seen as examples of the commodification of desire, of the channeling of individual values and longings, and the utopian impulses underlying those yearnings, into falsified images generated for mass consumption. The process of appropriation of mass cultural phenomena becoming a link between people is apparent in Carlos' association of the image of Mariana with the lyrics of the *bolero* "Obsesión," which expresses the romantic determination to overcome all obstacles to achieving individual self-realization through love. At the same time, the novel raises the question of the mediation of desire through banal images propagated by the mass media, the raison d'être of which is the sale of commodities. In the society emerging from *alemanismo*, then, love becomes another commodity in the international marketplace. The mass media use the *bolero*'s myth of romantic love to sell other commodities and, albeit unwittingly, to mediate the way that consumers textualize their experiences, including the way that the adult Carlos remembers and recounts his first love and disillusionment.

Carlitos' punishment for his nonconformity, together with changes in his family's social status, combine to empty these romantic images of their utopian content. His blind devotion to Mariana, like his dream of an equitable and just society, has been repressed by the time of his accidental encounter with Rosales, in which he explicitly denies his own responsibility for—and by implication, his class' complicity in—the expansion, impoverishment, and political disenfranchisement of the lower classes. The widening gap between his own ascendant middle class and Rosales' impoverished working class, the lumpenized sectors of the proletariat, is apparent in the open-ended denouement of *Las batallas en el desierto*. Thirty years later the narrator is still not certain of the truth of Rosales' story about Mariana's suicide and her lover's subsequent coverup. The internal contradictions of the story, as well as Carlos' inability to find definitive corroboration of it, raise doubts as to its veracity. Yet their neighbors' denial that Mariana and Jim ever existed supports the theory that there has indeed been a deception; that they are lying to avoid having problems with "el Señor," who owns the building. Moreover, it suggests the efficacy of bourgeois ideological hegemony and, perhaps more to the point, of the corruption and co-optation of Mexican society as a whole. The suspicion that remains in Carlos' mind, linked to a sense of guilt over his own insensitive behavior toward Rosales, is that Rosales may have invented the story in order to save face and to retaliate against him for selling out to the ruling class and refusing to accept social responsibility.

When Carlos visits Mariana's former apartment, he is confronted with conflicting images of modernity, on the one hand, and traditionalism, on the other. When Mariana and Jim had lived there the apartment had been neat and tidy, suggesting the ordering and compartmentalization of interior space that accompanied the development of the marketplace.[21] Neither the new furniture from Sears and Roebuck, the snapshots of "el Señor" in Mexico's service, nor any other object in Mariana's apartment had linked it to its context, a lower-middle-class Mexican neighborhood. With the apartment's change of tenants, this image of international modernity has now given way to one of preindustrial clutter and mestizo culture, not unlike Carlos' own household before his father's precipitous success. The elegant photographs have been replaced by tacky icons of Christian and indigenous myths: Carlos finds "una sala distinta, sucia, pobre, en desorden. . . . La Ultima Cena en relieve metálico y un calendario con el cromo de La Leyenda de los Volcanes" (a different living room: dirty, poor, disorderly. . . . The Last Supper in metallic relief and a calendar with pictures from The Legend of the Volcanoes) (66). As Carlitos wanders around the building, he smells the pungent odors of traditional Mexican cooking instead of Mariana's perfume, scents associated with family and tradition rather than with sexuality and technology. The boy's reaction to this reappropriation of the apartment building by popular culture is one of embarrassment and even revulsion. In his white tennis outfit, carrying a Perry Mason mystery, he now identifies totally with the U.S.-oriented bourgeoisie, as against his lower-middle-class Mexican origins.

Carlitos' behavior at this point in the story clearly represents the postrevolutionary ruling class' co-optation of potential opposition within the middle classes, mirroring Mariana's co-optation and defeat by "el Señor." By contrast, her alleged suicide represents a refusal to continue participating in a corrupt system. Although its finality suggests that effective opposition is impossible, her willingness to confront a representative of state and patriarchal power is nevertheless a reaffirmation of integrity and social responsibility as positive values. This is her legacy to Carlitos, the message of the alleged suicide note (perhaps written in English, like the note she left for Jim?), which he never received.

The ironic, self-critical dimension of Carlos' narrative implies that, in the three decades that have passed since the time of Mariana's alleged death, he has in some measure learned from her example and resumed his striving toward authenticity, an effort that is documented by the very existence of his autobiographical text. The utopian element implicit in the contradictory image of Mariana has been repressed in his personality but not eradicated; his childhood sense of alienation has been pacified but continues to lurk beneath the surface of his consciousness, ready to be elicited by memories of his (and Mexico's) Golden Age before the Fall. The final monologue synthesizes Carlos' ambivalent feelings toward the society that has shaped him:

> Qué antigua, qué remota, qué imposible esta historia. Pero existió Mariana, existió Jim, existió cuanto me he repetido después de tanto tiempo de rehusarme a enfrentarlo. . . . Demolieron la escuela, demolieron el edificio de Mariana, demolieron la colonia Roma. Se acabó esa ciudad. Terminó aquel país. No hay memoria del México de aquellos años. Y a nadie le importa: de ese horror quién puede tener nostalgia. Todo pasó como pasan los discos en la sinfonola. Nunca sabré si aún vive Mariana. Si viviera tendría sesenta años. (68)

> (How ancient! How remote! What an impossible story! But Mariana existed; Jim existed; everything I went over in my head existed even after such a long time of refusing to confront it. . . . They demolished the school; they demolished Mariana's building; they demolished my house; they demolished the Roman Quarter. That city came to an end. That country was finished. There is no memory of the Mexico of those years. And nobody cares: who could feel nostalgia for that horror? Everything came to an end just like the records on the jukebox. I will never know if Mariana is still alive. If she is, she would be sixty years old.)

There is an additional, perhaps less obvious, implication of this episode as well. If in narrating his story the adult Carlos recognizes the selfish and hypocritical nature of his own past behavior toward Rosales, symbolic of his own growing alienation from social responsibility, in one sense he repeats this type of behavior in the act of narrating. His almost exclusive concern in remembering the past is the welfare of Mariana, the personification of his individual desire, rather than the fate of the "Mexican Miracle"'s most direct victims. If Rosales' story *is* a malicious rumor, and Mariana didn't really commit suicide, she would now be sixty years old, as the narrator wistfully observes. In other words, the image of seemingly eternal beauty, sexuality, and modernity in fact would have aged, would have lost its value as object of male desire or exchange. Yet, even if we assume that she did kill herself, Mariana's status as victim only masks a parallel crime of greater proportions. Given the material reality of their class situation and the impossibility of advocacy, the literal or at least figurative death of Rosales and his family is virtually assured.

Thus, the novel's ending is ambiguous; if on the one hand it suggests that Carlos has not renounced his striving toward authenticity, toward a utopian ideal, it also hints that, despite the ironic self-criticism that permeates his narration, Carlos' values are still distorted by the ideological forces that shaped his generation. He still cherishes an objectified image of ideal femininity and romantic love; and he still allows his personal concerns to blind him to intolerable social problems. This adds a final touch of irony to Carlos' implicit denial that the "horrors" of the past continue in the present; his discourse painstakingly proves the falsehood of this assertion.

The Earthquake: From Nostalgia to Despair to Solidarity

Pacheco's next to last collection of poems, *Miro la tierra* (1986), transforms the bitter nostalgia of *Las batallas en el desierto* into despair. In the wake of Mexico's deepening economic crisis and the devastating earthquake of 1985, the apocalyptic Catholic discourse of Carlitos' mother in the novel (Mexico City as hell, as Sodom and Gomorra awaiting the rain of fire) has become increasingly insistent. In "Altar barroco" ("Baroque Altar") we read that "la tierra / es nuestro paraíso y la hemos vuelto infierno" (the earth / is our paradise and we have turned it into hell).[22] With the earthquake Mexico City has finally achieved its destiny as the "capital del vacío" (the capital of the void):

Esta ciudad *no tiene historia,*
sólo martirologio.
El país del dolor,
la capital del sufrimiento,
el centro deshecho
del inmenso desastre interminable. (29)

(This city *has no history,*
only martyrology.
The country of pain,
the capital of suffering,
the unravelled center
of the immense, unending disaster.)

Recent events have only made the hell of contemporary Mexican society more unbearable; they constitute a sort of coup de grace for a process begun much earlier: "La ciudad ya estaba herida de muerte. / El terremoto vino a consumar / cuatro siglos de eternas destrucciones" (The city was already mortally wounded. / The earthquake came to consummate / four centuries of eternal destructions) (22). In the ruins of the earthquake the poet finds that his country has been reduced to "un hoyo negro / . . . Me acerco a ver qué arde amargamente en la noche / y descubro mi propia calavera" (a black hole / . . . I approach to see what burns bitterly in the night / and I discover my own skull) (25). In "Los vigesémicos," from Pacheco's latest collection of poetry, *Ciudad de la memoria* (1989), the poetic speaker reflects on the coming millennium and affirms halfheartedly:

> Sin duda hay esperanza
> para la humanidad.
> Para nosotros en cambio
> no hay sino la certeza de que mañana
> seremos condenados.[23]

> (No doubt there is hope
> for humanity.
> For us, on the other hand,
> there is only the certainty that tomorrow
> we shall be condemned.)

Nevertheless, the impulse toward hope, however faint, is present in the concluding section of both recent books of poetry. At the end of *Miro la tierra*, the poetic speaker calls on his compatriots to dry their tears and set about rebuilding their country, in both a material and a moral or spiritual sense:

> No quiero darle tregua a mi dolor
> ni olvidar a los que murieron
> ni a los que están a la intemperie.

> Todos sufrimos la derrota,
> somos víctimas del desastre.
> Pero en vez de llorar actuemos:

> Con piedras de las ruinas hay que forjar
> otra ciudad, otro país, otra vida. (41)

> (I will not let my pain subside
> nor forget those who died
> nor those without shelter.

> We all suffered defeat,
> are victims of the disaster.
> But rather than cry, let us act:

With stones from the ruins we must forge
another city, another country, another life.)

This glimmer of hope in the midst of despair is also present in the
final poem of *Ciudad de la memoria*, which compares humans to
"Live Bait," worms squirming on the fishhook of life, helplessly
waiting to be eaten by death:

Y no obstante
creo en ti,
enigma de lo que existe;
terrible, absurda, gloriosa vida
que no cambiamos (ni en el anzuelo) por nada. (59)

(And yet
I believe in you,
enigma of that which exists;
terrible, absurd, glorious life
that we wouldn't trade [not even on the hook] for anything.)

The belief in civic activism, in the possibility of converting vic-
timization into agency, seems to have subsided in the three years
between the publication of these two books, giving way to an existential conception of perseverance against all odds. Perhaps this corresponds to the continuing undermining and frustration of attempts
to organize civil society in the years following the earthquake. If the
new political opposition movements and grassroots social movements do manage to make headway in the coming years, it will be
interesting to see if Pacheco's apocalyptic vision is further attenu-
ated. For now, the truth that he has to tell is still fundamentally one
of retribution for contemporary civilization's crimes against humanity. For José Emilio Pacheco, Mexico's disasters—natural, economic,
and political—are punishment for the sins of *desarrollismo* and all
that it entails: social injustice, violence, ecological destruction, commodification, and corruption.

5. Apocalypse and Patricide: *Cerca del fuego* (1986), by José Agustín

Era un gran rancho electrónico con nopales automáticos, con sus charros cibernéticos y serapes de neón.

—RODRIGO GONZÁLEZ ("ROCK-DRIGO") "TIEMPO DE HÍBRIDOS," *EL PROFETA DEL NOPAL*, 1986

It was a big electronic ranch with automatic cactuses, with its cybernetic cowboys and neon serapes.

—RODRIGO GONZÁLEZ ("ROCKDRIGO") "TIME OF HYBRIDS," *THE PROPHET OF THE CACTUS*, 1986

The novels and short stories of José Agustín (b. 1944), like the lyrics of his friend Rockdrigo, the rock balladeer who was killed in the 1985 earthquake, are somewhat postmodernist, aesthetically hybrid compositions. While his early writings employed lumpen slang to portray a middle-class existential posture strongly reminiscent of U.S. counterculture, his recent works, particularly the novel *Cerca del fuego* (*Near the Fire*, 1986) and the short-story collection *No hay censura* (*There is No Censorship*, 1988), combine these qualities with a political critique and a more profoundly psychological dimension. *Cerca del fuego* parodies U.S. imperialism (portrayed as an invasion of Mexico by the U.S. marines) and the inefficiency and corruption of the bourgeois party that has monopolized Mexican politics for the past half-century, the PRI (Party of the Institutional Revolution). This apocalyptic scenario, a fictional representation of the crisis in hegemony that came to a peak two years after the publication of Agustín's novel, parallels a spiritual crisis on the part of the protagonist of the novel, Lucio. In both cases, the problem is shown to be a crisis in patriarchy, occasioned by the physical or psychosocial absence of the father. In symbolic terms, the U.S. economic empire is portrayed in terms that parallel the presentation of the female principle in the novel. On the one hand, it is tyrannical

José Agustín. Photograph courtesy of Elena Poniatowska.

and invasive, absorbing Mexico's resources and identity; on the other, it is remote and diffuse, leaving an ineffectual Mexican puppet president ("father") as its figurehead. On a psychological level, the problem is posed as one of masculine maturation and acceptance of family responsibility; that is, of stepping into a power vacuum and assuming the paternal role. The solution posed by the novel, in both the public and private spheres, therefore involves a restoration of the patriarchal family unit.[1]

Rock Aesthetics and the Politics of the *Albur*

At the end of the 1970s Mexican writers and critics began announcing, with varying degrees of scorn and satisfaction, the demise of La Onda, that current of narrative that had emerged in the mid-1960s to capture, in all their vitality and banality, the everyday lives of urban middle-class teenagers, the "youth culture" of the same name that developed in Mexican cities, especially the capital, parallel to the countercultural movement in the United States and the student movement in both countries. The term that has been applied both to the counterculture and its narrative equivalent derives from the slang term *estar en onda*, "to be with it" or "in," suggesting its connection with a yearning to be contemporary, to not be *fresa* ("straight, "uptight," bourgeois), even—or perhaps especially—in the midst of underdevelopment.

As Monsiváis has noted, La Onda was fundamentally apolitical; its rebellion was not essentially against political or social institutions per se but rather against the dominant middle-class morality, characterized at once by an exacerbated sense of nationalism and a hunger for modernity along the lines established by the United States.[2] In addition, conventional morality circumscribed sexuality within the narrow boundaries of the Catholic family and the bordello and gave the Catholic Church a monopoly on spirituality. In rejecting their elders' false patriotism, parochialism, and repression, middle-class Mexican teenagers of the 1960s embraced the countercultural experiments of their U.S. peers through sexuality, consciousness-altering drugs, Eastern religions, Jungian psychology, and rock music. They recorded music in English, published a Spanish version of *Rolling Stone* magazine, and even staged Avándaro, a Mexican Woodstock. According to Monsiváis, the most significant legacy of the *jipitecas* (members of the Mexican counterculture, a conflation of *hippies* and *aztecas*) were certain "generational conquests," notably more permissive attitudes toward female sexual activity and use of sexual language.[3]

Early critical reactions to these novels were generally condescending. Juan Rulfo, for instance, referred to La Onda as "literatura payasa" (clown literature).[4] The authors' personal scandals and, especially, their outspoken irreverence toward their literary predecessors, in an ambience that valorizes discretion and respect for tradition, have contributed to this tendency of the literary establishment to not take them seriously, a trend which has continued into the late 1980s, even as writers not associated with La Onda have prematurely celebrated its demise.[5]

In a seminal article that appeared in 1977, Jorge Ruffinelli identified the formal characteristics of the Onda narrative and examined some of their ideological implications. In addition to their irreverent tone, he highlighted their particular use of language: "Se opta por el 'discurso intranscendente,' esto es, se lo desnuda de todo ademán literario, se lo 'desprestigia' para adoptar el coloquialismo, se lo aproxima al discurso ordinario de la comunicación" (They opt for "insignificant discourse," that is, they strip it of all literary pretense, they humble it by adopting colloquialisms, they bring it close to the ordinary discourse of communication). The authors also experimented with literary structure, creating collages of letters, tape recordings, personal diaries, and dialogues.⁶ As for its ideology, "la Onda no ataca teóricamente los bastiones de la cultura mexicana dominante en la década del sesenta, y menos aún establece una plataforma política, pero actúa a su margen en la práctica literaria, en su idea del país, y en vez de asumir el nacionalismo imperante, se hace cosmopolita" (the Onda doesn't theoretically attack the bastions of dominant Mexican culture in the decade of the sixties, much less establish a political platform; rather, it acts on its margins in literary practice, in its idea of the country, and instead of assuming the ruling nationalism, it becomes cosmopolitan).⁷ What for Ruffinelli is cosmopolitan discourse is, in the last analysis, colonial for Monsiváis: "Los jipitecas . . . fracasan al no captar que a la imitación no se le opone la imitación en un medio donde el proceso colonial ha ido de la admiración elitista por la cultura frances o inglesa a la admiración multidinaria por Norteamérica" (The Hippitecs . . . failed because they didn't realize that imitation cannot be opposed by imitation, in a context in which the colonial process has gone from the elitist admiration of French or English culture to the mass admiration of North America).⁸ However, Elena Poniatowska counters that "Si la Onda tuvo un origen colonial, se nacionalizó en el camino" (If La Onda had colonial origins, it has been nationalized along the way).⁹

Fredric Jameson sees more positive aspects in the "youth culture" of the 1960s. The problem with the countercultural aesthetic, as he sees it, arose when it did not surpass the individual dimension, when it did not "invent ways of uniting the here-and-now of the immediate situation with the totalizing logic of the global or Utopian one. . . . The right to a specific pleasure, to a specific enjoyment of the potentialities of the material body . . . must always in one way or another also be able to stand as a figure for the transformation of social relations as a whole."¹⁰

Although La Onda had no explicit theoretical program, it did attack—in practice if not through a coherent theory—certain "bastions of dominant Mexican culture," precisely in its rejection of both the false bourgeois nationalism fomented by the PRI and the exaggerated populist nationalism promoted by the traditional Mexican Left, as well as of the social realist aesthetic and solemnity characteristic of the Novel of the Mexican Revolution and the Muralist movement. Following the sixties dictum to "challenge authority,"

La Onda writers violated an important cultural code in steadfastly refusing to respect either official ideology or the literary canon.

In a context in which Juan Rulfo has been treated with universal reverence, widely being considered the greatest Mexican novelist, José Agustín dared to poke fun at the morbidity and solemnity of this legendary writer's works: "¡Tequila Ruco Rulfo, de Jalisco! ¡Usted caminará en su propia guácara!" (Old Man Rulfo Tequila, from Jalisco! You'll walk in your own barf!).[11] Such literary in-jokes have become a staple of Agustín's prose and a constant source of friction with other writers and intellectuals. *Cerca del fuego* contains similarly irreverent jokes about writers as diverse as Salvador Elizondo and Elena Poniatowska. The only apparent criterion for such treatment is that the author in question be a member of the current literary establishment or at least enjoy widespread popularity and/or critical acclaim.

Characters in Onda fiction are portrayed as shallow and narcissistic. As Margo Glantz has noted, by the mid-seventies these authors' lampooning of the middle class had become a parody of a parody, since "se es consciente de su banalidad, pero se sigue inmerso en él" (one is aware of its banality, but one continues immersed in it).[12]

Agustín has fashioned what Ruffinelli has termed "intranscendental discourse" out of the dialect of his own social group, combined with popular sources as diverse as lumpen slang and English rock lyrics. The irreverence that Agustín has so skillfully captured in his dialogue constitutes what Ruffinelli calls "a camouflaged act of parricide."[13] Yet, at the same time, in both *Cerca del fuego* and *No hay censura*, his defiance of the government, the Church, the bourgeoisie, and dominant Mexican literary culture is undercut by his unquestioning deference to two other sources of authority: Jungian psychology and the European literary canon.

In appropriating lumpen or subproletarian *caló* (slang) peppered with *albures*, which Octavio Paz has defined as "the verbal combat made of obscene allusions and double-entendres," Agustín enriches the novel with the irony and inventiveness of inner-city and border culture. But along with this he adopts its machismo. His texts portray love and sex as male combat and conquest; they partake of the *albur's* "eternal delight in defeating the adversary and forcing him into the role of passive homosexual, or of perennially putting down women."[14] Also, they linger on the female body as the object of male desire and the extremely perilous map over which the protagonist's body must move in the male journey toward transcendence (Jungian individuation). The male sexual organs are portrayed as the center of all perception, the essential tool for aesthetic creativity. Perhaps more than any other contemporary Mexican author, José Agustín has constructed what might be termed a testicular (texticular) narrative.

John Kirk has divided José Agustín's literary production into three stages: "the 'apprenticeship' period," including the author's first four books, "the *ondero* or '*chingodélica*' phase," constituted by *Se está haciendo tarde* and *El rey se acerca a su templo* (*The King Approaches His Throne*, 1978), and "the early literary maturity stage," covering *Círculo vicioso* (*Vicious Circle*, 1974), *La mirada en el centro* (*The Gaze in the Center*, 1977), and *Ciudades desiertas* (*Deserted Cities*, 1982).[15] The third stage of Agustín's production would also include *Cerca del fuego* and *No hay censura*, which had not yet been published at the time Kirk was writing. The chronological divisions of Agustín's work, then, would be roughly 1964 to 1969, 1973 to 1978, and 1982 to 1988 (at least), falling rather neatly into five- or six-year periods in discrete decades.

In the second, *ondero* phase, the seventies, the pursuit of pleasure is revealed as narcissistic, obsessive, self-deluding, and empty, yet there seems to be no preferable alternative. The car, a symbol of affluence, mobility, and independence from adult supervision, frees its occupants to make the pilgrimage from the middle-class neighborhoods of Mexico City to the middle-class playground of Acapulco and back again. It is a pilgrimage emptied of conventional religious significance and striving for an amorphous spirituality that the characters never fully achieve. In Agustín's most recent works, those written during the eighties, the circumstances of the search have changed; here multiple sexual relationships and "the tribe," or communal family, cede to the couple and traditional family as a context for self-knowledge and transcendence. The first novel in this stage, *Ciudades desiertas*, features a male protagonist's efforts to reconcile with his estranged wife, culminating in the reinstatement of the couple, while *Cerca del fuego* focuses on another male character's reconciliation with both his nuclear and extended family. Agustín said recently that his next novel will complete the trilogy of the "vuelta a casa" (homecoming) by centering on the parent-child relationship.[16]

After the Invasion: Apocalypse Now

While in his earlier books there was scant reference to the broader social and political context of the characters' lives, *Cerca del fuego* is situated squarely within the economic catastrophe and the crisis of hegemony of the 1980s, five years after an imagined invasion of Mexico by the U.S. marines. As a character explains:

> Nos invadieron los gringos, según ellos, muy decente, muy democráticamente, vinieron a ayudarnos a instaurar una verdadera democracia después de los mil siglos del PRI, que para esas fechas era considerado por los gringos y por la oligarquía nacional como El Más Abominable Monstruo Comunista, cuando en realidad hace seis años el pinche PRI ya era un gusano adiposo, apestoso, parchado por todas partes.[17]

> (The gringos invaded us, according to them, very decently, very democratically. They came to help us install a true democracy after the thousands of centuries of the PRI, which by then was considered by the gringos and by the national oligarchy as The Most Abominable Communist Monster, when actually six years ago the goddamned PRI was a greasy, stinking worm, covered with patches.)

Following a period of widespread torture and massacres, the United States oversaw national elections, resulting, ironically but perhaps not unpredictably, in the election of yet another president from the ranks of the PRI. After installing this "new" government, the marines withdrew, but not without leaving behind

> millones de asesores, e industrias al ciento por ciento, con mano de obra regalada, nos tienen agarrados de los huevos, y al parecer estamos condenados a trabajar para ellos hasta quién sabe cuándo. Lograron lo que siempre quisieron: tenernos de surtidores de materias primas a precios de risa y consumidores de todas sus mierdas desnatadas, libres de calorías, a precios de oro. (41)

> (millions of advisers, and industries by the hundreds, with practically free labor. They have us by the balls, and it looks like we're condemned to work for them until who knows when. They achieved what they always wanted: having us as suppliers of raw materials at laughable prices and consumers of all their low-fat shit, calorie-free, at gold-plated prices.)

As the novel begins, the protagonist, Lucio, has had amnesia for six years or a *sexenio*, the period of a presidential administration; his last memory therefore antedates the invasion. Among his first experiences in his journey back to the present, and then home, is an encounter with a president described, in characteristic Onda style, as "el mismísimo Gran Tlatu Lento, el Galán de Traje Oscuro, el de Camisa Estratégicamente Grisperla y Vigoroso, Patriótico, Nudo de Corbata. Una raya en la boca, casi rictus, lo parapetaba del ruidero" (the Great Slow Tlatu himself, the Gent in the Dark Suit, the man with the Strategically Pearl-Gray Shirt and Vigorous, Patriotic Necktie Knot. A line of the mouth, almost a rictus, barricaded him against the uproar) (18). The society that this empty-eyed puppet oversees is plagued by gross economic inequality resulting in abject poverty as well as systemic corruption and police brutality. Moreover, these problems have accelerated a process of widespread moral degeneration. In other words, the urban landscape portrayed in the novel is not unlike that of the Mexican capital during the 1980s.

At the same time, the last memory that Lucio has is of traveling by plane six years ago, from Ciudad Juárez to Mexico City, where his brother was to meet him at the airport and he was then to consult with some army officers for an unknown purpose. (Ciudad Juárez is, of course, on the border with the United States and is in Chihuahua, probably one of the fifteen states that declared themselves neutral and allowed the invaders to pass through their territory [40]). Earlier we learned that Julián is himself a captain in the army and that his two sons, significantly named Julián and Lucio (like Lucio's children, Julián and Lucero), have recently been killed in a drug-related shoot-out with the police. We also find out that Lucio's family had enlisted him in the army to straighten him out but that his military career was very short-lived and that, subsequently, his first novel was critical of the army. The purpose of Lucio's mysterious journey of six years ago is never clarified, but the fact that it coincided with the U.S. invasion raises the possibility of his collusion with the U.S. and Mexican governments in reestablishing the hegemony of the PRI and of North American investors. Could his amnesia, then, be brought on by a sense of guilt over his political corruption? Or might it have been related to drug trafficking?

The influence of the PRI rests not only on the upper class but also on the middle classes to which Agustín and his readers belong—specifically, the middle-middle class of petty bureaucrats and professionals that inhabit neighborhoods like the Colonia Narvarte, where Agustín and the other Onderos were raised. In Agustín's devastating satire of social types, this class is characterized by machismo, racism, jingoism, and *cursilería*, or pretentious bad taste. Some of these caricatures include the opportunistic film industry bureaucrat and second-rate movie director; the has-been director, who courts much younger women, unaware that he is a pathetic remnant of the

Golden Age of Mexican Cinema (the 1940s); the bland insurance company lawyer, whose sole passion is for dominoes (in which he immerses himself at his weekend home in Cuernavaca); the lawyer's domineering wife, who worships both femininity and the military (and who attempts to improve herself by participating in a journalism workshop taught by Elena Poniatowska—a characteristic Agustinian jab at a fellow writer). At the lower end of the socioeconomic spectrum there is the lower-middle-class housewife, doña Chona, who epitomizes *cursilería* and right-wing Catholicism. Doña Chona's interaction with her maid (whose name, Yésica, also suggests a poor imitation of North American culture) can be read as a humorous variant on the unhealthy mistress-servant dynamics so poignantly captured in Elena Poniatowska's short stories.

While social critique of the middle class is constant in Agustín's work, the direct treatment of political and economic problems and the extensive incorporation of working-class and lumpen characters represent a significant thematic change from the first twenty years of his career. One character in *Cerca del fuego* seems to some extent to represent the author's views in calling for "the true Marxist-Leninist-Hegelian-Gramscian-Kunderian revolution," that is, one that takes into account issues of personal, spiritual, and libidinal, in addition to economic and political, liberation (34). Recently Agustín has defined his position as follows:

> I place myself decisively on the side of the poor, the exploited, the oppressed, the marginal. I believe that we need a socialism with liberties and with the highest cultural level. But to get on with the task of sensitization, of humanization, of culturization is urgent; just as necessary as political action. Hence, a profound cultural development is essential. Without it, our politics can easily be diverted toward regrettable positions. What I've written reflects this. I also keep in mind that any revolutionary transformation cannot be only external and social but must be also internal and individual. Revolution must be propitiated simultaneously from the outside and from within; not one without the other.[18]

Statements like this one, as well as Agustín's outspoken advocacy of Cuauhtémoc Cárdenas, the popular-front candidate for president in the July 1988 elections, suggest that the author has, in recent years, become more politicized or perhaps has returned to his socialist ideals and political activism of the early 1960s, when he participated in Cuba's literacy campaign. Yet, in the realm of narrative, he is no political writer in any simple sense. As we shall see below, in spite of this attempt to treat the problem dialectically, the ferocious political and social satire of the opening pages of the novel is overshadowed by, and in effect subordinated to, the narration of a process of psychological and literary individuation, understood in orthodox Jungian terms. If *Cerca del fuego* is a novel about an individual spiritual crisis set against the backdrop of Mexico's economic and political crisis of the 1980s, the presentation of context ultimately is consumed by the writer's internal demons.

The Novel as Mandala

As Lucio, the protagonist, awakens to political knowledge (his name and those of his wife and daughter, Aurora [Dawn] and Lucero [Star], all connote light or enlightenment), he also comes to grips with a personal crisis, described in Jungian terms.[19] The novel consists of three major sections, labeled White, Black, and Red, the three colors of alchemy, as described by Jung in *Psychology and Alchemy*. A note by Agustín in the penultimate section of the novel explains the symbolism of these colors: "Nigredo es la inmersión en la sombra, la negrura; albedo, paso al blanco, a la primara luz; rubedo, el fuego, el rojo que se obtiene magnificando el calor del fuego a la máxima intensidad" (*Nigredo* is immersion in the shadow, blackness; *albedo*, the passage to white, to the first light; *rubedo*, the fire, the red that is obtained by magnifying the heat of the fire to the maximum intensity) (307–308). For Jung the stages of alchemy were comparable to the psychological process of individuation, in which the individual undertakes a spiritual journey culminating in wholeness or the integration of the self, as a result of encountering and coming to terms with various archetypes of the collective unconscious. Blackness, then, is associated with immersion in the subconscious and contact with the archetype of the shadow, while white represents the beginning of self-knowledge and encounter with the anima or animus, and red suggests wholeness or the self, the purifying fire that completes the transformation of the personality. As he reverses the order of the first two colors, Agustín also inverts the narration of the psychological stages associated with them, so that if one recreates the chronological order of the events in the novel, the order of symbolic colors becomes, properly, Black-White-Red. Agustín has explained the color symbolism of his novel in the following terms: The first major section, entitled "Blanco," corresponds to the external, political, and social reality of imperialism and state violence; the second, "Negro," to internal, psychological issues as known

through dreams; and the final section, entitled "Rojo," is "el enfren-
tamiento de esos mismos sueños ante la realidad, la cristalización
del mundo que te da lo onírico ante una realidad muy inmediata"
(the confrontation of those same dreams with reality, the crystalli-
zation of the world that dreams give you with a very immediate
reality).[20]

The cover of the novel, which, like the covers of most of Agustín's
books, was designed by his brother, painter Augusto Ramírez, depicts a man standing on his hands on the *zócalo* (the civic space par
excellence) in front of the National Palace, which is flying the U.S.
flag. Out of the man's body emanates a gigantic nude male figure
that is swathed in flames, which, in turn, envelop the seat of government, representing the Mexican nation. The implication is clear:
Out of individual self-knowledge and transformation there can
evolve an overarching social and political transformation. The cover
of this first edition is deep blue, a color that Jung associates with
spirituality.

The three major sections of the book are, in turn, divided into
sixty-four fragments, the number of hexagrams in the *I Ching* and
the square of the number four, which Jungian theory considers to be
the perfect number. According to Jung, the self expresses itself in
quaternity symbols or mandalas which help the individual psyche
to heal and become "whole" or integrated by imposing an ordered
structure. Agustín's novel returns obsessively to the number four.
The opening fragment of the text, which alludes elliptically to insomnia and the writing process, is entitled "Four in the Morning."
In the course of his travels around Mexico City, Lucio remembers
walking with a four-year-old boy (his son); he buys four pieces of a
lottery ticket (with which he wins either four or eight million
pesos); he recalls seeing the original film "Metropolis," with its four
girl protagonists representing springtime; and he repeatedly dreams
that he wakes up in Room 404 of the Gran Hotel Cosmos. He also
alludes to "the four by four," Jung's zen cure for insomnia (letting
the mind go blank), and he speaks of mounting "el gran dragón de
sesenta y cuatro cabezas que despide llamaradas ante el pasmo del
mundo" (the great sixty-four-headed dragon which snorts flames before the astonishment of the world) (126). During the car trip to
Yautepec, which I will discuss in detail below, Aurora, echoing the
Beatles, asks Lucio if he will still need her when she's sixty-four. I
think these examples suffice to demonstrate the systematic manner
in which Agustín has laden his text with Jungian symbolism.

But what is the significance of a Mexican writing a Jungian novel
in the late 1970s and early 1980s?[21] For one thing, it indicates a con-

tinuing rejection, by Agustín and at least some of his readers, of the sufficiency of traditional, rational ideologies in explaining reality and investing it with meaning. Neither Catholicism (the church) nor the PRI ("el Gran Tlatu Lento") nor Marxism (Salazar Saldaña) has all the solutions for Lucio or for Agustín. Yet the answers offered by Jungian archetypes are essentialist and aggressively ahistorical and therefore have the effect of pulling the narrative away from the historical specificity in which Agustín initially anchors his narrative problems. Moreover, as we shall see, these archetypes tend to coincide with racial, class, and, especially, gender stereotypes.

Traveling through the "Defecal Detritus"

The automobile, the favored vehicle of the middle-class adolescent "trip" (psychedelic, musical, sexual, and, at least in Agustín's novels, spiritual) figures prominently in the works of La Onda. Agustín's earlier novel *Se está haciendo tarde* features a trip to Acapulco, which had been the favored resort of the U.S. and Mexican bourgeoisie during the 1950s and 1960s but which, by the 1970s, had become a polluted paradise catering to a middle-class clientele. The journey in *Se está haciendo tarde* documents the banality and vacuousness of Mexico's *jipitecas,* as well as of alienated North American and European tourists who seek connection and transcendence in "exotic" settings. Rather than end on an optimistic note, like *Cerca del fuego*, this novel ended with a symbolic boat journey with a guide named Virgil on a Pacific Ocean become the River Styx.[22]

At other points in the novel Lucio experiences a sense of profound well-being and belonging, in spite of the relative physical discomfort, while traveling by bus or subway and immersing himself in "the anonymity of the masses." For instance, the narrator describes Lucio's fragmented perception of his fellow passengers on the subway:

> Veía fragmentos de rostros, de hombros, que inevitablemente se confundían cuando trataba de aislarlos, la victoria de la uniformidad, pincelazos exactos de la masa anónima, me tragó la ballena y encontré una muchedumbre de bellos miserables. Bendita masa anónima, pensé: ellos me sostenían, allí mismo, me tenían de pie. Advertí también que mi cuerpo estaba acostumbrado a todo eso . . . me sorprendí . . . de que la gente pudiera absorber tantas incomodidades. Podían leer, dormir, cantar, alguien incluso ya se había cagado, anunciar, vender y platicar en las mismísimas barbas congeladas de Satanás. (117–118)[23]

(I saw fragments of faces, of shoulders, which inevitably became confused when I tried to isolate them, the victory of uniformity, exact pencil strokes of the anonymous masses, the whale swallowed me and I found a crowd of beautiful poor people. Blessed anonymous masses, I thought: they held me up, right there, they kept me on my feet. I realized also that my body was used to all this . . . I was surprised . . . that people could absorb so many discomforts. They could read, sleep, sing, someone had even shit on himself, advertise, sell, and chat right in the frozen beard of Satan.)

As for the motif of the journey, in Agustín's recent works, the falsely "liberating" car trips of the early 1970s are replaced by aimlessly purposeful forays (the goal of which is recuperation of the couple or the family unit, as we shall see) into the land of the Other, understood in terms of nationality or class. In *Ciudades desiertas* this is the "provincial," midwestern United States (that is, Iowa City and Chicago, rather than New York and Los Angeles); in *Cerca del fuego*, it is poor, especially lumpen, neighborhoods of Mexico City, where much of the dialect appropriated by La Onda originated. Thus, the claustrophobic, middle-class homogeneity of the Colonia Narvarte and tourists' Acapulco has been opened both outward (from Mexico, the periphery, understood in hemispheric or global terms, to the peripheral regions of the United States, the center or metropolis) and inward (to the inner-city slums—from the socioeconomic "center" of the periphery, middle-class neighborhoods, to its own socioeconomic periphery, the slums, located in its geographic center). In *Cerca del fuego*, as we shall see, car travel, which is portrayed as solitary, alienating, and even destructive, alternates with travel on public transportation, buses, and subways, in which the masses are the source of extreme discomfort but also of survival and revitalization, understood in both individual and societal terms.

Lucio's Virgil, his initial guide through the city under siege and into the inferno of Mexico City's slums, is Juan José Salazar Saldaña, an old man whom he encounters first on a crowded bus and then, coincidentally, at a lunch counter. Salazar Saldaña, an alcoholic, lives in a filthy, book-lined shack near the Merced Market, which is littered with a postmodernist assortment of garbage: "tripas de rata, programas de televisión, mierda seca" (rat guts, TV guides, dried shit) (32). In keeping with Agustín's running commentary on political corruption, we eventually learn that the old man is both a doorman at the Supreme Court and a cocaine dealer. It becomes clear early on that this derelict is a variant on the archetype of the "Wise

Old Man," or guru, and that he is evoked unconsciously by Lucio in a moment of profound spiritual disorientation, which is symbolized by the amnesia. The implication seems to be that, in a degraded society, not even gurus are devoid of vulgarity and pathos. It is also characteristic of Agustín's self-irony that he has Lucio describe the characters' spiritual bond in irreverent terms: "Ese viejo era parte mía. . . . él y yo formábamos parte de un espíritu, o tal vez de un pedo, que siempre había soplado en el mundo" (That old man was a part of me. . . . He and I formed part of one spirit, or maybe of one fart, which had always blown in the world) (51).

It is Salazar Saldaña who, in a drunken spell of oratory, calls for "the true revolution." Immediately afterward he ironically cites the iconoclastic Marxist writer José Revueltas (1914–1976) regarding "the earthly paradise" (34–36). Revueltas, a major writer and activist, served as the intellectual guide to the student movement of 1968, and, in the wake of the massacre at Tlatelolco, he spent two and a half years in prison after assuming sole responsibility for the movement. For succeeding generations of Mexican writers, Revueltas has come to be the prototype of the committed intellectual. More pointedly, he was one of José Agustín's mentors from the time that they met as inmates in Lecumberri Prison. Juan José Salazar Saldaña's second name and political stance, as well as his alcoholism and his association with the lumpenproletariat, clearly allude to the Marxist theoretician. Revueltas, like Malcolm Lowry, another literary model that Agustín alludes to repeatedly, was an alcoholic who frequented lower-class cantinas and led a rather dissolute life. He was also the first Mexican novelist to populate his novels with lumpen characters. Salazar Saldañas' self-immolation in the name of humanity, which brings the second chapter of the novel to a dramatic conclusion, recalls the self-sacrifice of Revueltas' political imprisonment. The name Salazar alludes to Rubén Salazar Mallén, the quintessential social realist writer. Agustín has said that his intention in naming his character after Revueltas and Salazar Mallén was to show that an orthodox Marxist position is insufficient—it leads to the old man's pointless self-destruction; although he believes that, if Revueltas were still alive, he would be Kunderian.[24]

The names "Juan José" (in addition to coinciding with those of the author) bring to mind Agustín's other literary mentor, Juan José Arreola, in whose writing workshop he participated for several years, and may also allude to Juan Rulfo. Shortly before this section of the novel, Agustín indulges in a parodic combination of the titles of two Rulfo short stories, "No oyes ladrar los perros" ("Don't You Hear the Dogs Bark") and "Diles que no me maten" ("Tell Them Not to Kill

Me"] and thus pays ironic tribute to an additional literary model for this initiatory phase of Lucio's spiritual journey: "¡No oyes ladrar los canes? ¡Mi amor, diles que no me capen!" (Don't you hear the dogs bark? My dear, tell them not to castrate me!) (27). In view of the motifs of the spiritual journey to origins and purification by fire in *Cerca del fuego*, it is perhaps not accidental that Agustín should thus acknowledge a debt to the author of *Pedro Páramo*, the quintessential search for the father, and of *El llano en llamas* (*The Burning Plain*), the title of which seems to be echoed in Agustín's title.

As for the allusions to Malcolm Lowry, Agustín, who collaborated on the screen adaptation of *Under the Volcano*, repeatedly evokes Lowry's masterpiece, even entitling a segment of *Cerca del fuego* "Frente al volcán" ("Facing the Volcano"). At one point Lucio proposes to escape from a haunted house by staying at the Hotel Casino de la Selva in Cuernavaca, which Lowry frequented: "Es preferible ver al fantasma del viejo Malcomio, chance hasta nos invita un mezcalito" (It's preferable to see the ghost of the old man Malcomio [a word play on Malcolm and *manicomio*, "insane asylum"]; maybe he'll even buy us a mezcal) (218). Later, during a bout of insomnia, Lucio rejects the British novelist's battles with demons: "¿Cómo decía Lowry? ¿no tiene el alma sus Moctezumas y sus noches tristes? Me carga el carajo. Chingue a su madre el pendejo de Malcolm Lowry, sáquense los aburridos y modositos demonios lowrianos" (How did Lowry put it? Doesn't the soul have its Montezumas and its Tragic Nights [an allusion to the fall of the Aztec empire]? The hell with it. Screw stupid Malcolm Lowry, the hell with Lowry's boring and well-behaved demons) (231). The oneiric section of the novel features a visit to Cortés' palace in Cuernavaca, which also figures in *Under the Volcano* and has now been converted into an art museum.

Finally, the village of Yautepec, located between Mexico City and Cuernavaca in the state of Morelos, is the setting for key scenes in both novels (as well as in Lowry's posthumous novel *Dark as the Grave Wherein My Friend is Laid*). In *Under the Volcano*, the consul is on a bus to Yautepec that happens upon a dying Indian, whom the driver and passengers are legally forbidden from helping; instead, another peasant from the bus robs the man. This macabre incident comes to symbolize the absence of solidarity and morality. At the end of the novel, as the consul himself lies dying and is also being robbed, he identifies not with the Indian victim but with the thief from the bus. As we shall see, Yautepec is also the setting for Lucio's aggressive behavior, leading to a spiritual crisis and the process of purification that forms the backbone of *Cerca del fuego*.

Juan José Salazar Saldaña's second last name, as well as his act of self-destruction, also bring to mind Parménides García Saldaña, the third founding member of La Onda (along with Agustín and Sáinz) and—both personally and literarily—the most outrageous of the three. García Saldaña's excessive, anarchistic life (provoking fist fights at literary cocktail parties, interrupting a meeting of the Unified Mexican Socialist Party [PSUM] with accusations that the party had betrayed Stalin, twice attempting to murder his wife) ended prematurely, apparently as the result of a drug overdose. At least one other Onda writer met a similar fate.[25] Agustín is suggesting that these talented contemporaries, like Lucio's guru and like the author himself during an earlier period of his life, consumed themselves in a blaze of intense living ("made a funeral pyre of their lives," as Poniatowska writes), rather than passing through the purifying flame of introspection and creation.

According to Jung, the archetype of the Wise Old Man may also take the form of a child. After Salazar Saldaña's death, Lucio encounters Consuelo (the negative anima, who will be discussed below), some less symbolic characters, and then Homero Baldomero, a street vendor of lottery tickets whose given name is at once silly and wise. The boy's nickname is "don Pimpirulando," a character in the repertoire of Cri-Cri, a children's comedian. Don Pimpirulando, a dog trainer, sings a song entitled "The School for Animals," which includes the following verse. "Don Pimpirulando los está enseñando, los perritos quieren aprender" (Don Pimpirulando is teaching them, the little dogs want to learn). Thus, both of the child's names suggest that he is to serve as a guide or teacher for Lucio in his spiritual journey. Agustín has described the vendor as "niñito que sabe todo, e igualmente . . . niñito inocente, inocente, inocente" (a little boy who knows everything, and equally . . . an innocent, innocent, innocent little boy).[26]

In the segment of the novel that he narrates ("Oh yo no sé" [Oh I don't know]), in the lumpen slang of Mexico City's inner-city slums, Baldomero plays street-wise operator to Lucio's (intentionally) gullible innocent. This "Homer," who is proud of his skills as a con artist and of his jail record, will, for a price, sing a song by Rockdrigo. Alternately, Homero will sing a version of the Mexican national anthem rendered as a series of sexual puns, proving his agility with the *albur* that is a mainstay of elite culture's portrayal of the working-class and lumpen male: "Mexicanos al grito de hueva, a la verga aprestad el condón" (Mexicans, at the balls' cry, prepare the condom for the cock) (80).

Lucio, who is less naive than Baldomero assumes, is willing to pay the child's price, and more, but requires something in exchange: that Baldomero listen to the story of how he was mugged and then came face to face with his own shadow, in the shape of a cruel and cynical policeman identical to himself. In an inversion of the usual writer-reader relationship, Lucio pays Baldomero, his audience, to "read" a segment of his novel-in-progress, which, as we later learn, is to become the text we are reading, *Cerca del fuego*. In exchange for his attention, Lucio buys four pieces of a lottery ticket from the boy and then gives him two of them. That Lucio "profits" from this experience, and therefore has the truer philosophy, is made clear when his lottery ticket wins the jackpot. By the time this happens, however, Baldomero has resold, out of a combination of necessity and cynicism, the portions that Lucio gave him, and, as a result, his only "reward" is the physical abuse of his father, who is ironically the one who taught him *la transa* (the con game). As Monsiváis has noted regarding the *nacos*, a derogatory term for the lower-class youths of Mexico City, "su aprendizaje de la pequeña corrupción . . . [es una] defensa contra la Corrupción" (their apprenticeship in petty corruption . . . [is a] defense against Corruption).[27]

Physical brutality has been a constant in the boy's life. Lucio (in the role of "the U.S. Cavalry") rescues Baldomero from a policeman who uses him to rob jewelry stores, then beats him. Also, the child shows Lucio his reform-school drawings of policemen being tortured, clearly a projection of his own experiences and a suggestion that he has learned from the example of this antifather as well. In his haste to get away from Baldomero's father, who is threatening him with violence, Lucio apparently runs over Baldomero; but fear and irresponsibility impel him to speed up, keep driving, never know if he has killed his young friend. In Jungian terms, he has destroyed an earlier, less mature form of his Self. What he has learned from this second guide into his own psychic recesses is a sense of accountability for his actions—of social responsibility—that he has been lacking. This is not stated in so many terms; rather, Agustín's presentation of the scene is grotesque and revolting, first distancing the reader and then daring her to form a puzzle of the narrative pieces.[28]

Hit-and-run automobile accidents, like police brutality and interpersonal violence, are important leitmotifs of *Cerca del fuego*. The accident involving Baldomero is followed by a description of an incident in which Lucio, as a boy, was run over by a car immediately after a confrontation with his brother Julián, who was envious of their father's affection for Lucio. After Lucio has been reconciled with his wife and children in Tepoztlán, a car accelerates to hit his two-year-old daughter Lucero, then speeds away. This incident, at least, appears to be a nightmare, since Lucio mentions his family matter-of-factly in succeeding segments. Thus, we are to understand that Lucio's criminal irresponsibility toward Baldomero conjures up, first, childhood memories of sibling aggression, then dreams of alienated urban society's revenge against his own family. The motif of the hit-and-run driver appears in one additional context. When Lucio meets his negative anima, ironically named Consuelo (Consolation),[29] she tells him that, a week after her sexual awakening with her brother Memo (significantly, as we shall see, during a bus trip to Acapulco), the boy was run over by a car and killed. She apparently interprets this tragedy as divine punishment for incest.

The entire second section of the novel, "Negro," which contains this episode, is conceived as a series of dreams, many of them nightmares. For Jung the type of vehicle that appears in dreams is significant in that it "illustrates the kind of movement or the manner in which the dreamer moves forward in time—in other words, how he lives his psychic life, whether individually or collectively, whether on his own or on borrowed means, whether spontaneously or mechanically."[30] This may be an additional reason, then, why Agustín has chosen the automobile, that icon of industrial civilization, as a symbol of individual alienation and aggression.

Gender and Class as Other: Queen of the Subway

The raw psychic material provided in "Yautepec," which is probably the key chapter in the novel, allows us to more fully understand how issues of authority (both psychological and narrative) are implicated in the text. An earlier chapter, "La Reina del Metro (y otros cuentos)" ("The Queen of the Subway [and Other Stories]") is presented as a series of waking events, with more tools for analysis.

In his travels through the underbelly of the city, Lucio encounters his negative anima, Consuelo, or "La Reina del Metro" (The Queen of the Subway). Her gender and lower-class origins allow her to personify exotic Otherness: what is portrayed in the novel as the female principle or what Julia Kristeva has termed "the phallic Mother who gathers us all into orality and anality, into the pleasure of fusion and rejection."[31] Before encountering her on a subway platform, Lucio has been reading T-shirts that read, among other things, "IF YOU CAN'T SHIT, DON'T EAT" and "Coma Caca" (Eat Caca). He has overheard a passenger on a train say, "Hombre vamos a bajar hasta el fondo de la mierda" (Man, we're going down to the bottom of hell [literally, of shit].) Now he comes face to face with someone who personifies " el horror casi sagrado . . . la belleza de la caca" (the nearly sacred horror . . . the beauty of caca) (117–124):

> ¡Qué imagen portentosa! Era una chava de rostro horripilante, picoteado por años de barros . . . pobrecita: narizona, bocona, de dientes chuecos, ojos pequeñitos, pestañas ralas, orejas de duende y pelos parados como dobles signos de interrogación. Lo maravilloso era que ese horror, la máscara de seiscientos sesenta y seis de la Bestia (esto es, la bestia de la Bestia), no intentaba cubrir su fealdad; de hecho la ostentaba: si la cara la tiraba la buenez la levantaba. El cuerpo alto de la nena era . . . sublime . . . cachondísimo . . . la tajante perfección del cuerpo le daba una dignidad insospechada, altivez natural, la fineza de la aristocracia de la sensualidad . . . era capaz de ocasionar catástrofes y de traer graves peligros . . . rostro de Coatlicue agorgonada y kaliesca. (121)

> (What a portentous image! It was a chick with a horrifying face . . . scarred by years of pimples . . . poor thing: big nose, big mouth, crooked teeth, little eyes, sparse eyelashes, goblin's ears and hair standing straight up like double question marks. The marvelous thing was that that horror, mask number 666 of the Beast (that is, the beast of the Beast), didn't try to cover up her ugliness; in fact, she showed it off; if her face pulled her down, her sexiness held her up. The chick's tall body was . . . sublime . . . sexy as hell . . . the cutting perfection of her body gave her an unsuspected dignity, a natural haughtiness, the refinement of the aristocracy of sensuality . . . that was capable of occasioning catastrophes and of bringing grave dangers . . . the face of Coatlicue, infested with worms, and of Kali.)

Lucio, the "peasant poet," "rescues" the lumpen queen from a gang of would-be rapists of her own class, in order to seduce her himself. He takes her to the Gran Hotel Cosmos, where they engage in oral sex and she tells him her life story, corroborating his intuition of the danger that she represents for men. Consuelo's life has been marked by her father's premature death, her initiation into sex through incest with her brother (who was run over and killed shortly thereafter), and a gang rape by sons of the bourgeoisie. Her self-defense through biting the buttocks of one of her rapists reiterates her connection with both aspects of "female" pregenitality.

When Lucio next meets her, she has been transformed into the positive anima, into pleasure without danger. Perhaps not coincidentally, she is now employed and married. Thus, she has also undergone the transition from lumpen whore to plump proletarian wife, complete with an apron and a maternal air. However, her husband's name, Mephisto, perpetuates her association with evil. Consuelo offers Lucio a shell/eye/breast to eat: "Dentro de la concha rosada que se abre, como guiño, aparece la masa blanca, firme y temblorosa, del marisco" (Inside the pink shell that opens like a wink, the white meat of the seafood appears, firm and trembling). Later a vision of her firm, white breasts, which invite him to suckle "the perfect death," prevents Lucio from killing a manifestation of his shadow (241–243).

Gender and Authority: The Devouring Mother

After the death of his two spiritual guides, Juan José Salazar Saldaña and Homero Baldomero, and the sexual encounter with his negative anima, representing his passage through two stages of individuation, Lucio encounters additional archetypes, his shadow and the Terrible Mother. According to Jung, the shadow, like the anima,

> appears either in projection on suitable persons, or personified as such in dreams. The shadow coincides with the "personal" unconscious (which corresponds to Freud's conception of the unconscious). . . . The shadow personifies everything that the subject refuses to acknowledge about himself and yet is always thrusting itself upon him directly or indirectly . . . that hidden, repressed, for the most-part inferior and guilt-laden personality. The shadow tends to manifest itself through uncontrolled emotions and lack of moral judgment, as projected unconsciously onto others.[32]

The chapter entitled "Yautepec," which opens the middle, "black" section of the novel (and which was first published as a short story in 1980), recounts Lucio's dream. By spending the weekend at a friend's house in the village of Yautepec, he and his wife, Aurora, set out to escape the "esperpento esmagangoso que se ha vuelto el Detrito Defecal" (the smoggified *esperpento* [a grotesque form of theater] that the Defecal Detritus [Federal District, Mexico City] has become) (213). Lucio's behavior turns increasingly aggressive and *machista*. His reckless driving almost results in a head-on collision with a truck, and his speech becomes more and more hostile. At one point he suggests that, if Aurora doesn't stop nagging him to slow down, he will "slice off one of her tetiux," implying that he will make her physically resemble the Amazons or castrating females whose behavior she is presumably emulating. Aurora counters by telling Lucio a story a la Scheherazade, offering her husband the pleasure of narrative in an attempt to calm his reckless driving and thus, perhaps, save her life.[33] The story she chooses is apparently designed to flatter his ego by corroborating his fears of female insatiability and evil.

In this ghost story, which is associated with the house where they are to spend the weekend, Victoria's great-aunt became a merry widow—more specifically, a "Devoradora Dhombres" (Man-Devourer) whose nymphomania drove her first to adopt disguises, preferably as an Amazon, then to practice sadism, and finally to seduce her own son. The incestuous son, Tachito, filled with remorse, killed his mother in a drunken Oedipal rage by hitting her over the head with a fireplace poker. He then became a serial killer, so a cousin purged the family of yet another "crazy" by killing Tachito. However, the cousin, in turn, was murdered by a lynch mob, composed of townspeople who were fed up with the family's escapades.

During the course of Aurora's narration, the issue of narrative authority is foregrounded, first by the third-person narrator's repeated doubts regarding certain names ("Yautepec" and "Aurora"), and then by Lucio's scoffing at the truthfulness of various details in Victoria's story, as related by Aurora. At one point he suggests that Victoria had obviously borrowed it from "Poe Poe" and that she should read more accomplished gothic writers, like E. T. A. Hoffman and Gustav Meyrink. (Actually, it reads like the misogynist Oedipal plot from *Psycho*.) Thus, the question of female versus male narrative authority becomes intertwined with conflicting interpretations of Lucio's machismo, that is, whether he is in control of the automobile and thus of their lives. At one point a truck from the Aurrerá (suggesting Aurora) supermarket chain almost crashes into them, providing another indication that Lucio is projecting his fear of women onto his wife.[34] Later he projects his dread of the Devouring or Terrible Mother (which, according to Jung, is a projection of incestuous impulses and the fear they create) even more clearly onto Aurora when he imagines that she is going to attack him with a poker, the very weapon with which Tacho allegedly murdered the Devoradora Dhombres. Lucio says to himself, "Esa mujer es la imagen viviente de la maldad" (That woman is the living image of evil) (224).

This is not the first time that Agustín's narrative has evoked a male protagonist's fear of having his identity obliterated by women. It is personified by Lucrecia Borges, a witchlike older servant who

terrifies the young protagonist of *De perfil*. (Her name obviously alludes to Lucrezia Borgia, the sixteenth-century Italian libertine and
alleged criminal, and, since her face is compared to a labyrinth, perhaps it refers to Jorge Luis Borges as well.) Immediately after "reas-
suring" the boy that she isn't going to eat him, she stands on the
toilet and shows him her "hoyo, lleno de pelos secos, erizados, pol-
vosos . . . su vagina gigantesca" (hole, full of dry, bristling, dusty
hairs . . . her gigantic vagina).[35] The association between orality,
anality, and the *vagina dentata*, the fear of being ingested through
the female mouth/vagina/anus, is underlined when the protagonist
finds images of Lucrecia everywhere, even in his scrambled eggs. (In
addition to their traditional Mexican association with the testicles,
the eggs are prepared by Lucrecia, the cook who would devour him.)

The specific fear of castration at the hands of the Terrible Mother
appears in *Se está haciendo tarde*. Here she is Cornelia (who is ironically named after the ideal of the Roman mother), a sadist and a
hysteric, with the face of a model and the body of a monster or a
corpse. (As we shall see, she is the inverse of Consuelo in *Cerca del
fuego*.) Her breasts are like "socks with marbles" and her vagina is as
"heavily traveled" as the Pan American highway, returning us once
again to the female body as sexual map. The threat of castration
proves to be literal, as the screaming Cornelia digs her fingernails
"like machetes" into Virgil's body, then whips his erect penis.[36] The
motif of the earth-mother as filicide recurs in the story that concludes *No hay censura*, in which a character compares the devastating earthquake of 1985 to a maternal orgasm.

In *Cerca del fuego*, Lucio links orality, anality, and maternity
when he complains that the soup at the restaurant in Yautepec must
have been cooked in a septic tank (like the rudimentary one in the
Devoradora Dhombres' mansion). Earlier, when the protagonist was
attempting to leave Homero Baldomero's home, Homero's mother
chased after Lucio with an "enormous onion knife" from the
kitchen. Since Homero was a projection of himself, this image suggests the connection between maternal castration, orality, and re-
tention (annihilating the son's identity in order to keep him with
her). Furthermore, when Lucio ran over the boy with his car, he in-
advertently assisted his own mother in annihilating him (107–108).

As for Lucio's mother, she, like almost all mothers in the novel, is
described as a domineering figure, a tyrannical earth-mother: "Su
personalidad tenía un magnetismo insólito, estaba aliada a la tierra,
era hermana de las raíces, las lombrices y de los espíritus del bos-
que. . . . Mi hermano Julián . . . la amaba hasta el postero paro-
xismo. . . . Aún casado, y con hijos, Julián habría abandonado todo e

incluso se habría esclavizado a ella, porque mi sagrada jefecita . . .
también esclavizaba. . . . Podía ser tiránica" (Her personality had a
surprising magnetism, she was allied with the earth, sister of the
roots, the worms, and the spirits of the wood. . . . My brother Julián
. . . loved her up to the final paroxysm. . . . Even though he was married, with children, Julián would have abandoned everything and
even would have enslaved himself to her, because my sacred little
boss-lady . . . also enslaved. . . . She could be tyrannical) (72). Interestingly, in spite of the control that she exerts over his brother and
sisters, Lucio denies that she has a similar hold over him. After their
mother's death, his sister Mary, like her house (which was their
mother's house), has "curative properties" (161). She is married to a
mild man, Francisco Madero, who, like his namesake, the father of
the Mexican Revolution, is "the martyr of the household."[37] Moreover, Aurora's parents fit the same mold of a weak father (whose sole
passion is dominoes) and domineering mother (who worships femininity and socializes with the upper echelons of the PRI and the
military).

Lucio and Aurora's courtship is portrayed as a male conquest. He
describes her as "una verdadera peste: cortante, sin llegar a ser
grosera. Jamás quiso salir conmigo, y yo tenía que hacerme el es-
túpido para encontrármela" (a real plague: curt without quite being
rude. She would never go out with me, and I had to make a fool of
myself in order to run into her) (189). Lucio's behavior in the early
stages of their relationship, in which he suffers physical and psychological pain over several months while she teases him sexually and
goes out with an older director, suggests masochism on his part:
"No tienes idea de cómo me *asqueó* que me hicieras eso porque
nadie, nadie, ni siquiera mi papá o algún jefe . . . nadie me había tra-
tado así" (You have no idea how *sick* it made me that you would do
that to me, because no one, no one, not even my dad or some boss
. . . no one had treated me like that) (194). Yet, in looking back on
their early relationship after they are married, Lucio describes their
roles in terms of characters from Mexican cinema that embody male
sadism and female masochism: "En el fondo, my dear Aurora, te
gustó, no finjas delirios. Si bien estoy de acuerdo en que en mí vive
Pedro Armendáriz, no es menos verdadero que en ti también subyace
el prototipo de la abnegada cabecitablanca, ¿o no?" (In the last analysis, my dear Aurora, you liked it, don't fake delirium. While I agree
completely that Pedro Armendáriz lives inside me, it's no less true
that inside you there lies the prototype of the long-suffering Mexican mother, no?) (194). Modleski situates male masochism "at the
heart of man's relation to his mother and to subsequent love ob-

jects," but warns that, unlike female masochism, it may easily be rejected by the subject, with possibly dire consequences for the woman in question.[38] Thus, Aurora's sexual teasing almost leads Lucio to rape her, but her screams save her by attracting a "lynch mob" (196)—like the one that intervened against Tacho's cousin and, as we shall see, the one that nearly executes Lucio in Yautepec.

Women are also associated with the feminine/maternal element and filth or pollutants. Just before Lucio's mother dies, her face resembles that of someone "recién llegada del Apocalipsis" (recently arrived from the Apocalypse), and she and his sisters vomit "largas y viscosas fibras de algo negro y muy pegajoso . . . [una] masa aceitosa, negra y pestilente" (long, viscous fibers of something black and very sticky . . . [an] oily, black, stinking mass). Lucio attempts to burn this filth but finds that it will only catch fire when mixed with his own blood; it can only be purified when tempered with the masculine element. He carries the black marble left by the flames in his pocket as a reminder of his mother/the maternal (174). A similar case of female purification by vomiting occurs at the end of *Se está haciendo tarde*. This insistence on women's expulsion of pollutants from the mouth underlies the aforementioned fear of female orality. After Lucio's reconciliation with his family, he resists the temptation of becoming sexually involved with a young American blonde by eating a dying rat that he finds in a bathroom, causing him to vomit and thus purify himself. He then gets an erection but provokes a horrified reaction in his potential sexual partner when she sees his vaginalike "boca . . . llena de una sangre oscura, con hilillos de carne cruda y pelos en los labios" (mouth . . . full of dark blood, with shreds of raw flesh and hairs on the lips) (283). In Agustín's latest book, *No hay censura*, the image of female danger and filth will explicitly become a *vagina dentata*, then an "unbearably desirable" female corpse. This instance of necrophilia may be read as an attempt to possess, and therefore control, the most extreme form of female pollution, even as Lucio carries his mother's vomit, condensed and purified by the flames of his blood, safely ensconced in his pocket.

The Shadow and Literary Patricide

When Lucio and Aurora arrive in Yautepec, his aggressive behavior is exacerbated by finding his brother and a friend there and by the dilapidated condition of the house. He proceeds to alienate both relatives and neighbors, kicking Julián out of the house and insulting Victoria (by telephone) and several residents of the village, in-

cluding a waitress in the restaurant and a grocer, whom he (ironically) accuses of discriminating against Mexican tourists by not
carrying foreign wines. He and Aurora also entertain themselves by
sitting in the village kiosk and making fun of the local *campesinos*
who pass by. If, on a psychological level, Lucio's aggressiveness is an
acting out of repressed aspects of his personality, on a social level his
sexism, racism, and false nationalism are a critique of middle-class
machista behavior, particularly of the arrogance of *chilangos* (capital dwellers) in the provinces.

Lucio displays particular hostility toward Dr. Salvador Elisetas, a
neighbor and retired psychiatrist who keeps an eye on Victoria's
house. This character, an even more dissolute version of Salazar Saldaña, immediately sets himself up as a tyrannical and unreliable
authority figure, admonishing Lucio (as both Aurora and Salazar Saldaña will later do) that he should see a psychiatrist, since his behavior isn't normal, and offering him "tranquilizers" which actually
turn out to be amphetamines. Agustín has suggested that the novel
be read as a process of individuation. If we read it this way, then Elisetas represents the archetype of the shadow, while at the same time
it is yet another example of the patricide that we will encounter repeatedly in the novel. Nearly all the fathers of the story are either
dead, like Lucio's and Consuelo's fathers, or ineffectual, like Aurora's father, Pancho Madero, and the "puppet president of Mexico,
father of the nation" (which the narrator refers to as the *matria*, the
"motherland"). In the course of the narrative, three of Lucio's father-
figures will die, two of them at his hands. When he has been restored
as head of his household, he will complete the series of patricides by
sacrificing himself for his family's (and his nation's) survival.

With the figure of Dr. Elisetas, Agustín is once again poking fun at
a fellow writer, in this case Salvador Elizondo, a well-known novelist and Mexico's leading practitioner of La Escritura, which Margo
Glantz identified as the other leading tendency of Mexican narrative
during the 1960s. As its name suggests, this tendency was a self-
reflexive, nonreferential style heavily influenced by *l'écriture* in
France. While Agustín and other writers of La Onda have been called
the first generation of gringos born in Mexico, Elizondo is sometimes referred to as the Mexican Bataille. Agustín has repeatedly
pointed to Elizondo, who held a scholarship at the Centro Mexicano
de Escritores at the same time as he, as a key proponent of conservatism in Latin America: "The politicization of many writers such
as García Márquez, Cortázar, Benedetti, and Revueltas has sparked
an enormous interest in politics and in the necessity for revolution-

ary change in Latin America. Likewise, the ideas of Octavio Paz, Mario Vargas Llosa, and Salvador Elizondo have reinforced the conservative position of just as many other readers."[39] While he acknowledges that he and Elizondo get along well personally, Agustín has also noted the other novelist's impatience with his style of writing: "Cada vez que Elizondo me ve . . . me dice: 'Oye, ya, entra en la Academia' porque sé que lo que escribo le molesta hasta la locura" (Every time Elizondo sees me . . . he says to me, 'Hey, enough already, enter the Academy' because I know that what I write drives him crazy with irritation).[40]

The name Salvador Elisetas is an obvious parody of Salvador Elizondo; moreover, the first name suggests that the character is a false savior, and *setas* are mushrooms, foreshadowing the psychiatrist's overindulgence in drugs and alcohol. The connection between the character and the real-life novelist is made even clearer when the narrator changes "Elisetas" to "Elishongos"; *hongos* is the synonym for *setas* used for psychedelic mushrooms. In making the doctor a retired psychiatrist, Agustín has said that he was alluding to the exploration of psychological phenomena in Elizondo's early novels, which the author has since abandoned. Moreover, his narrative language "es muy suave, es una jerga doctoril, fría" (is really "cool," it's a doctorish, cold slang).[41] Thus, Elisetas' attempts to send Lucio to a psychiatrist and, later, to a psychiatric hospital can be read as a comment on Elizondo's efforts to convince Agustín to "enter the Academy," to follow his own literary example.

This chapter contains a number of anal metaphors and allusions. (Just two examples are Lucio's repeated complaints about the rudimentary toilet and septic tank and the comparison of soup to the water in this tank.) He and Aurora are engaged in anal intercourse (attempting to expel his psychic pollutants or *defecal detritus*?) when Elisetas barges in. He locks the door to prevent Lucio from escaping before the arrival of an ambulance that will take him to the local veterinary hospital, where he is to undergo six months of daily electroshock therapy. In the ensuing struggle, Lucio finds it necessary to kill the old man—his shadow and yet another of his literary fathers—in self-defense. The weapon he finds for this purpose is a rusty nail, reinforcing the association of this "Salvador" with a (deteriorated) Christ figure. (Elisetas is the second potential "savior" that has appeared on the scene; the friend of Lucio's brother that Lucio ran out of the house was also named Salvador.) Aurora gleefully finishes the job with the fireplace poker once belonging to the Devoradora Dhombres (at which point Lucio fears that she will attack him instead). Faced with the horror of his action and of Aurora's sadistic pleasure, Lucio decides that he is dreaming and wills himself to wake up.

He does awaken but, as we and he soon realize, it is into another dream, also set in Yautepec. He finds himself on a cot in a white room (an infirmary? a mental hospital?) and, to his horror, finds the nail oozing blood. After seeing his image quadrupled in a mirror (suggesting a fragmented, schizophrenic identity, but also the striving for wholeness), he sees his other self walking outside and knows that his double, like Tachito in the ghost story, will continue murdering until he is stopped. Lucio therefore takes a silver dagger, shaped like a cross, and kills his alter ego (himself). The imagery of martyrdom associated with Elisetas' death is thus reinforced.

Subsequently Lucio, like Tachito's avenging cousin, is chased by a lynch mob of angry campesinos. On a psychological level these characters represent evil, as we shall see below. At the same time, on a social level they may be taken to represent the rebellion of the peasantry of Morelos, Zapata's homeland, against the weekend expatriates from the smog-filled city who are their latest class enemy. Agustín has described them thus: "La clase media idiota es la que ha venido a crear los fraccionamientos, es la que ha venido a crear un tipo de vida que le ha partido la madre a los campesinos, que fragmentó sus ejidos, que los convirtió en empleados de la clase media" (The idiotic middle class is the one that has come to create housing developments, is the one that has come to create a way of life that has screwed the peasants, that split up their *ejidos* [collective farms], that turned them into employees of the middle class).[42] Agustín's interpretation of this episode of his novel is sustained by Lucio's arrogant and insulting behavior toward the peasants earlier in the chapter. In view of Lucio's extremely *machista* behavior toward Aurora, it seems reasonable to interpret her act of turning on him as a similar reaction, a feminist rebellion parallel to the peasants' class revolt. From Lucio's (Jungian) point of view, however, she thus corroborates his deepseated fear of female treachery.

Unlike Tacho, Lucio is saved by two policemen, whose uniforms are the same color as his own skin. As in the story that he told Baldomero, figures of authority resemble—emanate from—himself. If, in the other incident, Lucio the policeman let the muggers beat him mercilessly and escape, here the policemen (he) intervenes in time to save him(self). The implication is that Lucio's own vital forces are responsible for protecting his well-being. After standing trial for Elisetas' murder, Lucio—like Agustín—goes to prison, where he undergoes a process of profound introspection and self-purification: "Está convencido de que todo eso ha sido necesario para que se purifique, y pague" (He is convinced that all that has been necessary in order for him to purify himself, and pay) (227). The autobiographical dimension of this episode is inescapable. Agustín writes in his autobiography that, although he didn't deserve punishment for marijuana use, he did deserve to go to prison for the state of "extreme confusion" that led him to behave irresponsibly in his personal relations and his work.[43]

Upon leaving prison Lucio is drawn irresistibly into a sixteenth-century church; he nevertheless must combat a powerful force of resistance in order to finally cross the threshold: "Esa es la batalla de su vida" (That is the battle of his life) (228). George McMurray, in his critique of the short story which became the chapter entitled "Yautepec," interprets the dagger, the prison cell, and the church as representing psychological withdrawal. The ending, then, represents, on a personal level "Lucio's personal withdrawal from reality," even as it symbolizes, "in more universal terms, . . . a submersion into the collective unconscious of the Mexican psyche" (108). The author has denied this interpretation of the chapter:

> Para mí era una forma de señalar que la vuelta a la religión, en el sentido tradicional, para el personaje está degradada. Cuando él trata de encontrar a la iglesia como salida, lo único que encuentra es un oscurecimiento total. Es un *black-out*, un apagón, un negro total, por ahí no es el camino. . . . El camino va a ser bajo procedimientos no ortodoxos desde el punto de vista cristiano de la religión, que son los que se adelantan en esa parte negra. Es la redención de la sombra. Condena San Agustín las partes negativas de la Iglesia Católica o el cristianismo. El dice de la negatividad, "El diablo es la ausencia del bien . . ." En ese sentido no soy ortodoxo. Yo sostengo que la redención es solamente a través de la comunicación directa con los elementos del mal, o lo que se considera tradicionalmente como el mal, porque . . . es muy relativo. El rechazo total hacia lo que se consideran elementos negativos no funciona. . . . Y la novela juega con la idea de que lo que le pasa a Lucio es lo que le pasa a la nación.[44]

(For me it was a way to show that the return to religion, in the traditional sense, is degraded for the character. When he tries to find the church as an escape, the only thing he finds is a total darkening. It's a black-out, a total blackness, that isn't the way. . . . The way is going to be under nonorthodox procedures, from a Christian point of view, which are what come forward in that black part. It's the redemption of the shadow. Saint Augustine condemns the negative parts of the Catholic Church or Christianity. He says of negativity, "The devil is the absence of goodness . . ." In that sense I'm not orthodox. I maintain that redemption is only through direct communication with the elements of evil, or what is traditionally considered evil, because it's very relative. . . . The total rejection of what are considered negative elements doesn't work. . . . And the novel plays with the idea that what happens to Lucio is what happens to the nation.)

On another level, perhaps the colonial church, in a village that is not far from Sor Juana Inés de la Cruz's convent in Amecameca, also represents Agustín's immersion in the Hispanic literary tradition. While Sor Juana inaugurated Mexican literature in the seventeenth century, the Spanish Golden Age flowered a century earlier. Agustín has spoken of the significance of Golden Age literature for his development as a writer.[45] Later in *Cerca del fuego*, he plays explicit homage to the Spanish classics in the climactic baseball game.

Texticular Narrative

In this third phase of Agustín's prose, eroticism generally is placed in the context of love, commitment, and domestic tranquility, the conventional romantic ideal. Sex, then, serves as a vehicle of communication and bonding with the loved one, as well as a gateway to the spiritual experiences that hallucinogens had provided during the sixties and seventies. If this conception of sexuality is far from revolutionary (in fact, it recalls a more pluralistic version of Octavio Paz's erotic poetry of the 1950s), the insistent and explicit presentation of sexual themes and obscene language indicates a departure from canonical Mexican gender stereotypes. In the first place, they break a taboo. Previous male writers, such as Rulfo and Fuentes, had described heterosexual, genital sex to some extent in their narratives; but Agustín defies previous standards of decorum in his explicit language and graphic descriptions, and he incorporates a polymorphous approach to sexuality that includes homosexuality, bisexuality, and varieties of nongenital and perverse sex (such as sadomasochism). Nevertheless, Lucio's return home coincides with the shift from polymorphous sexuality to a more conventional view of sex within marriage.

Many Latin American women writers have focused on the female body during the seventies and eighties (a task which Fernando del Paso assumes from a male perspective in *Noticias del imperio*). Agustín obsessively describes the male body, creating a sort of testicular narrative, in which the male sexual organs serve as the central metaphor for literary creativity and spiritual transcendence, both of which are portrayed as eminently male endeavors. This is especially pronounced in *Cerca del fuego* and *No hay censura*, in which he seems to test the validity of his title with frequent, detailed descriptions of erections, testicular pain, and various forms of sexual intercourse focusing on the phallus, and in which he uses rape and necrophilia as figures for spiritual disintegration and transcendence.

Jean Franco has noted, in Latin American male narrative of the sixties and seventies, the recurrence of the ideologeme or collective fantasy of monstrous birth and births of monstrosities, which "was intended to resolve the problem of 'feminizing values' and criticizing machismo, while at the same time reserving true creativity for the male author."[46] In *Cerca del fuego*, the birth of Aurora and Lucio's first child, told from the point of view of Aurora, is counterposed with the completion of the book manuscript, as narrated by Lucio. Childbirth is portrayed as painless, indeed pleasurable: "Con todo, era un verdadero placer estar allí, ese nacimiento era un gozo" (Taking everything into account, it was a true pleasure to be there, that birth was enjoyable) (253). The writing of the novel, however, is nightmarish and painful, its conclusion signalling the completion of the process of literary individuation:

Cuando trataste de escribir la novela había algo nuevo: el brazo
. . . te dolía . . . el dolor aumentaba, cada vez costaba más trabajo
mover la pluma . . . tus testículos se endurecían, se comprimían
con tanta fuerza que no lo podías soportar, detestaste la frases
que se te vinieron encima. . . . En ese momento supiste que . . .
todas esas noches que habías estado en peligro . . . era por lo que
escribías. . . . Todo había sido acercarte paulatinamente a esta
última implosión del fuego, y sobrevivirla significaría despertar,
liberarte para siempre. (288–89)

(When you tried to write the novel there was something new:
Your arm . . . hurt you . . . the pain grew, it was harder and
harder to move the pen . . . your testicles hardened, they shrank
so powerfully that you couldn't stand it, you detested the sen-
tences that piled on top of you. . . . At that moment you knew
. . . all those nights that you had been in danger . . . were because

of what you wrote. . . . it had all happened in order to bring you
gradually closer to this final implosion of the fire, and to survive
it would mean to awaken, to free yourself forever.)

If male genital pain, which is associated elsewhere in the novel with
insomnia and writer's block, is a necessary element in the male creative process, so is female sexuality. Aurora is the reservoir of liquid
light into which Lucio dips his pen(is): "A mi esposa le emana una
sustancia dorada de la vagina: deja gotas a cada paso. . . . En mi cuar-
tilla blanca se derraman gotas de luz, como diamantes líquidos que
mojan el papel" (A golden substance emanates from my wife's vagina:
She leaves drops with each step. . . . Drops of light spill onto my
white notebook, like liquid diamonds that wet the paper) (307–309).

Their sex life had begun, after many false starts, with Lucio's
newly completed second novel (about the Mexican army) serving
as an aphrodisiac (197). (He had burned his first, autobiographical
novel, a collage of film plots.) Similarly, their reunion following Lucio's amnesia leads to love-making, followed by pillow talk revolving around his third novel (the one which we are reading): "Por el
momento, no había nada que decir, . . . salvo . . . volar juntos en un
cogidón que si no representaría una marca, sí un buen averaje, como
dicen los cubanos. Después, hablaríamos y hablaríamos sin cansan-
cio, y ella me diría todo lo que yo necesitaba saber, en especial lo
relacionado con mi novela" (For the time being, there was nothing to
say, . . . just . . . to fly together in a fuck which, if it wasn't a record,
it was a good average, as the Cubans say. Afterward, we would talk
and talk without tiring, and she would tell me everything I needed to
know, especially things related to my novel) (209).

Agustín has acknowledged that a weakness of *Cerca del fuego* is
its failure to develop Aurora's character.[47] Lucio's female sexual partner is an assistant or facilitator for his writing, a sort of sexual and
metaphysical batboy, as is suggested by the baseball metaphor. At
the same time, this metaphor foreshadows the baseball game that
will form the "climax" of the novel, during which Lucio will wield
his bat/pen/phallus to hit a home run (another "vuelta a casa"), thus
claiming his place among his opponents, the all-stars of world literature. (The line-up is conceived in terms of the Western and U.S. literary canon; it excludes not only women, but also Latin American
writers of either gender.) Lucio appropriates the other players for his
discourse (and Agustín attempts to downplay the reverence in which
he holds them) by christening them with Hispanized versions (or,
in the case of one Spanish author, a scatological version) of their
last names, the names that mark patriarchal lineage; for instance,

Bodeler, Rambó, Guete, Yits, Juxlei, Paund, Yínsber, el Calderón de la Mierda (the Kettle of Shit), and the manager, Shespir (Baudelaire, Rimbaud, Goethe, Yeats, Huxley, Pound, Ginsberg, Calderón de la Barca, and Shakespeare).

However, the process of social, personal, and literary individuation is not yet complete. The automobile, symbol and nemesis of contemporary urban civilization, will follow Lucio to Tepoztlán and disrupt his domestic bliss, his "portion of normalcy," by taking his daughter's life. At the same time, the political crisis in Mexico will worsen, leading to a stage of siege and curfew that will trap Lucio at the house of María and Pancho Madero. Here Lucio realizes that his only true friends, the only people he can trust implicitly, are the members of his extended family. The one way to save his loved ones from the political repression, Lucio concludes, is to follow the example posed by Isaac and sacrifice himself: "La única manera de despertar consistía en que le cortaran la cabeza" (The only way to wake up was for them to cut off his head) (289). In spite of the superficial resemblance to Salazar Saldaña's self-immolation, we are meant to understand Lucio's suicide, by slashing his wrists, as a valid act of purification, leading to his subsequent immersion in flames and phoenixlike rebirth, which is simultaneous with finishing his novel. Individuation has allowed his blood/fire/semen/ink to fix reality on the pages of the text that we read, where it will "burn eternally" (312).

This concluding section is preceded by a visit that Lucio, finally reunited with his wife and children, makes to Chapultepec Castle, to watch a phallic "volcano" of fireworks: "Se está formando . . . un volcán, está agrupando un hervidero de luces en la boca superior, estalla ahora la erupción, es una infinidad de luces" (A volcano . . . is forming; it is clustering together an ebullition of lights in the upper entrance [literally, mouth]; it explodes now in an eruption; it is an infinity of lights) (311). The castle is at once a redeemed version of the perversely haunted "palace" of "Yautepec" and a metaphor for the restoration of the national family. Chapultepec, after all, had been the site of Moctezuma's summer palace and became the residence of Mexico's first two invaders, a Spanish viceroy and the French emperor, Maximilian, as well as housing Porfirio Díaz and, subsequently, the revolutionary fathers—including "Pancho Madero"—who ousted the domestic tyrant. Moreover, the fireworks indicate that the occasion is Mexican Independence Day, suggesting that Mexico's newest colonial power, the United States in collusion with the PRI, has been expelled. In view of the centrality of the family to the symbolism of *Cerca del fuego*, it is significant that the setting is an executive residence converted into a national monument, rather than the more public seat of government, the National Palace, with which the story opened; the "vuelta a casa" or "homecoming" is thus complete. The novel ends, then, with the reconstitution of the *patria*, in the dual sense of the "fatherland" and the patriarchal family. The Devouring Mother has ceded to the Angel of the House/ Muse, and a series of absent and weak fathers have been replaced by the male novelist as hero, savior, and patriarch.

6. Out of the Rubble: Mexican Narrative and Social Movements of the Late 1980s

Hundo esta ciudad en mis entrañas como si fuera un sable roto,
para saborearme en los perfumes ambiguos del naufragio

—y la ciudad responde, rayos, insultos, masivas devastaciones,
innúmeras catástrofes. . . . Y yo, después de tanto silencio de
escribir a solas, yo de pie, a deshoras, sin fuerza, junto al teléfono
que no suena y la puerta más muda, alguien puede llegar, un dios

o una persona tristemente vestida o un sol con rostro y mucha,
mucha luz para mis venas al borde, cerca, junto al abismo.

(I plunge this city into my entrails as if it were a broken saber, in
order to relish the ambiguous perfumes of the shipwreck

—and the city responds, lightning bolts, insults, massive
devastation, countless catastrophes. . . . And I, after so much
silence from writing alone, I on my feet, at odd hours, without
strength, next to the telephone that doesn't ring and the ever-so-
silent door, someone might come, a god

or a sadly dressed person or a sun with a face and lots and lots of
light for my veins on the edge of, near, next to the abyss.)

—DAVID HUERTA, *INCURABLE* (1987)

En los poetas zapotecas contemporáneos . . . no hay temática
individual, angustias personales; la angustia es social porque se
trata de sociedades en donde el destino del individuo está sujeto a
las necesidades de la colectividad . . .

(In contemporary Zapotec poets . . . there are no individual themes,
personal anguish; The anguish is social because these are societies
in which the individual's destiny is subject to the needs of the
collective . . .)

—VICTOR TOLEDO, *LA FLOR DE LA PALABRA* (1983)

Marcha política/Political March [Hermila, widow of a disappeared political leader from Juchitán, Oaxaca]. Photograph by Graciela Iturbide.

Cuauhtémoc Cárdenas and Super Barrio Gómez. Photograph courtesy of Elena Poniatowska.

Dibujo en el aire una Guía Rojí que contenga avenidas y calzadas del porvenir. Red de coordenadas para apresar al alma escurridiza.

(I draw in the air a Rojí Map that contains avenues and highways of the future. A network of coordinates to capture the slippery soul.)

—CARMEN LEÑERO, *GAJES* (1988)

New Social Actors

The second half of the 1980s in Mexico has been characterized by a plethora of political opposition and grassroots social movements on a scale not seen since the Revolution.

On the one hand, student activism of this period has been much more conciliatory and modest than the movement of 1968. In 1986 the CEU, or University Student Council, was formed around the issues of equal opportunity and the quality of education (including financial support for universities and class size). This movement has mobilized demonstrations of up to 200,000 people and organized university strikes. In contrast with the movement of 1968, the demands are more modest and the mood more subdued, partly because, this time, the authorities are willing to enter into dialogue with the students and, for the most part, the level of police repression is considerably lower.[1] Decisions made during the first University Congress in 1990 suggest that the elected student representatives are willing to compromise with the administration to the extent of jeopardizing their constituency's interests.

On the other hand, movements originating in the popular classes have tended to be more militant and forceful. One significant catalyst was the earthquakes that devastated large sections of Mexico City on September 19 and 20, 1985. The response to this catastrophe exposed endemic corruption in the government and private sectors and provided continuing demonstrations of government negligence, inefficiency, and dishonesty. Committees were formed by inhabitants of the capital who had lost their homes, particularly residents of the poor and working-class neighborhoods—including Tlatelolco—that were affected most severely. The "Sindicato 19 de septiembre" (September 19 Union) was formed by the thousands of female garment workers whose exploitation was revealed by the earthquake. Many of their colleagues had died in sweatshops that were death traps, where the earthquake had caught them as they began work an hour earlier than most Mexicans. While the tens of thousands of middle-class citizens who were mobilized by the rescue efforts during the ensuing weeks and months have, for the most part, withdrawn from involvement, the working-class and lumpen people who remain homeless or inadequately housed are continuing their struggle through the Asamblea de Barrios (Assembly of Neighborhoods). This organization, which includes a feminist contingent with a sophisticated program for dual militancy, is spearheaded by a new Mexican folk hero, Super Barrio Gómez, discussed below.

The widespread anger toward the government that surfaced in the aftermath of the earthquakes found a political voice in the presidential elections of 1988. A significant cross-section of Mexican society (in which the very wealthy, the rural and urban poor, and intellectuals figured prominently) expressed its dissatisfaction with the current political structure by mobilizing opposition movements of both the right and the left. The July 6 elections presented the PRI with the first real challenge it had encountered in its sixty-year monopoly over political power. Even the widely disputed official results conceded that the right-wing PAN (National Action Party) had won a large following in the northern states, and the left-populist National Democratic Front (which has since become the PRD, or Democratic Revolutionary Party) had won three states plus Mexico City, home of one-fourth of all Mexicans and the political, economic, and cultural heart of the nation. The leader of this new left coalition is Cuauhtémoc Cárdenas, a former governor of Michoacán and son of the beloved populist president Lázaro Cárdenas (1934–1940). The younger Cárdenas had left the PRI because of its refusal to democratize its political procedures, including the autocratic selection of its presidential candidate (whose triumph has—until last year—been a foregone conclusion from the time his candidacy is announced). Not surprisingly, in a country that has not had clean elections in thirty years, opposition parties of the right and left agree that the elections and the vote count were marred by massive fraud. (For a *cardenista* analysis, see *Radiografía de un fraude* [*X-Ray of a Fraud*], or the documentary film *Crónica de un fraude* [*Chronicle of a Fraud*], which has been banned by the government from public exhibition in Mexico.) On September 1, when President-elect Carlos Salinas de Gortari delivered the state-of-the-nation address to the Chamber of Deputies, he was interrupted by a member of the opposition; the right- and left-wing parties united in staging walk-outs and other protests of the electoral fraud. These events underlined that Mexico had become a different nation, one in which both the political hegemony of the PRI and the extraordinary power of the president had been seriously damaged; one in which political pluralism had become a reality.

During the first year of his presidency, President Salinas de Gortari met the challenge of recuperating some measure of presidential authority and the PRI's influence by jailing prominent union and financial leaders who are notoriously corrupt, as well as the alleged assassins of a prominent opposition journalist, Manuel Buendía. In the eyes of critics, these are symbolic gestures that remove particularly offensive individuals without changing a system that tolerates and even promotes the concentration and abuse of power. It is also standard practice for new Mexican presidents to roll a few heads from the previous administration as a strategy for distancing the new regime, in the public's mind, from officially sanctioned crimes.

At the same time, the two opposition movements have been weakened. Manuel Clouthier, the widely respected presidential candidate of the PAN, died in a car accident in 1989. Also, top *cardenistas* have committed political errors that have cost their party some degree of credibility, and there are rumors of divisions among the leaders. Meanwhile the PSUM (United Socialist Party of Mexico), which was recently formed when the Communist Party merged with several smaller leftist parties, has changed its name to the Democratic Revolutionary Party (PRD) in order to give Cárdenas' organization of the same name sufficient members to warrant its official registration as a party. This allows the PRD to run candidates in state and local elections. It is also very probable that Cárdenas will run for president again in 1994. Meanwhile, in recent months, frauds in municipal and state elections in Oaxaca, Michoacán, and Guerrero have been met with sit-ins and confrontations, and several labor unions have staged massive strikes, with mixed results.[2] It seems likely that the political climate of Mexico during the 1990s will continue to be characterized by instability and change as new social forces continue to coalesce and to press for democracy, self-determination, and a decent standard of living for all Mexicans, and as the ruling class continues taking shrewd measures to preserve its hegemony.

This changing social climate is being chronicled eloquently by some of Mexico's major contemporary authors. Carlos Monsiváis wrote recently that three writers, Elena Poniatowska, José Emilio Pacheco, and the poet Jaime Sabines (b. 1926), have earned such a widespread and enthusiastic following as to become part of Mexican popular culture; he might have included himself in the list as well. In the eighteen years since the publication of *Días de guardar*, Monsiváis has published several additional books and numerous essays that have established him as the foremost Mexican critic of popular culture and one of the most incisive analysts of the current social and political scene. His recent book *Entrada libre: Crónicas de la sociedad que se organiza* (*Free Admission: Chronicles of the Society that Is Getting Organized*) (1987) is indispensable for understanding the social movements of the 1980s and the emergence of a civil society. Moreover, Monsiváis has continued to live in a working-class neighborhood and has maintained close ties with various sectors of the popular urban community. As a top advisor to Cuauhtémoc Cárdenas, he is one of the few leftist writers who is integrally involved in the political process. (The other outstanding example is the short story writer and consummate storyteller Eraclio Zepeda [b. 1937], who served as a representative of the United Socialist Party of Mexico in the House of Deputies and ran for president in the 1987 primary elections. He will soon be running for the Senate, this time for the PDR.) Poniatowska has recently written: "Some Latin American writers inscribe our literature within a collective project. In this respect I consider Carlos Monsiváis exemplary. His country is Mexico, his life and literature are Mexico, his cause, that of the poorest Mexicans, the ones that fill the *zócalo* during demonstrations. For him the popular movements, the multitudes that are getting organized, the civil society that is finally demanding its rights, every gathering of young people, are all liberating."[3]

While Poniatowska has not directly collaborated with the PRD, she has frequently lent her extremely influential voice and pen to supporting this and other new social movements. Also, she has been instrumental in the organization and support of the garment workers' union. When she began to participate in the rescue brigades following the 1985 earthquake, Monsiváis convinced her that she could make the greatest contribution by doing what she does best: writing. The results were daily chronicles and interviews published in the newspaper over a three-month period, which subsequently were edited and shaped into her latest book, *Nada, nadie: Las voces del temblor* (1988). Nearly two decades after offering her fellow Mexicans the essential book about the student movement, Poniatowska has given them the definitive interpretation of the earthquake and reconstruction. Both are profoundly disturbing works that insist on recalling national traumas that the psyche would prefer to forget; yet they document injustices and celebrate the everyday heroism of people who, to paraphrase the author, are superior to their leaders. The two books are also a document of how twenty years of history have changed the outlook of Mexican society; while *La noche de Tlatelolco* ended with an image of cadavers, *Nada, nadie* concludes with a description of popular mobilization and rebuilding, even in the midst of overwhelming shock and grief. The very process of writing the book was collective as well, since several members of Poniatowska's fiction workshop gathered testimonies that were incorporated into the text.

Another example of an organic intellectual in contemporary Mexico is Super Barrio Gómez. Super Barrio, who calls himself "defender of tenants, scourge of greedy landlords," rushes to the scene of evictions in his Barriomobile, dressed in a costume combining elements of two pillars of popular culture, Superman and the wrestler (red-and-yellow cape, hood and mask). He steadfastly refuses to reveal his other name—thus maintaining an anonymous, collective identity—or to remove his mask, in keeping with the belief that a wrestler cannot be defeated unless he is unmasked. In September 1988, he began publishing his own newspaper, *El Pichicuás de Super Barrio* (*Super Barrio's Rattler*), which informs poor people of their rights and is distributed free in slums and shantytowns. Since his first appearance on behalf of the urban housing movement in mid-1987, Super Barrio has also been identified with other progressive movements and issues, including the anti-AIDS campaign, the plight of

Mexican workers in the United States, and *neocardenismo*. In 1991 the ruling class has come up with its own response to Super Barrio, a character named Super Pueblo, who appears regularly on the powerful multinational television network Televisa. The appropriation of avant-garde and popular art forms is an increasingly common strategy of the right in these postmodern times.

Cultural Decentralization

The eighties have seen the emergence of an increasing number of intellectuals from popular backgrounds, although, predictably, most of them are not novelists. An outstanding example are the Zapotecs who run the Casa de la Cultura, or House of Culture, in Juchitán. The Casa has published numerous books about Zapotec culture, including literature, as well as a bilingual literary magazine (in Spanish and Zapotec) entitled *Guchachi' reza/Iguana Rajada* (*Sliced Iguana*). It is associated with the militant COCEI (Committee of Workers, Peasants, and Students from the Isthmus [of Tehuantepec]). Thus, the artists and writers who collaborate with the Casa are organic intellectuals; by virtue of their immersion in Zapotec culture and their political commitment and activism, they are equipped to represent the interests of contemporary Zapotecs on the Isthmus of Tehuantepec. Theirs is the sort of literature that makes the *indigenista* novel, that genre cultivated by mestizo leftist intellectuals of the 1930s and 1950s, nearly obsolete, with a few intriguing exceptions.[4]

Francisco Toledo (b. 1940), who was instrumental in establishing the Casa and launching its ambitious cultural activities, is Mexico's most eminent contemporary artist, along with his fellow Oaxacan Rufino Tamayo. He extensively incorporates the Zapotec world view of his native Juchitán into his paintings, engravings, and sculptures. Toledo moved to Europe in 1984, removing himself from the COCEI activities, and recently he has returned to Mexico City. There he founded his own publishing company in 1989, Ediciones Toledo, which has produced handsome art books of photography, painting, and poetry focusing on Zapotec culture and working-class struggles, as well as a substantial new series of poetry by young writers based in Mexico City. Probably more than any other contemporary Mexican intellectual, Toledo has contributed enormous creative energy and material support to the promotion of talented younger artists, photographers, and writers.

During the second half of the 1980s, there has been a growing interest in Mexico City in regional cultures and identities, responding to the local patriotism of writers from the provinces and an interest in alterity on the part of capital dwellers. For instance, Federico Campbell's novel *Pretexta* (*Pretext*, 1979) and his short story collection *Tijuanenses* (*Tijuanans*, 1989) take place in Baja California, while the celebrated novellas and short stories of Jesús Gardea (b. 1939), Juan Rulfo's closest literary descendant, are all set in Delicias, a fictitious town in Chihuahua. Many works by Inés Arredondo, Héctor Aguilar Camín, and the playwright Oscar Liera are set in their native Sinaloa. Other recent books have taken Sonora and Chiapas as their subjects.[5] Moreover, in a culture that could not have been more centralized during the 1950s and 1960s, well-known writers now reside and, in many cases, direct workshops in Chihuahua (Jesús Gardea); Cuaútla (José Agustín); Guadalajara (Dante Medina); Zirahuén, Michoacán (María Luisa Puga); Oaxaca (Leonardo Da Jandra, Margarita Dalton, and Víctor de la Cruz); San Luis Potosí (David Ojeda); Xalapa (Luis Arturo Ramos); and Zacatecas (Alberto Huerta).

Along with Juan Villoro and Carmen Boullosa, Hernán Lara Zavala (b. 1946) is one of the best new narrators working in Mexico today. Both his first short story collection, *De Zitilchén* (*On Zitilchén*, 1981), and his first novel, *Charras* (*Union Leader*, 1990), are set in the Southeast, where his family has roots. This novel carries forward the documentary tradition of Leñero and Poniatowska in narrating the 1974 political assassination in Mérida, Yucatán, of the author's cousin, Efraín Calderón Lara, an honest labor leader nicknamed "Charras." While a man named Carlos Francisco Pérez Valdés was convicted of the murder, the novel suggests that Carlos Loret de Mola, who was governor of Yucatán at the time, gave the order. Loret died in 1986 (in a suspicious car accident), but his son has denied Lara Zavala's implicit accusation and has in turn pointed the finger at two other prominent politicians, including the current secretary of agrarian reform, Víctor Cervera Pacheco. In a recent interview Lara Zavala, who holds a prominent administrative position at the National University (UNAM), explained that the changing political climate gave him the freedom to write and publish this highly controversial novel: "Si verdaderamente aspiramos a una democracia ya llegó el momento en que pueda hablarse abiertamente de los protagonistas que intervienen en los crímenes, sobre todo de orden político, sin que importe su jerarquía" (If we truly aspire to a democracy, the moment has now arrived in which one can speak openly about the perpetrators of crimes, especially of a political nature, regardless of their [place in the] hierarchy.)[6]

A very recent trend is toward autobiographical texts and fiction based on travel, both foreign and domestic. Jorge Aguilar Mora, José Agustín, Humberto Guzmán, Héctor Manjarrez, Silvia Molina, María Luisa Puga, and Juan Villoro have all written about Mexican characters residing in the United States, Europe, or Asia. In Hernán Lara Zavala's (b. 1946) excellent second short story collection, *El mismo cielo* (*The Same Sky*, 1987), many of the protagonists are themselves English or Chicano. The effect of these works is to expand the cultural territory that Mexican literature can embrace and to emphasize the cosmopolitan dimension of contemporary letters. The danger of such works lies in their potential, in the absence of a critique of cultural dependency, for perpetuating Mexican intellectuals' traditional fascination with French, British, and North American culture, which has at times masked a sense of cultural inferiority. On the other hand, both María Luisa Puga and Verónica Volkow (b. 1955) have implicitly explored connections between colonialism in Mexico and in other Third World nations. Puga's first novel, *Las posibilidades del odio*, explores colonialism in Kenya, while Volkow recently published a political travel memoir entitled *Diario de Sudáfrica* (*Diary of South Africa*, 1988).

In the realm of domestic journeys, Puga and Mónica Mansour (b. 1946) have co-authored *Itinerario de palabras* (*Itinerary of Words*, 1987), a book of memoirs based on their experiences while traveling around Mexico to give public lectures about literature as part of an outreach program sponsored by the ministry of public education. Juan Villoro's intriguing diary of his search for family roots and popular music in the Southeast, *Palmeras de la brisa rápida: Un viaje a Yucatán* (*Palmtrees of the Brisk Breeze: A Journey to Yucatán*, 1989), and Rafael Ramírez Heredia's *Por los caminos del sur, vámonos para Guerrero* (*Along Southern Roads, Let's Go to Guerrero*, 1990) inaugurated a new collection of travel literature that will be published by Alianza Editorial Mexicana.

Contemporary writers have also collaborated with photographers on some of the most interesting books of photography that have been published during the last few years, many of which document aspects of rural Mexico. This is especially true of Elena Poniatowska, who has written the text for several books by Mexico's two leading women photographers, Mariana Yampolsky (b. 1933) and Graciela Iturbide (b. 1942). Yampolsky and Poniatowska traveled widely to document rural houses of southern Mexico; haciendas in the state of Hidalgo; and the Creole town of Tlacotalpan, Veracruz. Iturbide has also traveled throughout rural Mexico to take photographs (see *Sueños de papel* [*Paper Dreams*, 1985]), and she lived in

Juchitán, Oaxaca, while preparing *Juchitán de las mujeres* (*Juchitán, a Town of Women* [Ediciones Toledo, 1989]), which has a prologue by Poniatowska. The photographers Lourdes Grobet (b. 1940), Rafael Doniz (b. 1948), and Flor Garduño (b. 1957) have also centered their work during the 1980s on the Indian cultures of rural Mexico. Grobet's *Bodas de sangre* (*Blood Wedding*, 1987) captures a Chontal production of the Lorca play by the Laboratorio de Teatro Campesino e Indígena (Laboratory of Peasant and Indian Theater); and Garduño's *Magia del juego eterno* (*Magic of the Eternal Game*, 1985) and *Bestiarium* (1987) document various Indian cultures, especially those of Oaxaca, Chiapas, and Michoacán.

At present several of these photographers are taking their interest in popular female culture into urban contexts. Yampolsky's current project, entitled *Flor de maíz* (*Flower of Maize*), studies the lives of Mazahua women both in their native villages in the state of Mexico and in Mexico City, where they frequently immigrate to support their families as street vendors. Grobet is completing a book on women wrestlers in Mexico City, and Iturbide has been photographing the female members of Chicano street gangs on the U.S.-Mexican border. What these projects have in common is an interest in how women adapt to change by inverting traditional gender roles in both the economic sphere and the realm of cultural icons.

These literary and photographic projects reflect an increasing interest in documenting and preserving folk and popular cultures, and they come at a time of growing frustration with the poor quality of life in the overpopulated, seriously polluted, and violent capital. The growing sense of a need to decentralize Mexican culture (along with politics and the economy) is beginning to be implemented in federal policy. For instance, the budget recently allotted by the National Institute of Fine Arts for provincial cultural activities is significantly larger than in previous years. On the other hand, some state governments are undermining these efforts. For instance, the Laboratorio de Teatro Campesino e Indígena of Oxolotán, Tabasco, mentioned above, achieved international acclaim during the last administration with the support of the experimental novelist Julieta Campos (b. 1932), wife of the former state governor. However, with the change of administrations and in spite of strenuous protests from the actors and their many supporters in the intellectual and artistic community, the peasant theater collective has received no further funding or commitment of support. The state official in charge of cultural activities has been quoted by the press as asking, "If peasants devote themselves to theater, who's going to till the fields?"[7]

The New Feminism

In addition to the interdisciplinary collaborations between women writers and photographers listed above, the late 1980s have seen the development of a new stage of feminist activism and writing. On the one hand, middle-class women's movements have been joined by popular movements (such as the garment workers' union and the feminist wing of the urban housing movement), as well as collaborations across classes, such as Mujeres en Acción Sindical, or MAS (Women in Union Action). On the other hand, these political developments have not given rise to an increased number of literary texts characterized by militant or committed feminism of the sort associated with Poniatowska. Rather, a new group of women writers is emerging who explore the roots of psychosocial issues associated with gender in childhood and the patriarchal family and the politics of interpersonal relationships.

Ayer es nunca jamás (*Yesterday Is No More,* 1988), by Vilma Fuentes, offers an original perspective on the student movement. Women's points of view have been notoriously lacking since *La noche de Tlatelolco,* which examines female activism in the movement to some extent and focuses on maternal grief and mobilization following the massacre. Fuentes' is the first Mexican novel to explore the contradiction between female power in the private sphere and disempowerment in the public sphere in the context of sixties activism. This story is narrated, in retrospect, by the wife of a student activist who sympathized with the movement and was profoundly affected by it but who felt doubly marginalized by virtue of gender as a pregnant woman. Still, she was the dominant partner in her troubled marriage, which, like the student movement, Fuentes portrays as haunted by the specter of madness.

Fuentes deals extensively with the protagonist's intimate relationships, political ideas, and struggles with creativity. Interestingly, in a tradition that tends to idealize the mother (as in Poniatowska's text), she neither idealizes maternity nor portrays it as troublesome; it is simply not an issue. Once her daughter is born, the character seems to nearly forget she exists. In fact, all the female characters are either absent or deformed. Even the protagonist's female maid is a dwarf. During the crisis of her marriage, the protagonist finds female connections, of a sort, in the distorted mirror of her fellow inmates in a mental hospital. Nor is sanity presented as a male prerogative; the principal male characters are a homocidal lumpen who is recruited to attack students and two suicidal intellectuals. In addition to evoking the poisonous atmosphere of defeatism following

Tlatelolco, these characterizations suggest limitations imposed by patriarchal constructions of gender (articulated as possessiveness, paternalism, and objectification) and the spiritual deformity that they provoke in women and men alike.

Carmen Boullosa (b. 1954) and Carmen Leñero (b. 1959), now in their early to mid-thirties, are the best representatives of the new generation of feminist narrators. Leñero is the author of *Birlibirloques* (*Magic Acts*, 1986) and *Gajes* (*Fees*, 1988). The latter, which provides one of the epigraphs to this chapter, is a surreal text that straddles the borders between prose and poetry and which openly explores the issues of female sexuality and creativity as well as women's struggles against Oedipal relations, Catholic ideology, and commodification. Here the city map becomes a metaphor for the utopian project of reinventing the Mexican woman's soul. Boullosa, author of the novel *Mejor desaparece* (*Better It Vanishes*, 1986) and the poetry collection *La salvaja* (*The Savage Woman*, 1989), received the coveted Xavier Villaurrutia Prize for her second novel, *Antes* (*Before*, 1989). Another extremely talented, younger feminist writer is the playwright Jesusa Rodríguez, who has written and directed several acclaimed experimental plays and performance pieces during the last few years, many of which question traditional gender roles.

The musical counterpart to these younger authors would not be the "new song" performers of the seventies and early eighties, whose repertoire draws heavily on folk music, political poetry, jazz, and the blues. Rather, it is the postmodernist style of the rock singer Eugenia León, whose music incorporates various international pop rock forms, including reggae, as well as icons of Mexican elite and mass culture (from the poet Ramón López Velarde to the popular composer Agustín Lara).

In the area of cinema, women are among the most promising younger directors; they form part of the first generation to be trained at the National University's new film school. Two talented directors of fiction films who share the concerns of younger women novelists are María Novaro and Busi Cortés. Novaro has directed several acclaimed shorts and features, including *Una isla rodeada de agua* (*An Island Surrounded by Water*), which explores the subjectivity of an abandoned girl searching for her guerrilla parents in Guerrero, and *Lola*, a highly praised feature portraying the perspective of a young mother who lives on the streets of Mexico City. Busi Cortés' movie *El secreto de Romelia* (*Romelia's Secret*) retells Rosario Castellanos' story "El viudo Román" from the points of view of three generations of women.

Lesbian literature was only beginning to appear at the end of the 1980s, primarily in the areas of poetry and drama. The best book of lesbian erotic poetry to have appeared is *Lunas* (*Moons*, 1988), by Sabina Berman (b. 1956), a leading contemporary playwright. Homoeroticism and transvestitism are present in some of Jesusa Rodriguez's performance pieces and plays, along with parodies of traditional gender roles and stereotypes (including La Malinche and the Aztec goddess Coatlicue). Mexico's first lesbian fiction has also just appeared in the last few years; it includes *Amora* (*Love*, 1989), by Rosamaría Roffiel; *México 1956* and *Recuento para recuerdo* (*Inventory to Remember*), by Carmen Rosenzweig; and *Dos mujeres* (*Two Women*, 1990), by Sara Levi Calderón.

La novela negra

If lesbian literature is on the rise, gay male literature seems to be receding. *Lo peor ocurre al atardecer* (*The Worst Happens at Sundown*, 1990), a novel by Olivier Debroisie (b. 1952), a prominent young art critic, combines homoeroticism with the detective genre (*la novela negra*), which had become extremely popular in Mexico, as in the rest of the Hispanic and the Anglo-American worlds, at the end of the 1980s. Reviving a genre begun in Mexico by Rafael Bernal with *El complot mongol* (*The Mongol Plot*, 1969), Paco Ignacio Taibo II (b. 1949), president of the International Association of Detective Writers, has written some thirty such novels, of which the most recent is *Cuatro manos/Four Hands* (1990), which brings together current events, popular culture, and the everyday life of Mexican intellectuals, into an entertaining yarn. Recently Vicente Leñero and ten younger Mexican narrators that he more or less mentors (Marco Aurelio Carballo, Joaquín Armando Chacón, Gerardo de la Torre, Hernán Lara Zavala, David Martín del Campo, Silvia Molina, Aline Pettersson, Rafael Ramírez Heredia, Bernardo Ruiz, and Guillermo Samperio) collaborated on a collective detective novel, *El hombre equivocado* (*The Wrong Man*, 1988). By the authors' own acknowledgment, the literary product is less interesting than the experiment itself. The instigator of this project, David Martín del Campo (b. 1952), has recently published several novels, including two well-received murder mysteries, *Isla de lobos* (*Island of Wolves*, 1987) and *Dama de noche* (*Lady of the Night*, 1990).

Aside from Debroisie's book, few gay male novels had been published in the second half of the decade; perhaps this is a response to the AIDS epidemic, which has been more widespread in Brazil and Mexico than in any other Latin American countries, and is spreading rapidly. Luis González de Alba and other intellectuals have begun elaborating a scientific and journalistic discourse around the illness and its sociocultural impact. Perhaps the 1990s will see the emergence of an AIDS literature, similar to what has happened recently in various other countries affected by the crisis, including the United States, France, and Brazil.

Feminism and Popular Movements: Marching into the Twenty-first Century

In spite of the plethora of younger women writers, it is the "foremother" of these women, Elena Poniatowska, whose works best frame the overall trajectory of Mexican narrative of the past twenty years, in its textualization of political and gender critiques and its advocacy of a new subjectivity. Her recent characterizations of urban geography in the autobiographical essay "A Question Mark Engraved on My Eyelids" (1990) and her autobiographical novel *La "Flor de Lis"* (*The "Fleur de Lis"*, 1988)[8] embrace some of the same popular public spaces as her works from the 1960s, *Todo empezó en domingo* and *Hasta no verte Jesús mío*. Yet Jesusa Palancares' pessimism over the deterioration of the city, an index of her defeatist ideology based on her difficult life experience, has been displaced here by Poniatowska's contagious optimism. The author pays homage to the city as public space, in which the common experience of urban culture, of the parks, streets, and subway stations of downtown Mexico City, provides a model for recuperating a sense of community and a sort of popular nationalism:

How much of me there is in these faces that don't know me and that I don't know, how much of me in the subway, in the steps that pile up, one on top of the other, until they finally come out into the great, white spout of light, how much of me in the last, weary steps coming out, how much of me in the rain that forms puddles on the pavement, how much of me in the smell of wet wool, how much of me in the rusted steel sheets, how much of me in the Colonia del Valle–Coyoacán buses that rush along until they crash and form part of the cosmos, in the graffiti on the walls, in the pavement, in the earth trod on a thousand times. How much of me in those worn-out benches, their flaking paint, how much in the hardware stores, in the little corner stores, how much in all those testosterone shots on those dusty pharmacy shelves, in those syringes that used to be boiled and that spread hepatitis, how much of me in the signs that used to hang all

along San Juan de Letrán: "All types of venereal diseases treated,"
how much in the newspaper stands, in the Fountain of the Little
Frogs, in the shoeshine boxes, in the rickety trees—just like
little sticks climbing up to the sky—in the man who sold
electric shocks, in the old people's wrinkles, in the young
people's legs.[9]

Poniatowska's vision of the city, and of the society it represents, is
not the predominant one of the 1980s; it is neither an idealized colonial neighborhood in decline nor a monstrous megalopolis in the
throes of catastrophe. Rather, it is a succession of familiar neighborhoods that are in a steady state of disrepair and disease occasioned
by poverty, but in which ordinary details are capable of inspiring joy.
Poniatowska's optimism derives from her conviction that she is
participating, in her creative work as in everyday life, in a collective project involving a coalition of intellectuals with the popular
classes, founded on a common culture and a passionate commitment to creating Mexico, as a utopian construct and a material
reality.

Notes

1. Of Pyramids and Fleas

1. The army claimed that it acted in response to fire by snipers sympathetic to the students. However, nongovernmental analysts concurred that the action must have been planned in advance by the government and that fire was opened by soldiers dressed as civilians but identified by white gloves, calling themselves the Olympia Battalion. An army captain signed an official notarized statement about his participation in this secret battalion (Poniatowska, *La noche*, 172). One issue that has never been clarified is who wounded Gen. Hernández Toledo, the commander of the paratroopers, as the first shots were fired; student leaders suspect that there was serious dissension among the army leaders (personal interview with Luis González de Alba, 1981).

2. As in the case of the U.S. equivalent, there has been a proliferation of studies of 1968 in México. Probably the definitive study to date is still Sergio Zermeño's *México: Una democracia utópica—el movimiento estudiantil del 68* (1978). Gilberto Guevara Niebla's *La democracia en la calle: Crónica del movimiento estudiantil mexicano* (1988) situates 1968 within the development of student movements from 1958 through 1984. Also see the two issues of the journal *Nexos* that focus on 1968: nos. 9 (Sept. 1978) and 121 (Jan. 1988).

3. Guevara Niebla, *La democracia en la calle*, 46.

4. Monsiváis, *Entrada libre*, 134.

5. For an incisive overview of social movements of the 1980s, see ibid. On the COCEI, see Felipe Martínez López, *El crepúsculo del poder: Juchitán, Oax. 1980–1982* (1983), Laurent Aubague, *Discurso político, utopía y memoria popular en Juchitán* (1985), and Moisés J. Bailón Corres and Sergio Zermeño, *Juchitán: Límites de una experiencia democrática* (1987). On the CEU, see no. 49–50 of the journal *Cuadernos Políticos* (Jan.–June 1987).

6. While this opinion coincides with one expressed by Alejandro Toledo at the Congreso de Novela Mexicana del Siglo XX, held in Jalapa in 1984, my thesis dates from a paper that I presented at the Latin American Studies Association meeting in Mexico City in 1982. For an opinionated account of the symposium and a rapid survey of novels focusing on Tlatelolco, see

Gonzalo Martré, *El movimiento popular estudiantil de 1968 en la novela mexicana* (1986).

7. Glantz, *Repeticiones,* 90.

8. Poniatowska, draft of "A Question Mark . . ."

9. For instance, in Oaxaca, the poorest state in Mexico, the average number of years of education completed is 3.4 (*La Jornada,* June 4, 1989).

10. Juan Villoro, one of Mexico's most highly regarded younger short story writers, has recently parodied the social chronicle as a genre in his book *Tiempo transcurrido (Crónicas imaginarias)* (1987), a "fictional document" of the period 1968 to 1985, as embodied by a gallery of social types that the author paints in broad, satirical strokes.

11. Job, "Women Novelists," 46.

12. On *indigenista* fiction, see my book *Narrativa indigenista en los Estados Unidos y México* (1985).

13. Sefchovich, *México,* 223.

14. Villoro, "Pasaportes," 118.

15. Ibid.

16. Malvido, "Ramos," 18.

17. For instance, in an interview that took place in connection with a 1984 symposium on the theory and practice of the short story, Guillermo Samperio explained that in his second short story collection, *Textos extraños (Strange Texts,* 1981), he adopted a more classic style and apolitical themes in order to prove to his critics that he was not naive and could write like them (Bravo, *El cuento,* 208–209). Eraclio Zepeda admits that he had done the same thing with his own second short story collection, *Asalto nocturno (Nocturnal Assault,* 1974), in order to escape the label of *indigenista* writer and prove that he could write like his critics (Bravo, *El cuento,* 282–283). As he tells Samperio, "La gran burla hubiera sido que les dijeras, ahora no" (The great joke would have been for you to have told them no) (ibid., 209).

18. This is Pacheco's third novel if we count *El principio del placer (The Pleasure Principle,* 1972) as a short novel. This categorization is probably warranted, since the length and narrative structure are very similar to those of *Las batallas en el desierto.* Critics have tended to consider the former text a short story because it was published in a collection together with several stories, while *Las batallas en el desierto* was published by itself.

19. Bravo, *El cuento,* 210. In the same interview, Samperio refers to his treatment of Mexico City as "muy pachequista, muy Pacheco. Pienso que vamos el desastre" (very Pacheco-like, very Pacheco. I think we're headed toward disaster) (212).

20. Brushwood, *Narrative Innovation,* 82.

21. Pacheco, "Noticias," 50. Pacheco also compares the two styles of writing, as exemplified by the works of Julio Torri and Alfonso Reyes, to an hors d'oeuvre versus a turkey *mole* dinner, with its thirty-two varieties of chiles; and to a bonsai versus an *ahuehuete* (Mexican cypress tree) ("Cien años de Julio Torri," 56–57).

22. See my "Hacia una fusión del rigor y el placer, de la responsabilidad y

el desmadre: Entrevista con José Agustín," in *Nuevo Texto Crítico* (forthcoming).

2. Gender, Genre, and Authority

1. *Hasta no verte Jesús mío* was published by Ediciones Era in 1969, then by the Secretaría de Educación Pública in 1986. The English translation, *Here's Looking at You, Jesus,* has been completed and will be published by Pantheon Books. *La noche de Tlatelolco* was also published by Ediciones Era in 1971; the English translation by Helen R. Lane, *Massacre in Mexico,* was published by the Viking Press in 1975 and is currently being reprinted. *Hasta no verte Jesús mío* will hereafter be cited in text.

2. Ediciones Era's latest edition of *Hasta no verte Jesús mío* consisted of four thousand copies, while the latest printing of *La noche de Tlatelolco* was of eight thousand.

3. Elena Poniatowska, personal interview, Mexico City, July 1987. Although Josefina Bórquez maintained that she was born in 1902 (and Palancares implies this in the novel [216, 220]), Poniatowska calculated that she was actually born in 1900.

4. Elena Poniatowska, personal interview, Mexico City, July 1984.

5. Poniatowska, "Hasta," 10.

6. Poniatowska, personal interview, September 1988.

7. Poniatowska, "Testimonies," 158.

8. Poniatowska, "Hasta," 10.

9. Ella hablaba mucho de su situación actual, de lo mal que estaba su vivienda, de la gente en la vecindad, de lo mal que estaba el país, era una visión muy pesimista. De a dónde íbamos a dar, que la comida era pésima, que la leche tenía agua, que las tortillas tenían papel periódico, que el pan costaba demasiado caro. Eso era una cosa que ella repetía mucho, mucho, mucho. Y claro que yo se lo quité, porque el estar hablando todo el tiempo de eso. . . . Para ella la novela habría sido sólo el espiritualismo, la carestía y la mala situación actual (She talked a lot about her present situation, about the bad shape her house was in, about the people in the slum, about the bad state the country was in; it was a very pessimistic vision. About where we were going to end up, about how the food was lousy, milk was watered down, tortillas were made from newspaper, bread was too expensive. That's what she repeated a lot, a lot, a lot. And of course I took it out; because the idea of talking all the time about that. . . . If it had been up to her, the novel would have been only spiritualism, shortages, the bad economic situation) (Poniatowska, "Entrevista," with author, 94–95).

10. Poniatowska, "Testimonios," 160.

11. Poniatowska, "Hasta," 7.

12. See Geiger, "Women's Life Histories"; Meese, "Languages"; and Langness and Frank, *Lives,* for an overview of these and other issues in current life history research.

13. Friedman, "Marginated Narrator," 182.

14. Ibid., 183.

15. Guillén, *Literature as System*, 84.
16. Ibid., 80.
17. Poniatowska, personal interview, Sept. 1988.
18. Guillén, *Literature as System*, 84–85.
19. Beverley, "Lazarillo," 36.
20. Ibid., 37.
21. Larissa Lomnitz has noted, among Mexican shantytown inhabitants, what she calls the "ideology of assistance": "When questioned, most informants are reluctant to describe their own requests for assistance; yet they are unanimous in claiming to be always ready to help out their own relatives and neighbors in every possible way. . . . The duty of assistance is endowed with every positive moral quality" ("Social and Economic Organization," 151).
22. Langness and Frank, *Lives*, 46–47.
23. Foucault, *History of Sexuality*, 58–59.
24. Ibid., 61.
25. Elena Poniatowska, personal interview, Mexico City, July 1984.
26. Fromm and Maccoby, *Social Character in a Mexican Village*, 111–114.
27. Lomnitz, "Social and Economic Organization," 137, 145, 143. Poniatowska's personal experience in Mexico City's shantytowns contradicts Lomnitz's observation; the author has found that it is not uncommon for elderly people to live alone.
28. Friedman, "Marginated Narrator," 181.
29. Ibid., 184–187, 261.
30. After Josefina Bórquez's death in 1987, Poniatowska had Héctor García make new prints of the photographs he had taken of her in 1963, which Bórquez had torn up when they did not conform to her own internalized image of herself as young. One of these photographs, of Bórquez with Poniatowska, is reproduced here.
31. See González and Iracheta, "La violencia en la vida," regarding the relationship between poverty and violence in rural Mexico at the turn of the century.
32. Fromm and Maccoby, *Social Character in a Mexican Village*, 115, 151.
33. See Rubin, "The Traffic in Women," on the sex/gender system.
34. Elsewhere in the narrative Palancares provides an alternative (or additional?) explanation for her cross-dressing. It allowed her to follow Pedro into combat at times when women were not allowed to accompany their husbands (109).
35. Compare the combination of submission and rebellion (expressed in a shift from the formal to the informal verb form, and by echoing the words from a popular love song) in this letter dictated by an illiterate turn-of-the-century peasant woman for the abusive husband she had fled:

Apreciable Sr.: . . . después de saludar a ud. con el respeto devido, . . . le doi las mas rendidas gracias por los dias que estube tomando un pan en su dichosa casa. . . . un millon de gracias por todo y por los porrasos que Ud.

me dio tanto que sufri con Ud. no podria estar ni un momento a gusto con Ud. tal vez porque era llo pobre. . . . En fin deje Ud. el mundo rodar y puede encontrar otra megor que llo. Ni llo para Ud. ni Ud. para mi. . . . Adiós ingrato. Dios quiera que te cases pronto para que maltrates a tu mujer y te aga lo mismo. (Cited in González and Iracheta, "La violencia en la vida," 141)

(My Dear Sir: . . . after greeting you with all due respect, I'd like to thank you for the days that I was breaking bread in your happy home. . . . a thousand thanks for everything and for the beatings that you gave me so often that I suffered with you I couldn't be at peace for a moment with you maybe because I was poor. . . . So let the world turn and you can find someone better than me. I wasn't meant for you and you weren't meant for me. . . . Good-bye ingrate. With God's will, may you marry soon so you can mistreat your wife and she can do the same with you.)

36. Shupe, Stacey, and Hazelwood, *Violent Men,* 36–37.

37. Gil, "Sociocultural Aspects," 128.

38. In her 1984 interviews with a group of women residing in Ciudad Nezahualcóyotl, which is located on the outskirts of Mexico City and is reputed to be the largest shantytown in Latin America, Gisela Espinosa Damián found that "more than half the women are beaten, and although many defend themselves with the same violence, the idea also prevails that if a woman 'behaves badly,' it's right to beat her" (in Davies, *Third World—Second Sex,* 40).

39. Fromm and Maccoby, *Social Character,* 186; González and Iracheta, "La violencia," 124.

40. Compare Poniatowska's description of the elderly Josefina Bórquez's habit of shutting up her animals when she went off to work: "En aquellos años Jesusa no permanecía mucho tiempo en su vivienda porque salía a trabajar temprano a un taller de imprenta en el que aún la empleaban. Dejaba su cuarto cerrado a piedra y lodo, sus animales adentro asfixiándose, sus macetas también" (During those years Jesusa didn't stay at home much because she would go out to work early in a print shop where she was still employed. She would leave her room shut up with rocks and mud, her animals inside suffocating, her plants too) ("Hasta," 5).

41. Sociologists concur that patterns of violence tend to be learned from one's parents in childhood. For instance, see McCall and Shields ("Social," 114) and Shupe, Stacey, and Hazelwood (*Violent Men,* 36).

42. Shupe, Stacey, and Hazelwood, *Violent Men,* 85.

43. Palancares dwells in rich detail, at several points in the narrative, on the pleasures of eating (36, 41, 67, 87–88).

44. Poniatowska, "Hasta," 10–11.

45. Foucault, *History of Sexuality,* 35–36.

46. "Novena," 6–8.

47. Personal interview.

48. Harwood, *Rx: Spiritist as Needed,* 190–191. In the *Vuelta* article Poniatowska identifies Bórquez's religion as Spiritualism and distinguishes

this from Spiritism on the basis of their association with the poor and the upper classes, respectively. The sociological sources that I have consulted consider the distinctive element of Spiritism to be reincarnation; unlike Spiritualism, it (like Jesusa Palancares) subscribes to the belief in multiple lives. Moreover, while it began in Latin America as an elite phenomenon, Spiritism "filtered to the urban lower class and the peasantry," where it was combined with folk Catholicism (Macklin, "Belief, Ritual, and Healing," 393, 415–417). Jesusa Palancares herself refers to her religion as "espiritismo" (160).

49. Harwood, *Rx: Spiritist as Needed*, 41–45.
50. Prince, "Psychotherapy," 33–34.
51. Ibid., 34.
52. Roberts, *Cities of Peasants*, 145.
53. Ibid., 145–146.
54. Fry, *Spirits of Protest*, 196.
55. In a recent interview, Poniatowska explained, "Siempre me han atraído los hombres que te descubren una verdad del mundo, por eso mi acercamiento a dirigentes obreros o a líderes intelectuales, mi estar siempre pendiente de alguien que te va a revelar una verdad que cambiará tu vida o tu modo de ser. Eso es verdad en mi carácter pero creo que lo es también en mi familia" (I've always felt attracted to men who uncover a truth about the world for you; that's why I've been drawn to working-class organizers or to intellectual leaders, I've always gravitated toward people who will reveal a truth to you that will change your life or your way of being. That's true of my character, but I think it's also true in my family) (Poniatowska, "Entrevista," with author, 98).

3. The Novel as Pyramid

1. Fiddian, "Fernando del Paso y el arte," 144.
2. Martínez, in Ocampo, *La crítica de la novela*, 204.
3. In an interview with Angeles Mastretta regarding *Noticias del imperio*, del Paso spoke of the difficulties he has limiting his discourse: "Tuve que sacrificar, hacer una síntesis. Eso es muy doloroso porque el escritor, en general, no hace una síntesis; lo que hace precisamente es explayarse, derramarse un poco" (I had to sacrifice, to make a synthesis. That was very painful because writers, in general, don't make syntheses; what they do is precisely to dwell on things, run over a little) (Mastretta, Diálogo, 8).
4. Personal interview.
5. Ruffinelli, "Fernando del Paso," 199.
6. Ibid., 191.
7. Ibid., 195.
8. Personal interview.
9. Ruffinelli, "Fernando del Paso," 193.
10. Fernando del Paso, *Palinuro de México*, 629. Hereafter cited in text.
11. Personal interview.
12. In my written interview with him in 1981, del Paso wrote,

El movimiento estudiantil me hace pensar en una frase cuyo autor no recuerdo, que se refería a la Revolución del 48, o mejor dicho, a esa serie de rebeliones, asonadas y revueltas que tuvieron lugar en varios países y lugares de Europa—Francia, Austria, Hungría, el Norte de Italia entonces dominado por los austriacos—, que le hicieron pensar a Carlos Marx que había llegado el momento de la revolución socialista internacional. La frase—la cito de memoria, y quizás no es textual—es, "a turning point in history in which history failed to turn." Creo que necesitan pasar años, varias décadas quizás, para que podamos contar con la perspectiva histórica suficiente para juzgar el Movimiento del 68. Para ver si ese momento, que parecía un momento culminante de la historia de México, cambió o coadyuvó a cambiar nuestro futuro. Por ahora, parece que fue un sacrificio inútil: la injusticia social, la pobreza y la opresión no han hecho sino aumentar, y a todo ello se ha agregado una paradoja: México, gracias al petróleo—cuyos veneros escrituró el diablo, como dijo López Velarde—, es ahora, al mismo tiempo, un país muy rico y un país muy pobre.

(The student movement brings to mind a phrase whose author I do not remember who referred to the Revolution of '48, or, rather, to that series of rebellions, mob attacks, and revolts that took place in various countries and places in Europe—France, Austria, Hungary, northern Italy, dominated by the Austrians at that time—, which made Karl Marx think that the moment of international socialist revolution had arrived. The phrase—I cite it from memory, and perhaps it is not exact—is, "a turning point in history in which history failed to turn." I believe that years, perhaps several decades must go by before we can judge the Movement of '68. In order to see if that moment, which seemed a climactic moment in the history of Mexico, changed or helped change our future. For now, it seems that it was a useless sacrifice: Social injustice, poverty, and oppression have only increased, and to all this there has been added a paradox: Mexico, thanks to oil—for which the devil drew up the deed, as López Velarde said—, is now, at one and the same time, a very wealthy country and a very poor country.)

13. In *The Devil's Dictionary* Bierce defined heaven as "a place where the wicked cease from troubling you with talk of their personal affairs, and the good listen with attention while you expound your own."

14. McWilliams, *Ambrose Bierce*, 316.

15. Ibid., 329.

16. Bierce, *Skepticism*, 130–131.

17. Fernando del Paso, *Noticias del imperio*, 269. Hereafter cited in text.

18. Del Paso, *Visiones* (1990), 15.

19. Del Paso, "Entre el hombre," 26.

4. Commodification and Desire in the Wasteland

1. Pacheco's novel in progress may deviate to some extent from this pattern, since published excerpts indicate that it is a lengthy historical novel.

2. Bakhtin, "The *Bildungsroman*," 23.

3. Cockcroft, *Mexico*, 152. The economic and media empire that Miguel Alemán founded continues through his son, Miguel Alemán Velasco, vice-president of the newspaper *Novedades* and owner of several other popular newspapers and magazines (*The News*, *Claudia*, and *Contenido*), as well as the *fotonovelas*. Since 1986, Alemán Velasco has been president of Mexico's most powerful television conglomerate, Televisa, and he now also owns Aeromar, one of several new privately owned airline companies that have risen from the ashes of the bankrupt national airline Aeroméxico (Trejo Delarbe, "Three Faces," and Vera, "Magnates"). At the moment (September 1990) he is the leading candidate for the governorship of the state of Veracruz.

4. Bakhtin, "The *Bildungsroman*," 20–21.

5. Ibid., 21–24.

6. Ibid., 25.

7. The children's games in the novel recreate the actual war games that were played in the author's school during the late 1940s, which were motivated by the presence of Jews and Arabs in the Colonia Roma.

8. Pacheco, *Las batallas en el desierto*, 51. Hereafter cited in text. English translations of excerpts from *Las batallas en el desierto* are by Katherine Silver; those of Pacheco's poetry are mine. (I have recently translated *Ciudad de la memoria* in its entirety for publication as *City of Memory*.)

9. Mattelart, *La comunicación masiva*, 40.

10. Bakhtin, "The *Bildungsroman*," 51.

11. Ulloa, *Historia general de México*, 13–17.

12. Franco, "Beyond Ethnocentrism," 505.

13. García Canclini, *Las culturas populares*, 15–18.

14. Willis, "El 'consumidorismo,'" 62.

15. Jameson, *The Political Unconscious*, 293.

16. Enzensberger, "Introduction," 1.

17. Doane, *The Desire to Desire*, 5.

18. De Lauretis in ibid.

19. Ibid., 22.

20. Kaplan, *Women and Film*, 58.

21. Tabloid Editorial Collective, *Tabloid*, 1.

22. Pacheco, *Miro la tierra*, 57. Hereafter cited in text.

23. Pacheco, *Ciudad de la memoria*, 25. Hereafter cited in text.

5. Apocalypse and Patricide

1. In the presentation ceremony for Agustín's short story collection *No hay censura*, on March 9, 1989, the distinguished Mexican critic Emilio Carballido said of the writer's work: "Aunque hasta hoy no se le ha dado el precio que merece, seguramente dentro de muchos años será objeto de estudio. Una obra de gran importancia para la conciencia política, y la identificación con lo que, muchas veces, resulta ajeno para el lector" (Although until now it hasn't been given the value that it deserves, certainly within a

number of years it will be the object of study. A work of great importance for political conscience, and the identification with what frequently is foreign to the reader) (González, "José Agustín," 19). On the jacket of *Cerca del fuego*, José Emilio Pacheco refers to Agustín as "uno de nuestros más serios novelistas" (one of our most serious novelists) and refers to this book as "la más ambiciosa y lograda de sus novelas" (the most ambitious and successful of his novels).

2. Monsiváis, "La naturaleza de la onda," in Monsiváis, *Amor perdido*, 227.

3. Ibid., 256–258.

4. Poniatowska, "La literatura de la Onda," in *¡Ay, vida, no me mereces!*, 205.

5. The reception of Agustín's works in Mexico has suffered from his sensational personal life. He was born José Agustín Ramírez Gómez in Acapulco, not in Huaútla, Oaxaca, Mexico's psychedelic mecca, as he told Carter and Schmidt. At age sixteen Agustín eloped to revolutionary Cuba with Margarita Dalton, a sister of Roque Dalton, the Salvadoran guerrilla poet; there they participated in the Revolution's literacy campaign and soon parted ways. Back in Mexico City, Agustín remarried but later left his second wife, Margarita Bermúdez, for the upcoming singer and actress Angélica María. While he sympathized with the student movement during this period, he did so as a spectator rather than a participant. After reconciling with Bermúdez, Agustín spent seven months in the infamous Lecumberri Prison for alleged drug trafficking (actually, according to Agustín, for having marijuana in his possession while visiting a friend whose roommate turned out to be a drug dealer). It was in Lecumberri that he befriended the Marxist writer and political prisoner José Revueltas. After leaving prison in 1971, Agustín remarried Bermúdez and started a family, spent two years as a visiting professor at U.S. universities, and then settled with his wife and three children in an elegant suburb of the sleepy town of Cuaútla, between Mexico City and Cuernavaca. In short, he has metamorphosed from *enfant terrible* into respectable family man (Poniatowska, "La literatura," 196). Still, the controversies surrounding him have not abated, as evidenced by his recent resignation as the host of a literary program on Televisa, over issues of censorship. (It is therefore no accident that Agustín's latest collection of short stories is ironically entitled *No hay censura*.) Moreover, his comments on this program and elsewhere, to the effect that the eighties have been dominated by power struggles between literary mafias of the left and the right (*Three Lectures*, 8), have also offended leftist intellectuals, even as he had earlier insulted centrist and right-wing literati during the 1960s and 1970s. In short, this is a respectable family man who continues to devote considerable energy to *épater le bourgeois*, in both literature and life. His brother, the painter Augusto Ramírez, has recently characterized him as a literary *ponchador*, or boxer, blocking the reader before the reality that he describes (González).

6. Ruffinelli, "Sainz and Agustín," 155–157.

7. Ibid., 158.

8. Monsiváis, "La naturaleza," 237.

9. Poniatowska, "La literatura," 213.
10. Jameson, *Ideologies of Theory*, 74.
11. Agustín, *Se está haciendo tarde*, 58.
12. Glantz, "La Onda diez años despues," in *Repeticiones*, 118.
13. Ruffinelli, "Sainz and Agustín," 157.
14. In opposition to standard wisdom that the *albur* is an invention of lower-class Mexican male culture, of the so-called *lépero, pelado,* or *caifán,* the terms different historical periods have used to denote the street-wise lumpenproletariat (see Glantz, "La Onda diez años después," 125), Monsiváis proposes that Mexicans owe these bawdy puns to "el ocio de curas lascivos, de abogados hartos del Código de Procedimientos, de literatos fallidos, de médicos de provincia ansiosos de disfrazar sus devaneos literarios, de periodistas forjados en el intercambio relampageante de cantina" (the free time of lascivious priests, of lawyers fed up with the Code of Procedures, of failed writers, of provincial doctors anxious to disguise their literary pursuits, of journalists forged in the lightning-fast exchanges of *cantinas*) (*Escenas*, 305).
15. Carter and Schmidt, *José Agustín*, 22–23.
16. Agustín, personal interview.
17. Agustín, *Cerca del fuego*, 40. Hereafter cited in text.
18. "Forty Archetypes Draw their Swords," in Carter and Schmidt, *José Agustín*, 25–26.
19. This crisis seems to parallel the author's psychological breakthroughs, as he describes them in *El rock de la cárcel*. With regard to this autobiographical dimension of the novel, Agustín comments, "*Cerca del fuego* is the book in which consciously—at least more or less so—I have plunged into my darkest and most dangerous areas. For me this work is a metaphor for an individuation via literature, which explains the overwhelming and infinite difficulties I have had in rounding out the text" (Agustín, "Forty," 27). In his autobiography Agustín acknowledges having studied closely first the *I Ching*, then Carl Gustav Jung's complete works, which "gave meaning and unity" to his experiences, and in turn led him to read the writings of Joseph Campbell, Erich Neumann, Mircea Eliade, and Carlos Castañeda (*El rock*, 72–73). Whether or not the reader accepts these authors' theories, Agustín's immersion in Jungian psychology has served as a source of powerful symbolism and imagery for his latest novel, imagery that, as we shall see, is nevertheless ideologically problematic.
20. Agustín, personal interview.
21. Agustín has said that he wrote the complete first draft of the novel in 1978 and then spent the next eight years revising it (personal interview).
22. From the beginning Agustín has demonstrated a predilection for archetypal names. In *La tumba* the protagonist is named Gabriel Guía (Gabriel Guide).
23. Agustín explained the symbolism of this episode for him:

Allí el metro . . . es una representación de la Ciudad de México por excelencia, creo que es el alma de México, representa la condición actual de

México. Es una incomodidad de la chingada, un apretujamiento horrible. Allí la gente nace, se muere, canta, se caga, hace millones de cosas, se roba, se vive, se explaya, y todo, y es perfectamente inconsciente de lo que está ocurriendo. Y además nadie puede huir de eso porque todos se sostienen el uno al otro. El apretujamiento es tal que no permite que nadie se caiga. Creo que eso es la Ciudad de México actualmente. El metro es el nuevo Leviatán, la nueva ballena, el Moby Dick que te oprime, que te tiene jodido, pero que al mismo tiempo te renueva, te permite estar en pie, estar unido con los demás, y que además es fuente de alimento de las clases populares. Yo soy muy metrónomo. (Personal interview)

(There the subway . . . is a representation of Mexico City *par excellence;* I think it's the soul of Mexico, that it represents current conditions in Mexico. It's fucking uncomfortable, a horrible squeeze. There people are born, die, sing, shit on themselves, do millions of things, steal, live, hold forth, and everything, and they're perfectly unconscious of what's happening. And anyway no one can get away from that because they all sustain each other. There is such a squeeze that it doesn't let anyone fall. I think that's Mexico City at this time. The subway is the new Leviathan, the new whale, the Moby Dick that oppresses you, that has you screwed, but at the same time it renews you, it allows you to stay on your feet, to be united with everyone else, and it's also a source of nourishment for the popular classes. I'm a big "metronome" [subway fan]).

24. Agustín, personal interview.
25. Poniatowska, "La literatura de la Onda," 190–191.
26. Agustín, personal interview.
27. Monsiváis, *Escenas,* 238.
28. Agustín has noted that this accident is also a representation of his own literary maturation: "Matar a don Pimpirulando fue también matar al niño Juan José Agustín infantil que narra cositas con un lenguaje muy fresco, muy coloquial, muy cotorro, pero que es un niño a fin de cuentas" (To kill don Pimpirulando was also to kill the little boy Juan José Agustín who tells things in a language that's very fresh, very colloquial, very clever, but who is a child, after all) (personal interview).
29. The "Reina del Metro," according to Agustín, "es el ánima pero dada en su condición más material, y lo que Jung llamaría el ánima negativa. La que todavía está muy involucrada en todos los procesos humanos, materiales y carnales" (is the anima but given in its most material mode, what Jung would call the negative anima. The one that's still very involved in all the human, material, and carnal processes) (personal interview).
30. Jung, *Psychology and Alchemy,* 117, vol. 12 in the *Collected Works.*
31. Kristeva, *Desire in Language,* 191.
32. Jung, *The Archetypes,* 284, *Aion,* 266, 9, vol. 9, parts 1 and 2 in the *Collected Works.*
33. This parallel was suggested to me by Donally Kennedy.
34. In *La tumba* a sports car whose driver had been racing with the protagonist, Gabriel Guía, crashed into a truck while rounding a curve and

went up in flames. Gabriel felt a sense of satisfaction and thought that the other driver deserved his fate for attempting to pass him (14).

35. Agustín, *De perfil*, 273.
36. Agustín, *Se está haciendo tarde*, 150–152.
37. Agustín, personal interview.
38. Modleski, *The Women Who Knew Too Much*, 70.
39. Agustín, "Forty," in Carter and Schmidt, *José Agustín*, 31.
40. Agustín, "Entrevista," 37.
41. Agustín, personal interview.
42. Ibid.
43. Agustín, *El rock*, 129.
44. Agustín, personal interview.
45. Agustín, "Entrevista," 34.
46. Franco, "Beyond Ethnocentrism," 510.
47. Agustín, personal interview.

6. Out of the Rubble

1. Monsiváis, *Entrada libre*, 272.
2. The national teachers' strike of April–May 1989 won schoolteachers a 25 percent pay raise—they had asked for a 100 percent increase—and, more significantly, toppled a corrupt, deeply entrenched union leader. However, the overlapping strike of Mexico City bus drivers led to mass firings.
3. Poniatowska, draft of "A Question Mark . . ."
4. These two publishing houses have tended to focus on works of art, poetry, photography, and history. For instance, see the following publications by the Popular Municipal Government of Juchitán: Víctor de la Cruz, *La flor de la palabra: Antología de la literatura zapoteca* (*Blossom of the Word: Anthology of Zapotec Literature*, 1983); Foto Estudio Jiménez, *Sotero Constantino, fotógrafo de Juchitán* (*Sotero Constantino, Photographer of Juchitán*, 1983); André Pieyre de Mandiargues, *La noche de Tehuantepec* (*The Night of Tehuantepec*, 1985), a travel story; and the two books of history and political analysis of the COCEI cited in chapter 1, note 5. By Ediciones Toledo (Mexico City), see Alfredo López Austin, *Una vieja historia de la mierda* (*An Ancient History of Shit*, 1988) and Graciela Iturbide and Elena Poniatowska, *Juchitán de las mujeres* (*Juchitán, a Town of Women*, 1989). Ediciones Era and the Galería López Quiroga have also published books of photographs of works by the Zapotec artist Francisco Toledo. For instance, see *Lo que el viento a Juárez* (*How the Wind Affected Juárez*, 1986), with a prologue by Carlos Monsiváis; *Toledo* (1987), with a prologue by Luis Cardoza y Aragón; and *Canto a la sombra de los animales* (*Song in the Animals' Shadow*, 1988), which includes poetry by Alberto Blanco. One interesting *indigenista* novel that has appeared is Jesús Morales Bermúdez's *Memorial del tiempo o Vía de las conversaciones* (*Memorial of Time or By Way of Conversations*, 1987). Morales, who lived in a Chol village for four years, recreates the villagers' testimony by reproducing their distinctive Spanish dialect.

5. On Sonora, see Francisco Luna's *Tres de asada y uno de machaca pa' llevar* (*Three Barbecued Steak Tacos and One Shredded Beef Taco, to Go,* (1989); on Chiapas, Roberto López Moreno's *El arca de Caralampio* (*El extraño mundo zoológico de Chiapas*), (*Caralampio's Ark* [*The Strange Zoological World of Chiapas*], 1983).

6. Ochoa Sandy, "Lara Zavala," 50.

7. Another woman photographer, Lourdes Grobet, has published a handsome book of photographs of the Teatro Campesino's version of *Bodas de sangre* (*Blood Wedding*), by Federico García Lorca. The book, which was published by the state government of Tabasco under the last administration, includes the heavily modified text, which adapts the Spanish rural tragedy to the situation of Mexican peasants of the Southeast.

8. This passage expands the ending of *La "Flor de Lis,"* in which the protagonist revels in the sunshine and the faces as she strolls through Alameda Park: "Me gusta sentarme al sol en medio de la gente, esa gente, en mi ciudad, en el centro de mi país, en el ombligo del mundo" (I like to sit in the sun in the midst of the people, those people, in my city, in the middle of my country, in the center of the world). She also compares the streets she has traveled on the Colonia del Valle–Coyoacán bus to the years she has lived (261).

9. Poniatowska, "A Question Mark," 122–123.

Bibliography

[In addition to works cited, primarily narrative and literary criticism of the period 1968 to 1988 and the literary theory that has guided my analyses, the following list includes key historical, sociological, and anthropological studies that have enhanced my understanding of contemporary Mexican culture and society. Works by the same author are listed in order of publication, rather than in alphabetical order, in order to convey a sense of the writer's development. Works by the four authors whose novels I analyze in detail are listed at the end of the bibliography.]

Abreu Gómez, Ermilo. "Un libro mil veces admirable: *Hasta no verte Jesús mío.*" Review in *La Cultura en México: Suplemento de Siempre!*, Feb. 4, 1970, 12–13.

Aguilar Camín, Héctor. "Sólo cenizas hallarás (Registros para la historia cultural de un sexenio, 1968–1976)." In *Cultura y dependencia.* Guadalajara: Departamento de Bellas Artes, Gobierno de Jalisco, 1977. 229–270.

———. *La decadencia del dragón.* Mexico City: Océano, 1983.

———. *Morir en el golfo.* Mexico City: Océano, 1985.

———. *La guerra de Galio.* Mexico City: Ediciones Era, 1991.

———, ed. *México mañana.* Mexico City: Océano-Nexos, 1986.

———. "Pensar el 68." Special issue of *Nexos: Sociedad, Ciencia, Literatura* (Jan. 1988).

Aguilar Mora, Jorge. *Cadáver lleno de mundo.* Mexico City: Joaquín Mortiz, 1971.

———. *Si muero lejos de ti.* Mexico City: Joaquín Mortiz, 1979.

———. *Una muerte sencilla, justa, eterna (Cultura y guerra durante la revolución mexicana).* Mexico City: Ediciones Era, 1990.

Aguilera, Gaspar. "La larga vigencia de *Morirás lejos.*" Review in *La Jornada Semanal*, Nov. 29, 1987, 14–15.

Aguirre, Eugenio. *Gonzalo Guerrero.* Mexico City: Universidad Nacional Autónoma de México, 1980; Secretaría de Educación Pública (Lecturas Mexicanas), 1986.

Alvarez, Ildefonso. "Fernando del Paso: De 'José Trigo' a 'Palinuro de México.'" *La Estafeta Literaria*, Jan. 1, 1978, 14–15.

Alvarez Abreu, Alvaro. "Tiempo de novela." *La Jornada*, Mar. 4, 1989.

Alvarez Chacón, Edgard. "*Palinuro de México.*" Review, in *Revista de Crítica Literaria Latinoamericana* 9.17 (1983): 255–257.

Anonymous. "Fernando del Paso expone sus ilustraciones en París." *La Jornada*, Jan. 21, 1989, 18.

Aponte, Barbara Bockus. "José Emilio Pacheco, cuentista." *Journal of Spanish Studies, Twentieth Century* 7 (1979): 5–21.

Argüelles, Juan Domingo. "José Emilio Pacheco: Recordar entre ruinas." Review of *Las batallas en el desierto*. *El Día*, June 3, 1981, 28.

Aridjis, Homero. *Vida y tiempos de Juan Cabezón de Castilla*. Mexico City: Editorial Diana, 1988.

———. *Memorias del Nuevo Mundo*. Mexico City: Editorial Diana, 1988.

Arizpe, Lourdes. *Indígenas en la ciudad de México: El caso de las 'Marías.'* Mexico City: Secretaría de Educación Pública (SepSetentasDiana), 1979.

———. *Historia de la Revolución Mexicana*. Vol. 20, *1940–1952, Civilismo y modernización del autoritarismo*. Mexico City: El Colegio de México, 1979.

———. *Campesinado y migración*. Mexico City: Secretaría de Educación Pública, 1985.

Arredondo, Inés. *Río subterráneo*. Mexico City: Joaquín Mortiz, 1979.

———. *Opus 123*. Mexico City: Océano, 1983.

———. *Los espejos*. Mexico City: Joaquín Mortiz, 1988.

———. *Obras completas*. Mexico City: Siglo XXI, 1988.

Arreola, Juan José. *Confabulario*. Mexico City: Fondo de Cultura Económica, 1952.

———. *La feria*. Mexico City: Joaquín Mortiz, 1963.

Aubague, Laurent. *Discurso político, utopía y memoria popular en Juchitán*. Oaxaca: Universidad Autónoma "Benito Juárez" de Oaxaca, 1985.

Avilés Fabila, Andrés. *El gran solitario de palacio*. Mexico City: Cía. Fabril Editora, 1971.

Azuela, Arturo. *El tamaño del infierno*. Mexico City: Joaquín Mortiz, 1974.

———. *Un tal José Salomé*. Mexico City: Joaquín Mortiz, 1975.

———. *Manifestación de silencios*. Mexico City: Joaquín Mortiz, 1979.

———. *El matemático*. Mexico City: Plaza y Valdés, 1988.

Azuela, Mariano. *Los de abajo*. 1924; Mexico City: Fondo de Cultura Económica, 1960.

Bailón Corres, Moisés J., and Sergio Zermeño. *Juchitán: Límites de una experiencia democrática*. Mexico City: Instituto de Investigaciones Sociales, Universidad Nacional Autónoma de México, 1987.

Bakhtin, M. M. *Rabelais and His World*. Trans. Helene Iswolsky. Cambridge: MIT Press, 1972.

———. "The *Bildungsroman* and Its Significance in the History of Realism (Toward a Historical Typology of the Novel)." In *Speech Act Genres and Other Late Essays*. Trans. Vern W. McGee. Austin: University of Texas Press, 1986. 10–59.

———. *The Dialogic Imagination: Four Essays*. Ed. Michael Holquist.

Trans. Caryl Emerson and Michael Holquist. Austin: University of Texas Press, 1981.

Balboa Echeverría, Miriam. "Notas a una escritora testimonial: *Fuerte es el silencio* de Elena Poniatowska." *Discurso Literario* 5.2 (Spring 1988).

Barberán, José, Cuauhtémoc Cárdenas, Adriana López Monjardín, and Jorge Zavala. *Radiografía del fraude: Análisis de los datos oficiales del 6 de julio.* Mexico City: Editorial Nuestro Tiempo, 1988.

Bartra, Roger. *La democracia ausente.* Mexico City: Grijalbo, 1986.

———. *La jaula de la melancolía: Identidad y metamorfosis del mexicano.* Mexico City: Grijalbo, 1987.

———. et al. "México: La democracia y la izquierda." *Cuadernos Políticos* 49–50 (Jan.–June 1987).

Bary, David. "Poesía y narración en cuatro novelas mexicanas." *Cuadernos Americanos* 234.1 (1981): 198–210.

Basurto, Jorge. *La clase obrera en la historia de México,* Vol. 14, *En el régimen de Echeverría: Rebelión e independencia.* Mexico City: Siglo XXI, 1983.

Bellinghausen, Hermann. *Crónica de multitudes.* Mexico City: Océano, 1987.

Bellinghausen, Hermann, and Hugo Hiriart, eds. "Pensar el 68." Special issue of *Nexos: Sociedad, Ciencia, Literatura* (Jan. 1988).

Benería, Lourdes, and Martha Roldán. *The Crossroads of Class and Gender: Industrial Homework, Subcontracting, and Household Dynamics in Mexico City.* Chicago: University of Chicago Press, 1987.

Berman, Sabina. *Lunas.* Mexico City: Katún, 1988.

———. *La bobe.* Mexico City: Planeta, 1990.

Bermúdez, María Elvira. *Muerte a la zaga.* Mexico City: Premiá, 1985.

———. *Encono de hormigas.* Xalapa: Universidad Veracruzana, 1987.

Bernal, Rafael. *El complot mongol.* Mexico City: Joaquín Mortiz, 1969.

Betancourt, Ignacio. *De cómo bajó Guadalupe a La Montaña y todo lo demás.* Mexico City: Instituto Nacional de Bellas Artes and Joaquín Mortiz, 1977.

Beverley, John. "*Lazarillo* and Primitive Accumulation: Spain, Capitalism and the Modern Novel." *Bulletin of the Midwest Modern Language Association* 15.1 (1982): 29–42.

Bierce, Ambrose. *Tales of Soldiers and Civilians.* Freeport, N.Y.: Books for Libraries Press, 1970 (1891).

———. *The Devil's Dictionary.* Owings Mills, Md.: Stemmer House, 1978.

———. *Skepticism and Dissent: Selected Journalism from 1898–1901.* Ann Arbor, Mich.: Delmas Books, 1980.

Blanco, José Joaquín. *La vida es larga y además no importa.* Mexico City: Premiá, 1979.

———. *La paja en el ojo: Ensayos de crítica.* Puebla: Universidad Autónoma de Puebla, 1980.

———. "Aguafuertes de narrativa mexicana, 1950–1980." *Nexos: Sociedad, Ciencia, Literatura* (Aug. 1982): 23–39.

———. *Las púberes canéforas.* Mexico City: Océano, 1983.

————. *Calles como incendios*. Mexico City: Océano, 1985.

————. *Cuando todas las chamacas se pusieron medias nylon*. Mexico City: Joan Boldó i Climent, Editores, 1988.

————. *Un chavo bien helado (Crónicas de los años ochenta)*. Mexico City: Ediciones Era, 1990.

Borinsky, Alicia. "José Emilio Pacheco: Relecturas e historia." *Revista Iberoamericana* 150 (Jan.–Mar. 1990): 267–273.

Boullosa, Carmen. *Mejor desaparece*. Mexico City: Océano, 1987.

————. *Antes*. Mexico City: Vuelta, 1989.

————. *La salvaja*. Mexico City: Fondo de Cultura Económica, 1990.

Bradu, Fabienne. "*Palinuro de México*: La picaresca de la desilusión." Review in *Revista de la Universidad de México* (Aug. 1979): 43–44.

Bravo, Roberto. *No es como usted dice*. Mexico City: Joaquín Mortiz, 1980.

————. *Vida del orate*. Mexico City: Joaquín Mortiz, 1990.

Bravo, Roberto, ed. *El cuento está en no creérselo*. Tuxtla Gutiérrez, Chiapas: Universidad Autónoma de Chiapas, 1985.

————. *Itinerario inicial (La joven narrativa de México.)* Tuxtla Gutiérrez, Chiapas: Universidad Autónoma de Chiapas, 1985.

Bruce-Novoa, Juan. "Subverting the Dominant Text: Elena Poniatowska's *Querido Diego*." In *Knives and Angels: Women Writers in Latin America*. Ed. Susan Bassnett. London: Zed Books, 1990. 115–131.

Brushwood, John. *La novela mexicana (1967–1982)*. Mexico City: Editorial Grijalbo, 1984.

————. *Narrative Innovation and Political Change in Mexico*. New York: Peter Lang, 1989.

Bustamante, Miguel. "José Emilio Pacheco en España." Review of *Alta traición, antología poética*. *Universidad de México* 411–412 (1985): 50–51.

Calva, José Rafael. *Utopía gay*. Mexico City: Editorial Oasis, 1983.

Campbell, Federico. *Pretexta*. Mexico City: La Máquina de Escribir, 1977; 2nd ed. rev. and enl., Fondo de Cultura Económica, 1979; Secretaría de Educación Pública (Lecturas Mexicanas), 1988.

————. *Tijuanenses*. Mexico City: Joaquín Mortiz, 1989.

Campos, Jorge. "'*Palinuro de México*,' de Fernando del Paso." Review in *Insula* 33.378 (1978): 11.

Campos, Julieta. *Celina o los gatos*. Mexico City: Siglo XXI, 1968.

————. *Tiene los cabellos rojizos y se llama Sabina*. Mexico City: Joaquín Mortiz, 1974.

Campos, Marco Antonio. "*Las batallas en el desierto*." Review in *Proceso*, May 4, 1981, 55–56.

Capistrán, Miguel. "La transmutación literaria." *La Vida Literaria* (Apr. 1970): 12–15.

Cárdenas, Cuauhtémoc. *Nuestra lucha apenas comienza*. Mexico City: Editorial Nuestro Tiempo, 1988.

Carter, June C. D., and Donald L. Schmidt, eds. *José Agustín: Onda and Beyond*. Columbia: University of Missouri Press, 1986.

Castañeda, Salvador. *¿Por qué no lo dijiste todo?* Mexico City: Grijalbo, 1979. Premio Grijalbo.

Castañón, Adolfo. "Tus hombres, Babel, se envenenarán de incomprensión (la narrativa mexicana en los setenta)." *La Cultura en México: Suplemento de Siempre!* May 4, 1976, 2–10.

Castellanos, Rosario. "La diversificación de la novela mexicana." *Diorama de la Cultura (Excélsior)*, Mar. 1, 1970.

Castillo, Heberto, et. al. *1968: El principio del poder.* Mexico City: Proceso, 1980.

Cervantes, Francisco. "El nuevo adiós a mamá Carlota." Review of *Noticias del imperio. La Jornada de Libros*, July 2, 1988, 1, 6.

Chacón, Joaquín-Armando. *Las amarras terrestres.* Hanover, N.H.: Ediciones del Norte, 1982.

———. *El recuento de los daños.* Mexico City: Diana, 1987.

Chavarri, Raúl. "El personaje en la moderna novela mejicana. A propósito de *José Trigo* de Fernando del Paso." *Cuadernos Hispanoamericanos* 82.215 (1967): 395–400.

Chevigny, Bell Gale. "The Transformation of Privilege in the Work of Elena Poniatowska." *Latin American Literary Review* 26 (1985): 49–62.

Chimal, Carlos. *Cuatro bocetos.* Mexico City: Martín Casillas, 1983.

———. *Escaramuza.* Mexico City: Fondo de Cultura Económica, 1987.

Clifford, James, and George E. Marcus, eds. *Writing Culture: The Poetics and Politics of Ethnography.* Berkeley: University of California Press, 1986.

Cluff, Russell. "*Morirás lejos:* Mosaico intemporal de la crueldad humana." *Chasqui* 8.2 (1979): 19–36.

———. "Immutable Humanity within the Hands of Time: Two Short Stories by José Emilio Pacheco." *Latin American Literary Review* 10.20 (1982): 41–43.

———. *Siete acercamientos al relato mexicano actual.* Mexico City: Universidad Nacional Autónoma de México, 1987.

Cockcroft, James D. *Mexico: Class Formation, Capital Accumulation, and the State.* New York: Monthly Review Press, 1983.

Collective Author. *El hombre equivocado.* Mexico City: Joaquín Mortiz, 1988.

Connolly, Cyril. *The Unquiet Grave.* New York: Harper and Brothers, 1945.

Córdova, Arnaldo. *La formación del poder político en México.* Mexico City: Ediciones Era, 1972.

Cortázar, Julio. *Rayuela.* Buenos Aires: Editorial Sudamericana, 1963.

Cypher, James M. *State and Capital in Mexico: Development Policy since 1940.* Boulder: Westview Press, 1990.

Da Jandra, Leonardo. *Entrecruzamientos.* 2 vols. Mexico City: Joaquín Mortiz, 1986, 1988.

Dalton, Margarita. *Larga sinfonía en D.* Mexico City: Diógenes, 1968.

———. ". . . Y la nube pasa." Oaxaca: Casa de la Cultura, Gobierno del Estado de Oaxaca, 1986.

Dalton, Margarita, and Roberta Zohn. *Poemas de amor y otras cosas.* Oaxaca: Casa Oaxaqueña de la Cultura, 1989.

Davies, Miranda, ed. *Third World–Second Sex.* Vol. 2. London: Zed Books, 1987.

Debroise, Olivier. *Lo peor ocurre al atardecer.* Mexico City: Cal y Arena, 1990.

Délano, Poli. "José Agustín entre la pluma y la pared." *Plural* (Jan. 1977): 59–66.

de Lauretis, Teresa, ed. *Feminist Studies/Critical Studies.* Bloomington: Indiana University Press, 1986.

Deleuze, Gilles. *Foucault.* Trans. Seán Hand. Minneapolis: University of Minnesota Press, 1988.

Delgado, Antonio. *A causa de los equinoccios.* Mexico City: Joaquín Mortiz, 1978.

———. *Figuraciones en el fuego.* Mexico City: Joaquín Mortiz, 1980.

del Palacio, Jaime. *Parejas.* Mexico City: Martín Casillas, 1981.

Díaz, Nancy Gray. "El mexicano naufragado y la literatura 'pop': 'La fiesta brava' de José Emilio Pacheco." *Hispanic Journal* 6.1 (1984): 131–139.

Díaz-Polanco, Héctor, et. al. *Indigenismo, modernización y marginalidad: Una revisión crítica.* Mexico City: Juan Pablos Editor, 1979.

Díez, Luis A. "La narrativa fantasmática de José Emilio Pacheco." *Texto Crítico* 2.5 (1976): 103–114.

Doane, Mary Ann. *The Desire to Desire: The Woman's Film of the 1940s.* Bloomington: Indiana University Press, 1987.

Domecq, Brianda. *La insólita historia de la Santa de Cabora.* Mexico City: Planeta, 1990.

Domínguez, Christopher. "Fernando del Paso o el banquete de la historia." Review of *Noticias del imperio. Proceso,* Feb. 3, 1988, 58–59.

Donoso Pareja, Miguel. "La caducidad del realismo." Review of *Hasta no verte Jesús mío. La Vida Literaria* (Apr. 1970): 10–11.

———. "*Las batallas en el desierto.*" Review in *El Día,* May 14, 1981, 14.

Dorra, Raúl. *La literatura puesta en juego.* Mexico City: Universidad Nacional Autónoma de México, 1986.

Dottori, Nora. "*José Trigo:* El terror a la historia." *Nueva novela latinoamericana.* Vol. 1. Ed. Jorge Lafforgue. Buenos Aires: Editorial Paidós, 1976. 262–299.

Duncan, Cynthia. "The Fantastic as a Vehicle of Social Criticism in José Emilio Pacheco's 'La fiesta brava.'" *Chasqui* 14.2–3 (1985): 3–13.

Duncan, J. Ann. *Voices, Visions and a New Reality: Mexican Fiction since 1970.* Pittsburgh: University of Pittsburgh Press, 1986.

Eckstein, Susan. *The Poverty of Revolution: The State and the Urban Poor in Mexico.* Princeton: Princeton University Press, 1977.

Ehrenberg, Felipe. "Entre el hombre genérico y el hombre cognoscitivo" (on Fernando del Paso's drawings). *Tierra Adentro* 47 (May–June 1990): 25–26.

Elizondo, Salvador. *Farabeuf.* Mexico City: Joaquín Mortiz, 1965.

———. *El hipogeo secreto*. Mexico City: Joaquín Mortiz, 1968.

Enzensberger, Hans Magnus. "Introduction." *Tabloid* 1 (1980).

Escudero, Roberto, et. al. *Cuadernos Políticos* 17 (1978). (Special issue on the student movement of 1968.)

Espejo, Beatriz. *Muros de azogue*. Mexico City: Editorial Diógenes, 1979; Secretaría de Educación Pública (Lecturas Mexicanas), 1986.

Esquivel, Laura. *Como agua para chocolate*. Mexico City: Planeta, 1989.

Faris, Wendy. "Desire and Power, Love and Revolution: Carlos Fuentes and Milan Kundera." *Review of Contemporary Fiction* 8.2 (Summer 1988): 273–284.

Fernández, Sergio. *Los peces*. Mexico City: Joaquín Mortiz, 1968.

———. *Segundo sueño*. Mexico City: Joaquín Mortiz, 1976.

Fernández Perera, Manual. "Prólogo o epílogo (todo depende): Onda y escritura, tronados e iluminados." *La Cultura en México, Suplemento de Siempre!*, July 5, 1978, 2–4.

Fernández Violante, Marcela. "Mexican Women Film Directors." *Voices of Mexico* 6 (Dec. 1987–Feb. 1988): 51–57.

Fiddian, Robbin. "A Case of Literary Infection: *Palinuro de México* and *Ulysses*." Unpublished essay, 1981.

———. "*Palinuro of México:* A World of Words." *Bulletin of Hispanic Studies* 58 (1981): 121–133.

———. "*Palinuro de México* and *Ulysses*." *Estudios Anglo-Americanos* (São Paulo, Brazil) 5–6 (1981–82): 50–56.

———. "Beyond the Unquiet Grave and the Cemetery of Words: Myth and Archetype in Palinuro de México." *Ibero-Amerikanisches Archiv* n.s. 8.3 (1982): 243–255.

———. "James Joyce y Fernando del Paso." *Insula* 455 (Oct. 1984): 10.

———. "Fernando del Paso y el arte de la renovación." *Revista Iberoamericana* 150 (Jan.–Mar. 1990): 143–158.

Fiscal, María Rosa. "Mystery Novels Prosper in Mexico." *Voices of Mexico* 5 (Sept.–Nov. 1987): 47–48.

Flanzer, Jerry P. *The Many Faces of Family Violence*. Springfield, Ill.: Charles C. Thomas Publisher, 1982.

Flori, Mónica. "Visions of Women's Symbolic Physical Portrayal as Social Commentary in the Short Fiction of Elena Poniatowska." *Third Woman* 2.2 (1984): 77–83.

Foster, David William. "Latin American Documentary Narrative." *PMLA* (Jan. 1984): 41–55.

Foucault, Michel. *Madness and Civilization: A History of Insanity in the Age of Reason*. Trans. Richard Howard. New York: Vintage Books, 1973.

———. *The Birth of the Clinic: An Archaeology of Medical Perception*. Trans. A. M. Sheridan Smith. New York: Vintage Books, 1975.

———. *Discipline and Punish: The Birth of the Prison*. Trans. Alan Sheridan. New York: Vintage Books, 1979.

———. *The History of Sexuality*, Vol. 1, *An Introduction*. Trans. Robert Hurley. New York: Vintage Books, 1980.

————. *Power/Knowledge: Selected Interviews and Other Writings 1972–1977*. Trans. Colin Gordon et al. New York: Pantheon Books, 1980.

Francescato, Martha Paley. "Onda y desonda: Narradores jóvenes mexicanos." *Revista Canadiense de Estudios Hispánicos* 2: 296–302.

Franco, Jean. "Del milenio efímero a la vanguardia que fue: La literatura latinoamericana 1959–1976." *Nexos: Sociedad, Ciencia, Literatura* (Jan. 1978): 13–18.

————. "The Critique of the Pyramid and Mexican Narrative after 1968." *Latin American Fiction Today*. Ed. Rose Minc. Tacoma Park, Md.: Hispamérica, 1979. 49–60.

————. "Beyond Ethnocentrism: Gender, Power, and the Third-World Intelligentsia." *Marxism and the Interpretation of Culture*. Ed. Cary Nelson and Lawrence Grossberg. Urbana: University of Illinois Press, 1988. 503–515.

————. *Plotting Women: Gender and Representation in Mexico*. New York: Columbia University Press, 1989.

Friedman, Edward H. "The Marginated Narrator: *Hasta no verte Jesús mío* and the Eloquence of Repression." *The Antiheroine's Voice: Narrative Discourse and Transformations of the Picaresque*. Columbia: University of Missouri Press, 1987. 170–187.

Fromm, Erich, and Michael Maccoby. *Social Character in a Mexican Village: A Sociopsychoanalytic Study*. Englewood Cliffs, N.J.: Prentice-Hall, 1970.

Fry, Peter. *Spirits of Protest: Spirit-Mediums and the Articulation of Consensus*. Cambridge: Cambridge University Press, 1976.

Frye, Northrop. *Anatomy of Criticism: Four Essays*. New York: Atheneum, 1969.

Fuentes, Carlos. *La región más transparente*. Mexico City: Fondo de Cultura Económica, 1958.

————. *Aura*. Mexico City: Ediciones Era, 1962.

————. *La muerte de Artemio Cruz*. Mexico City: Fondo de Cultura Económica, 1962.

————. *Cantar de ciegos*. Mexico City: Joaquín Mortiz, 1964.

————. *Cambio de piel*. Barcelona: Seix Barral; Mexico City: Joaquín Mortiz, 1967.

————. *Terra nostra*. Mexico City: Joaquín Mortiz, 1975.

————. *La cabeza de la hidra*. Barcelona, Seix Barral; Mexico City: Joaquín Mortiz, 1978.

————. *Una familia lejana*. Mexico City: Joaquín Mortiz, 1980.

————. *Agua quemada*. Mexico City: Fondo de Cultura Económica, 1981.

————. *Gringo viejo*. Mexico City: Fondo de Cultura Económica, 1985.

————. *Cristóbal nonato*. Mexico City: Fondo de Cultura Económica, 1987.

————. *Myself with Others: Selected Essays*. New York: Farrar, Straus and Giroux, 1988.

————. *Constancia y otras novelas para vírgenes*. Mexico City: Fondo de Cultura Económica, 1990.

Fuentes, Vilma. *Ayer es nunca jamás*. Mexico City: Joaquín Mortiz, 1988.

Galindo, Carmen. "Vivir del milagro." Review of *Hasta no verte Jesús mío. La Vida Literaria* (Apr. 1970): 8–9.

Galindo, Sergio. *El hombre de los hongos.* Xalapa: Universidad Veracruzana, 1976.

———. *Otilia Rauda.* Mexico City: Grijalbo, 1985.

García Canclini, Néstor. *Las culturas populares en el capitalismo.* Mexico City: Editorial Nueva Imagen, 1982.

———. *Culturas híbradas (Estrategias para entrar y salir de la modernidad).* Mexico City: Consejo Nacional para la Cultura y las Artes and Editorial Grijalbo, 1990.

García Ponce, Juan. *La casa en la playa.* Mexico City: Joaquín Mortiz, 1966.

———. *Crónica de una intervención.* 2 vols. Mexico City: Joaquín Mortiz, 1982.

García Saldaña, Parménides. *Pasto verde.* Mexico City: Editorial Diógenes, 1968.

Gardea, Jesús. *Los viernes de Lautaro.* Mexico City: Siglo XXI, 1979.

———. *La canción de las mulas muertas.* Mexico City: Oasis, 1981.

———. *El sol que estás mirando.* Mexico City: Fondo de Cultura Económica, 1981.

Garduño, Flor. *Magia del juego eterno.* Mexico City: Guchach' Reza A. C. Juchitán, Oaxaca, 1985.

———. *Bestiarium.* Zurich: Argentum, 1987.

Garibay, Ricardo. *La casa que arde de noche.* Mexico City: Joaquín Mortiz, 1971.

———. *Las glorias del Gran Púas.* Mexico City: Grijalbo, 1978.

———. *Acapulco.* Mexico City: Grijalbo, 1979.

Garro, Elena. *Andamos huyendo Lola.* Mexico City: Joaquín Mortiz, 1980.

———. *Testimonios sobre Mariana.* Mexico City: Grijalbo, 1981.

Geiger, Susan. "Women's Life Histories: Method and Content." *Signs* 11.2 (Winter 1986): 331–351.

Gelles, Richard J. *Family Violence.* Beverly Hills: Sage Publications, 1979.

Gil, David G. "Sociocultural Aspects of Domestic Violence." In *Violence in the Home: Interdisciplinary Perspectives.* Ed. Mary Lystad. New York: Brunner/Mazel, 1986. 124–149.

Gilly, Adolfo. *Nuestra caída en la modernidad.* Mexico City: Joan Boldó i Climent, Editores, 1988.

Giordano, Jaime. "Transformaciones narrativas actuales: *Morirás lejos,* de José Emilio Pacheco." *Cuadernos Americanos* (Jan.–Feb. 1985): 133–140.

Glantz, Margo. *Las genealogías.* Mexico City: Martín Casillas, 1981.

———. "Viajerías, VIII." Review of *Las batallas en el desierto. Uno Mas Uno,* May 27, 1981, 20.

———. *Síndrome de naufragios.* Mexico City: Joaquín Mortiz, 1984.

———, ed. *Onda y escritura en México: jóvenes de 20 a 33.* Mexico City: Siglo XXI, 1971.

———. *Repeticiones: Ensayos sobre literatura mexicana.* Xalapa: Universidad Veracruzana, 1979.

Goldsmith, Mary. "Trabajo doméstico asalariado y desarrollo capitalista."

Trabajadoras domésticas asalariadas en México: Lecturas seleccionadas de fem (4.16 [1980–1981]). New York: Women's International Resource Exchange, n.d. 1–9.

Gómez Montero, Sergio. "José Agustín y su literatura." Review of *El rey se acerca a su templo. Proceso,* Nov. 13, 1978, 52–54.

———. "José Agustín en su contexto histórico." *La Palabra y el Hombre* n.s. 53–54 (1985): 109–122.

González, Ana María. "José Agustín tiene el don del anarquismo: Carballido." *La Jornada,* Mar. 11, 1989, 19.

González Casanova, Pablo, and Enrique Florescano, eds. *México, hoy.* Mexico City: Siglo XXI, 1979.

González Casanova, Pablo, ed. *América Latina: Historia de medio siglo.* Vol. 2, *México, Centroamérica y el Caribe.* Mexico City: Siglo XXI, 1981.

———. *La democracia en México.* Mexico City: Ediciones Era, 1967.

González de Alba, Luis. *Los días y los años.* Mexico City: Ediciones Era, 1971.

González Rodríguez, Sergio. "Digamos que JEP, 1980." *Nexos: Sociedad, Ciencia, Literatura* (July 1980): 4, 7, 8.

González Solano, Bernardo. "Una joyita de las que no abundan." Review of *Las batallas en el desierto. El Sol de México,* May 10, 1981, 1, 3.

González, Soledad, and Pilar Iracheta. "La violencia en la vida de las mujeres campesinas: El distrito de Tenango, 1880–1910." In *Presencia y transparencia: La mujer en la historia de México.* Mexico City: El Colegio de México, 1987. 111–141.

Gordon, Samuel. "Los poetas ya no cantan ahora hablan." *Revista Iberoamericana* 150 (Jan.–Mar. 1990): 255–266.

Green, Martin. *The Triumph of Pierrot: The Commedia dell'arte and the Modern Imagination.* New York: Macmillan, 1986.

Grobet, Lourdes. *Bodas de sangre* (versión oxoloteca de la obra de Federico García Lorca, del Laboratorio de Teatro Campesino e Indígena). Mexico City: Gobierno del Estado de Tabasco, 1987.

Guerra-Cunningham, Lucía. "Luz y oscuridad: El dilema de la juventud mexicana en *El rey se acerca a su templo.*" *Nueva Revista del Pacífico* 10–11 (1978): 56–60.

Guevara Niebla, Gilberto. *La democracia en la calle: Crónica del movimiento estudiantil mexicano.* Mexico City: Siglo XXI, 1988.

Guillén, Claudio. *Literature as System.* Princeton, N.J.: Princeton University Press, 1971.

Guzmán, Humberto. *El sótano blanco.* Mexico City: Ediciones Injuve, 1972; Universidad Autónoma Metropolitana, 1984.

———. *Historia fingida de la disección de un cuerpo.* Mexico City: Joaquín Mortiz, 1982.

———. "Yo también hablo de la onda." *La Palabra y el Hombre* n.s. 53–54 (1985): 63–67.

———. *Los buscadores de la dicha.* Mexico City: Joaquín Mortiz, 1990.

Hancock, Joel. "Elena Poniatowska's *Hasta no verte Jesús mío:* The Remak-

ing of the Image of Woman." *Hispania* (Sept. 1983): 353–359.
———. "Perfecting a Text: Authorial Revisions in José Emilio Pacheco's *Morirás lejos.*" *Chasqui* 14.2–3 (1985): 15–23.
Harwood, Alan. R_x: *Spiritist as Needed: A Study of a Puerto Rican Community Mental Health Resource.* London: John Wiley and Sons, 1977.
Hellman, Judith Adler. *Mexico in Crisis.* 2nd ed. New York: Holmes and Meier Publishers, 1983.
Hernández, Luisa Josefina. *Nostalgia de Troya.* Mexico City: Siglo XXI, 1970.
Hiriart, Hugo. *Disertación sobre las telarañas.* Mexico City: Martín Casillas, 1981.
Hoeksema, Thomas. "José Emilio Pacheco: A Poetry of Extremes." In *Signals from the Flames.* José Emilio Pacheco. Trans. Thomas Hoeksema. Pittsburgh: Latin American Literary Review Press, 1980. 1–15.
Huerta, Alberto. *¡Ojalá estuvieras aquí!* Mexico City: Joaquín Mortiz, 1978.
Ibargüengoita, Jorge. *Los relámpagos de agosto.* Mexico City: Joaquín Mortiz, 1965.
———. *Las muertas.* Mexico City: Joaquín Mortiz, 1977.
———. *Dos crímenes.* Mexico City: Joaquín Mortiz, 1979.
———. *Los pasos de López.* Mexico City: Océano, 1981.
Iturbide, Graciela. *Sueños de papel.* Mexico City: Fondo de Cultura Económica, 1985.
Jácobs, Bárbara. *Doce cuentos en contra.* Mexico City: Martín Casillas, 1982.
———. *Las hojas muertas.* Mexico City: Ediciones Era, 1987.
Jameson, Fredric. *The Political Unconscious: Narrative as a Socially Symbolic Act.* Ithaca: Cornell University Press, 1981.
———. *The Ideologies of Theory: Essays 1971–1986.* Volume 2: *Syntax of History.* Minneapolis: University of Minnesota Press, 1988.
Jelin, Elizabeth. "Migration and Labor Force Participation in Latin America: The Domestic Servants in the Cities." *Signs* 3 (1977): 129–141.
Jiménez de Báez, Yvette, et al. *Ficción e historia: La narrativa de José Emilio Pacheco.* Mexico City: El Colegio de México, 1979.
Job, Peggy. "Women Novelists in Mexico Reflect Their Reality." *Voices of Mexico* 6 (Dec. 1987–Feb. 1988): 46–50.
Jung, Carl G. *Memories, Dreams, Reflections.* New York: Pantheon Books, 1963.
———. *Collected Works.* 2nd ed. 20 vols. Princeton, N.J.: Princeton University Press, 1967.
———. *The Essential Jung.* Ed. Anthony Storr. Princeton, N.J.: Princeton University Press, 1983.
———, ed. *Man and His Symbols.* New York: Dell Publishing Company, 1964.
Kaplan, E. Ann. *Women and Film: Both Sides of the Camera.* New York: Methuen, 1983.

Kardec, Allan, and H. J. Turk. *Diccionario espiritista y catequismo espiritista.* Trans. J. M. F. and Enrique Bosch. Barcelona: Edicomunicación, SA, 1986.

Karrel, Alex. *Ritual de magia divina.* São Paulo: Editôra Pensamento, 1963.

Kirk, John M. "En torno a *De perfil,* obra maestra de la nueva narrativa mexicana." *Hispanic Studies in Honour of Frank Pierce.* Ed. John England. Sheffield: University of Sheffield, 1980. 111–122.

Klahn, Norma. Review of *Signals from the Flames,* by José Emilio Pacheco, and *Tarumba,* by Jaime Sabines. *Review* 29 (1981): 85–87.

Krause, Ethel. *Intermedio para mujeres.* Mexico City: Océano, 1982.

———. *Donde las cosas vuelan.* Mexico City: Océano, 1985.

———. *El lunes te amaré.* Mexico City: Océano, 1988.

Kristeva, Julia. *Desire in Language: A Semiotic Approach to Literature and Art.* New York: Columbia University Press, 1980.

Kundera, Milan. *The Unbearable Lightness of Being.* Trans. Michael Henry Heim. New York: Harper and Row, 1985.

Laboratorio de Teatro Campesino e Indígena. *La tragedia del jaguar.* Mexico City: Instituto de Cultura de Tabasco, 1989. (See also Lourdes Grobet.)

Lagos-Pope, María Inés. "El testimonio creativo de 'Hasta no verte, Jesús mío.'" *Revista Iberoamericana* 150 (Jan.–Mar. 1990): 243–253.

Langness, L. L., and Gelya Frank. *Lives: An Anthropological Approach to Biography.* Novato, Calif.: Chandler and Sharp Publishers, 1981.

Lara Zavala, Hernán. *De Zitilchén.* Mexico City: Joaquín Mortiz, 1981.

———. *El mismo cielo.* Mexico City: Joaquín Mortiz, 1987.

———. *Charras.* Mexico City: Joaquín Mortiz, 1990.

Leal, Luis. "La nueva narrativa mexicana." *Nueva Narrativa Hispanoamericana* 2.1 (1972): 89–97.

———. "Tlatelolco, Tlatelolco." *Denver Quarterly* 14.1 (1979): 3–13.

Lemaitre, Monique J. "Jesusa Palancares y la dialéctica de la emacipación femenina." *Revista Iberoamericana* 51.132–133 (1985): 751–763. (An earlier version of this article appeared in *Hispamérica* 10.30 [1981]: 131–135.)

Leñero, Carmen. *Birlibirloque.* Mexico City: Fondo de Cultura Económica, 1987.

———. *Gajes.* Mexico City: Universidad Autónoma Metropolitana, 1988.

Leñero, Vicente. *Los albañiles.* Barcelona: Seix Barral, 1964.

———. *El garabato.* Mexico City: Joaquín Mortiz, 1967.

———. *Los periodistas.* Mexico City: Joaquín Mortiz, 1978.

———. *El evangelio de Lucas Gavilán.* Mexico City: Seix Barral, 1979.

———. *Asesinato.* Mexico City: Plaza y Janés, 1984.

Levi Calderón, Sara. *Dos mujeres.* Mexico City: Editorial Diana, 1990.

Lewis, Oscar. *Five Families.* New York: Basic Books, 1959.

Loaeza, Guadalupe. *Las niñas bien.* Mexico City: Océano, 1987.

———. *Las reinas de Polanco.* Mexico City: Cal y Arena, 1988.

Lomnitz, Larissa. "The Social and Economic Organization of a Mexican Shantytown." *Latin American Urban Research.* Vol. 4. Ed. Wayne A. Cornelius and Felicity M. Trueblood. Beverly Hills: Sage Publications, 1974. 135–155.

López-González, Aralia. "De un cuento propio a un cuerpo, una conciencia y una reflexión propios." *Blanco Móvil* 42–43 (May–June 1990): 3–12.

———. "Una obra clave en la narrativa mexicana: *José Trigo*." *Revista Iberomericana* 150 (Jan.–Mar. 1990): 117–141.

López-González, Aralia, Amelia Malagamba, and Elena Urrutia, eds. *Mujer y literatura mexicana y chicana: Culturas en contacto*. Tijuana: El Colegio de México and El Colegio de la Frontera Norte, 1988.

———. *Mujer y literatura mexicana y chicana: Culturas en contacto*. Volume 2. Mexico City: El Colegio de México, 1990.

López Moreno, Roberto. *El arca de Caralampio*. Mexico City: Editorial Katún, 1983.

Luna, Francisco. *Tres de asada y uno de machaca para llevar*. Hermosillo: Universidad de Sonora, 1989.

Lystad, Mary, ed. *Violence in the Home: Interdisciplinary Perspectives*. New York: Brunner/Mazel, 1986.

Macías, Anna. *Against All Odds: The Feminist Movement in Mexico to 1940*. Westport, Conn.: Greenwood Press, 1982.

Macklin, June. "Belief, Ritual, and Healing: New England Spiritualism and Mexican-American Spiritism Compared." In *Religious Movements in Contemporary America*. Ed. Irving I. Zaretsky and Mark P. Leone. Princeton: Princeton University Press, 1974.

Magnarelli, Sharon. *The Lost Rib: Female Characters in the Spanish-American Novel*. Lewisburg: Bucknell University Press, 1985.

Malvido, Adriana. "Ramos: *Luz interna*, es la obra central de José Agustín." *La Jornada*, June 10, 1989, 18.

Manjarrez, Héctor. "La indiscreción de Elena Poniatowska." Review of *Fuerte es el silencio*. *Cuadernos Políticos* 27 (1981): 102–114.

———. *Lapsus*. Mexico City: Joaquín Mortiz, 1971.

———. *No todos los hombres son románticos*. Mexico City: Ediciones Era, 1983.

Mansour, Mónica. *Los mundos de Palinuro*. Xalapa: Universidad Veracruzana, 1986.

Márquez Rodríguez, Alexis. "*Palinuro de México*: Novedad y tradición." Review in *Plural* (Jan. 1984): 26–28.

Martin, Gerald. *Journeys through the Labyrinth: Latin American Fiction in the Twentieth Century*. London: Verso, 1989.

Martín del Campo, David. *Las rojas son las carreteras*. Mexico City: Joaquín Mortiz, 1976.

———. *Isla de lobos*. Mexico City: INBA-Joaquín Mortiz, 1987.

———. *Dama de noche*. Mexico City: Joaquín Mortiz, 1990.

Martínez López, Felipe. *El crepúsculo del poder: Juchitán, Oax. 1980–1982*. Oaxaca: Universidad Autónoma "Benito Juárez" de Oaxaca, 1983.

Martré, Gonzalo. *El movimiento popular estudiantil de 1968 en la novela mexicana*. Mexico City: Universidad Nacional Autónoma de México, 1986.

Mastretta, Angeles. *Arráncame la vida.* Mexico City: Océano, 1985.
———. *Mujeres de ojos grandes.* Mexico City: Cal y Arena, 1990.
Mata, Oscar. "Fernando del Paso." *La Palabra y el Hombre* 53–54 (1985): 81–88.
Mattelart, Armand. *La comunicación masiva en el proceso de liberación.* Mexico City: Siglo XXI, 1973.
McAuslan, Patrick. *Urban Land and Shelter for the Poor.* London: Earthscan, 1984.
McCall, George M., and Nancy M. Shields. "Social and Structural Factors in Family Violence." In *Violence in the Home: Interdisciplinary Perspectives.* Ed. Mary Lystad. New York: Brunner/Mazel, 1986. 98–122.
McWilliams, Carey. *Ambrose Bierce: A Biography.* Hamden, Conn.: Archon Books, 1967.
Medina, Dante. "*Palinuro de México:* Un verdadero héroe nacional." Review in *El Universal,* Aug. 17, 1981, 24.
———. *Tola.* Barcelona: Tusquets Editores, 1987.
Medina, Luis. *Historia de la Revolución Mexicana,* Vol. 18: *1940–1952. Del cardenismo al avilacamachismo.* Mexico City: El Colegio de México, 1978.
Meese, Elizabeth A. "The Languages of Oral Testimony and Women's Literature." *Women's Personal Narratives: Essays in Criticism and Pedagogy.* Ed. Leonore Hoffman and Margo Culley. New York: Modern Language Association of America, 1985.
Melo, Juan Vicente. *La obediencia nocturna.* Mexico City: Ediciones Era, 1969.
Mendoza, María Luisa. *Con El, conmigo, con nosotros tres.* Mexico City: Joaquín Mortiz, 1971.
———. *De ausencia.* Mexico City: Joaquín Mortiz, 1974; Secretaría de Educación Pública (Letras Mexicanas), 1986.
Menton, Seymour. *Narrativa mexicana (Desde* Los de abajo *hasta* Noticias del imperio*).* Tlaxcala: Universidad Autónoma de Tlaxcala, 1991.
Mercado, Enrique. "Ya lo dijo el vate Velarde: Empitona la camisa el mujerío." Review of La *"Flor de Lis."* *La Jornada,* Apr. 30, 1988, 3, 6.
Mercado, Tununa. "Tristezas de Colonia Roma." Review of *Las batallas en el desierto. Claudia* (Aug. 1981): 137.
Miller, Beth. *Mujeres en la literatura.* Mexico City: Fleischer Editora, 1978.
Modleski, Tania. *The Women Who Knew Too Much: Hitchcock and Feminist Theory.* New York: Methuen, 1988.
Molina, Silvia. *La mañana debe seguir gris.* Mexico City: Joaquín Mortiz, 1977.
———. *Ascensión Tun.* Mexico City: Martín Casillas, 1981.
———. *La familia vino del norte.* Mexico City: Océano, 1987.
———. *Dicen que me casé yo.* Mexico City: Cal y Arena, 1989.
———. *Imagen de Héctor.* Mexico City: Cal y Arena, 1990.
Monsiváis, Carlos. *Días de guardar.* Mexico City: Ediciones Era, 1970.
———. "Clasismo y novela en México." *Latin American Perspectives* 2.2 (1975): 164–179.

———. "Notas sobre la cultura mexicana en el siglo XX." *Historia general de México*. Vol. 4, México: El Colegio de México, 1976. 303–476.

———. "Notas sobre la cultura mexicana en la década de los setentas." *Literatura y dependencia*. Guadalajara: Departamento de Bellas Artes, Gobierno de Jalisco, 1977. 197–227.

———. *Amor perdido*. Mexico City: Ediciones Era, 1977.

———. "En el estudio todo ha quedado igual." *La Cultura en México: Suplemento de Siempre!* July 12, 1978, 4–6.

———. "'Mira, para que no comas olvido . . .'": Las precisiones de Elena Poniatowska." *La Cultura en México: Suplemento de Siempre!*, July 15, 1981, 2–5.

———. *Nuevo catecismo para indios remisos*. Mexico City: Siglo XXI, 1982.

———. *Entrada libre: Crónicas de la sociedad que se organiza*. Mexico City: Ediciones Era, 1987.

———. *Escenas de pudor y liviandad*. Mexico City: Grijalbo, 1988.

Monsiváis, Carlos, et al. "¡¡¡ Duro, duro, duro!!! El movimiento estudiantil en la UNAM." (special issue of) *Cuadernos Políticos* 49–50 (1987).

———. Special issue of *Nexos: Sociedad, Ciencia, Literatura* on the student movement of 1968 (Sept. 1978).

Montemayor, Carlos. *Mal de piedra*. Mexico City: Premiá Editora, 1981.

———. *Las minas del retorno*. Barcelona: Argas Vergara, 1982.

Monterde, Francisco. "Cuadro vivo del pueblo." Review of *Hasta no verte Jesús mío*. *La Vida Literaria* (Apr. 1970): 5–7.

Monterroso, Augusto. *La oveja negra y demás fábulas*. Mexico City: Joaquín Mortiz, 1970.

———. *Movimiento perpetuo*. Mexico City: Joaquín Mortiz, 1972.

Montes de Oca, Marco Antonio. "*Palinuro de México* de Fernando del Paso." Review in *Vuelta* (Mar. 1980): 42–44.

Morales Bermúdez, Jesús. *Memorial del tiempo o Vía de las conversaciones*. Mexico City: Instituto Nacional de Bellas Artes and Editorial Katún, 1987.

Morán, Carlos Roberto. "José Agustín: La búsqueda de algo." *Texto Crítico* 2.5 (1976): 150–161.

Moreno, Hortensia. *Las líneas de la mano*. Mexico City: Joan Boldó i Climent, Editores, 1985.

Muñiz, Angelina. *Morada interior*. Mexico City: Joaquín Mortiz, 1972.

———. *Tierra adentro*. Mexico City: Joaquín Mortiz, 1977.

Muñoz, Humberto, Orlandina de Oliveira, and Claudio Stern. *Migración y desigualdad social en la ciudad de México*. Mexico City: El Colegio de México, 1977.

Navarrete, Sylvia. "Con tu lengua y con tus ojos, tú y yo juntos." Review of *Noticias del imperio*. *La Jornada de Libros*, Dec. 12, 1987, 1, 5, 6.

Neymet, Mónica de. *Las horas vivas*. Mexico City: Grijalbo, 1986.

Nicoll, Allardyce. *Masks, Mimes, and Miracles*. New York: Harcourt Brace and Company, 1931.

———. *The World of Harlequin: A Critical Study of the Commedia dell'arte.* Cambridge: Cambridge University Press, 1963.

"Novena y Triduo dedicados al milagrosísimo Niño de Atocha." N.p.: n.p., n.d. Purchased at a stand of Catholic literature in front of the cathedral, Mazatlán, Sinaloa, Sept. 23, 1988.

Ocampo, Aurora M., ed. *La crítica de la novela mexicana contemporánea.* Mexico City: Universidad Nacional Autónoma de México, 1981.

Ochoa Sandy, Gerardo. "Lara Zavala revive en su novela 'Charras' el asesinato del líder Efraín Calderón Lara en el Yucatán de Carlos Loret de Mola." *Proceso,* July 23, 1990, 50–53.

O'Hara, Edgar. "Pacheco: Un monumento a lo efímero." *Plural* (Oct. 1982): 15–22.

———. "Cuando tiembla la poesía." Review of *Miro la tierra* by José Emilio Pacheco. *Hora de Poesía* (Barcelona) 49–50 (Jan.–Apr. 1987): 169–171; repr. *Utopías* (Mexico City) (Mar.–Apr. 1989): 67–68.

Ojeda, David. *Las condiciones de la guerra.* La Habana, Cuba: Casa de las Américas, 1978.

Oreglia, Giacomo. *The Commedia dell'arte.* New York: Hill and Wang, 1968.

Orgambide, Pedro. "Vivir con los personajes." Review of *Las batallas en el desierto.* *Excélsior,* June 15, 1981, 3.

Orrantia, Dagoberto. "The Function of Myth in Fernando del Paso's *José Trigo.*" In *Tradition and Renewal: Essays on Twentieth-Century Latin American Literature and Culture.* Ed. Merlin H. Foster. Urbana: University of Illinois Press, 1975. 129–138.

Ortega, Julio. "Tres notas mexicanas" *(Morirás lejos). Cuadernos Hispanoamericanos* (Mar. 1982): 667–676.

Otero, Lisandro. "Otra corona para la nueva novela latinoamericana." Review of *Palinuro de México. Casa de las Américas* 23.136 (1983): 152–153.

Pacheco, Cristina. *Cuarto de azotea.* Mexico City: Secretaría de Educación Pública, 1986.

———. *Zona de desastre.* Mexico City: Océano, 1986.

———. *La última noche de "El Tigre."* Mexico City: Océano, 1987.

———. *El corazón de la noche.* Mexico City: Ediciones El Caballito, 1989.

Paley Francescato, Martha. "Acción y reflexión en cuentos de Fuentes, Garro, y Pacheco." *Kentucky Romance Quarterly* (Feb. 1986): 99–112.

Patán, Federico. *Nena, me llamo Walter.* Mexico City: Fondo de Cultura Económica, 1985.

———. *Ultimo exilio.* Xalapa: Universidad Veracruzana, 1986.

———. *En esta casa.* Mexico City: Fondo de Cultura Económica, 1987.

———. *Contrapuntos.* Mexico City: Universidad Nacional Autónoma de México, 1989.

Pavón, Alfredo, ed. *Paquete: Cuento (La ficción en México).* Tlaxcala: Universidad Autónoma de Tlaxcala, 1990.

———. *Te lo cuento otra vez (La ficción en México).* Tlaxcala: Universidad Autónoma de Tlaxcala, 1991.

Paz, Octavio. *Posdata*. Mexico City: Siglo XXI, 1970. (Translated as *The Other Mexico*, 1972.)

Pérez Cruz, Emiliano. *Tres de ajo*. Mexico City: Oasis, 1983.

———. *Borracho no vale: Crónicas*. Mexico City: Plaza y Valdés, 1988.

Pérez Gay, Rafael, and Alberto Román. "La maga y los cuarenta escritores: Novela y cuento en 1978." *Nexos: Sociedad, Ciencia, Literatura* 14 (Feb. 1979): 41–43.

Pérez Gay, Rafael. *Me perderé contigo*. Mexico City: Cal y Arena, 1988.

Perlman, Janice E. *The Myth of Marginality: Urban Poverty and Politics in Rio de Janeiro*. Berkeley: University of California Press, 1976.

Pettersson, Aline. *Círculos*. Mexico City: Universidad Nacional Autónoma de México (Punto de Partida), 1977.

———. *Casi en silencio*. Mexico City: 1980.

———. *Proyectos de muerte*. Mexico City: Martín Casillas, 1983.

———. *Los colores ocultos*. Mexico City: Grijalbo, 1986.

———. *Sombra ella misma*. Xalapa: Universidad Veracruzana, 1986.

———. *De cuerpo entero*. Mexico City: Universidad Nacional Autónoma de México, 1990 (autobiography).

———. *Piedra que rueda*. Mexico City: Joaquín Mortiz, 1990.

———. *Querida familia*. Mexico City: Diana, 1990.

Pitol, Sergio. *El tañido de una flauta*. Mexico City: Ediciones Era, 1972.

———. *Nocturno de Bujara*. Mexico City: Siglo XXI, 1981.

———. *Juegos florales*. Mexico City: Siglo XXI, 1982.

———. *El desfile del amor*. Madrid: Anagrama, 1984.

———. *Domar a la divina garza*. Barcelona: Editorial Anagrama, 1988.

———. *Cuerpo presente*. Mexico City: Ediciones Era, 1990.

———. *La vida conyugal*. Mexico City: Ediciones Era, 1991.

Pozas, Ricardo. *Juan Pérez Jolote*. Mexico City: Fondo de Cultura Económica, 1952.

Prado Oropeza, Renato, et al. "Análisis semiótico de 'El Castillo en la aguja' de José Emilio Pacheco." *Semiosis* 1 (1978): 5–20.

Prieto, Emma. *Los testigos*. Mexico City, 1985.

Prince, Raymond. "Psychotherapy and the Chronically Poor." *Culture Change, Mental Health, and Poverty*. Ed. Joseph C. Finney. Lexington: University of Kentucky Press, 1969. 20–41.

Puga, María Luisa. *Las posibilidades del odio*. Mexico City: Siglo XXI, 1978.

———. *Cuando el aire es azul*. Mexico City: Siglo XXI, 1980.

———. *Accidentes*. Mexico City: Martín Casillas, 1981.

———. *Pánico o peligro*. Mexico City: Siglo XXI, 1983.

———. *La forma del silencio*. Mexico City: Siglo XXI, 1987.

———. *Intentos*. Mexico City: Grijalbo, 1987.

———. *Antonia*. Mexico City: Grijalbo, 1989.

Puga, María Luisa, and Mónica Mansour. *Itinerario de palabras*. Mexico City: Folios Ediciones, 1987.

Quiroga Clérigo, Manuel. "La historia grande de un hombre sin historia"

(*Palinuro de México*). *Cuadernos Hispanoamericanos* (June 1979): 660–677.

———. "Notes on *Palinuro de México*." *Review* 28 (1981): 31–33.

Rama, Angel. *La novela latinoamericana 1920–1980*. Bogotá: Instituto Colombiano de Cultura, 1982.

Ramírez, Armando. *Chin Chin el teporocho*. Mexico City: Novaro, 1971; Grijalbo, 1985; Secretaría de Educación Pública (Lecturas Mexicanas), 1986.

Ramírez, Carlos. "José Agustín: La impotencia frente al edén perdido." Review of *El rey se acerca a su templo*. *Proceso*, Nov. 13, 1978, 54–55.

Ramírez, Michael D. *Mexico's Economic Crisis: Its Origins and Consequences*. New York: Praeger, 1989.

Ramírez, Ramón. *El movimiento estudiantil de México: julio–diciembre de 1968*. 2 vols. Mexico City: Ediciones Era, 1969.

Ramírez Heredia, Rafael. *Trampa de metal*. Mexico City: Joaquín Mortiz, 1979.

———. *El Rayo Macoy*. Mexico City: Joaquín Mortiz, 1984.

———. *Los territorios de la tarde*. Mexico City: Joaquín Mortiz, 1988.

———. *Por los caminos del sur, vámonos para Guerrero*. Mexico City: Alianza, 1990.

Ramos, Agustín. *Al cielo por asalto*. Mexico City: Ediciones Era, 1979.

———. *La vida no vale nada*. Mexico City: Martín Casillas Editores, 1982.

———. *Ahora que me acuerdo*. Mexico City: Grijalbo, 1985.

Ramos, Luis Arturo. *Violeta-Perú*. 1979; Mexico City: Leega Literaria, 1986.

———. *Intramuros*. Xalapa: Universidad Veracruzana, 1983.

Rábago Palafox, Gabriela. *Todo ángel es terrible*. Mexico City: Martín Casillas, 1981.

———. *La señorita*. Mexico City: Cultura-SEP, 1982.

———. *Estancias nocturnas*. Mexico City: Instituto Politécnico Nacional, 1987.

Revueltas, José. *Los errores*. Mexico City: Fondo de Cultura Económica, 1964.

———. *El apando*. Mexico City: Ediciones Era, 1969.

Reyes, Octavio. *Cangrejo*. Mexico City: Katún, 1984.

Reyes Nevares, Salvador. "Sí pero no: Combates en el desierto." Review of *Las batallas en el desierto*. *El Sol de San Luis*, May 25, 1981, B3.

Rivas, Humberto. *Falco*. Mexico City: Katún, 1984.

Roberts, Bryan. *Cities of Peasants: The Political Economy of Urbanization in the Third World*. London: Edward Arnold, 1978.

Robles, Martha. *La sombra fugitiva; Escritoras en la cultura nacional*. Vol. 1. Mexico City: Universidad Nacional Autónoma de México, 1985.

Rodríguez, Hipólito. "Del Paso y el desafío de la historia." *La Jornada*, May 13, 1989, 5.

Roffiel, Rosamaría. *Amora*. Mexico City: Planeta, 1989.

Rojas, Mario. "José Agustín y el 'rock' como poética." In *Spanish American*

Literature and Popular Culture. Ed. Rose Minc. Gaithersburgh, Md.: Ediciones Hispamérica, 1981.

Rollins, Judith. *Between Women: Domestics and Their Employers.* Philadelphia: Temple University Press, 1985.

Rubin, Gayle. "The Traffic in Women: Notes on the 'Political Economy' of Sex." In *Toward an Anthropology of Women.* Ed. Rayna R. Reiter. New York: Monthly Review Press, 1975.

Ruffinelli, Jorge, et al. "Los escritores ante su realidad." *Hispamérica* 4.11–12 (1975): 33–48.

Ruffinelli, Jorge. "Código y lenguaje en José Agustín." *La Palabra y el Hombre* 13 (1975): 57–62.

———. "Sainz and Agustín: Literatura y contexto social." *Texto Crítico* 3.8 (1977): 155–164.

———. "Fernando del Paso: La novela como exorcismo." In *El lugar de Rulfo.* Xalapa: Universidad Veracruzana, 1980. 191–200.

———. "Notas sobre la novela en México (1975–1980)." *Cuadernos de Marcha* n.s. 3.14 (1981): 47–59.

Ruiz, Bernardo. *Olvidar tu nombre.* Mexico City: Premiá, 1982.

Ruiz Abreu, Alvaro. "Las arenas de Alemán." Review of *Las batallas en el desierto.* *Nexos: Sociedad, Ciencia, Literatura* (Aug. 1981): 45–47.

Rulfo, Juan. *El llano en llamas.* Mexico City: Fondo de Cultura Económica, 1953.

———. *Pedro Páramo.* Mexico City: Fondo de Cultura Económica, 1955.

Ruy Sánchez, Alberto. *Los nombres del aire.* Mexico City: Joaquín Mortiz, 1987.

Saborit, Antonio. "Episodios imperiales mexicanos." Review of *Noticias del imperio.* *Nexos: Sociedad, Ciencia, Literatura* (July 1988): 57–60.

Sáinz, Gustavo. *Gazapo.* Mexico City: Joaquín Mortiz, 1965.

———. *La princesa del Palacio de Hierro.* Mexico City: Joaquín Mortiz, 1974.

———. *Compadre lobo.* Mexico City: Grijalbo, 1978.

———. *Obsesivos días circulares.* Mexico City: Joaquin Mortiz, 1979.

———. "New Trends in Mexican Literature: A Response to Change." In *Mexico: A Country in Crisis.* Ed. Jerry R. Ladman. El Paso: Texas Western Press, 1986.

———. *Muchacho en llamas.* Mexico City: Grijalbo, 1987.

Samperio, Guillermo. *Lenin en el futbol.* Mexico City: Grijalbo, 1978.

———. *Textos extraños.* Mexico City: Folios, 1981.

———. *Gente de la ciudad.* Mexico City: Fondo de Cultura Económica, 1986.

———. *Miedo ambiente y otros miedos.* Mexico City: Secretaría de Educación Pública, 1986.

Scherer Garcia, Julio. *Los presidentes.* Mexico City: Grijalbo, 1986.

Schwartz, Perla. "Fernando del Paso y los sitios mágicos de la ciudad." *La Brújula en el Bolsillo* (Dec. 1982): 5–11.

Sefchovich, Sara. *México: País de ideas, país de novelas.* Mexico City: Editorial Grijalbo, 1987.

————. *Demasiado amor.* Mexico City: Planeta, 1990.

Seligson, Esther. *Tras la ventana un árbol.* Mexico City: Editorial Bogavante, 1969.

————. *Otros son los sueños.* Mexico City: Editorial Novaro, 1973.

————. "'José Trigo': Una memoria que se inventa." *Texto Crítico* 2.5 (1976): 162–169. (Repr. in *La fugacidad como método de escritura.* Mexico City: Plaza y Janés, 1988. 91–102.)

————. *Luz de dos.* Mexico City: Joaquín Mortiz, 1978.

————. *La morada en el tiempo.* Mexico City: Arífice Ediciones, 1981.

Semo, Enrique, ed. *México: Un pueblo en la historia.* Vol. 4. Mexico City: Editorial Nueva Imagen and Universidad Autónoma de Puebla, 1982.

Showalter, Elaine, ed. *The New Feminist Criticism: Essays on Women, Literature and Theory.* New York: Pantheon, 1985.

Shupe, Anson, William A. Stacey, and Lonnie R. Hazelwood. *Violent Men, Violent Couples.* Lexington, Mass.: Lexington Books, 1987.

Smith, Winifred. *The Commedia dell'arte.* New York: Benjamin Blom, 1964.

Solares, Ignacio. *Puerta del cielo.* Mexico City: Grijalbo, 1976.

————. *El árbol del deseo.* Mexico City: Cía. Eds., 1980.

————. *Madero, el otro.* Mexico City: Joaquín Mortiz, 1989.

Sommers, Joseph. *After the Storm: Landmarks of the Modern Mexican Novel.* Albuquerque: University of New Mexico Press, 1968.

Spivak, Gayatri Chakravorty. *In Other Worlds: Essays in Cultural Politics.* New York: Methuen, 1987.

Steele, Cynthia. *Narrativa indigenista en los Estados Unidos y México.* Mexico City: Instituto Nacional Indigenista, 1985.

————. "La mediación en las obras documentales de Elena Poniatowska." In *Mujer y literatura mexicana y chicana: Culturas en contacto.* Ed. Aralia López-Gonzalez et al. Tijuana: El Colegio de México and El Colegio de la Frontera Norte, 1988. Vol. 1: 211–219.

————. "The Other Within: Class and Ethnicity as Difference in Mexican Women's Literature." In *Cultural-Historical Grounding for Hispanic and Luso-Brazilian Feminist Literary Criticism.* Ed. Amy Kaminsky and Hernán Vidal. Minneapolis: Institute for the Study of Ideology and Literature, 1989, 297–328.

————. "Entrevista con Elena Poniatowska." *Hispamerica* 53–54 (1989): 89–105.

————. "Hacia una fusión del rigor y el placer, de la responsabilidad y el desmadre: Entrevista con José Agustín." *Nuevo Texto Crítico* (forthcoming).

Tabloid Editorial Collective. *Tabloid: A Review of Mass Culture and Everyday Life* 1 (1980).

Taibo II, Paco Ignacio. *No habrá final feliz.* Mexico City: Lasser Press Mexicana, 1981.

————. *La vida misma.* Mexico City: Planeta, 1987.

————. *Cuatro manos/Four Hands.* Mexico City: Editorial Z, 1989.

Tamez, Elsa. *Against Machismo.* Oak Park, Ill.: Meyer Stone Books, 1987.

(Originally published in Costa Rica in *Teólogos de la liberación hablan sobre la mujer.*)

Tatum, Charles. "Elena Poniatowska's *Hasta no verte Jesús mío.*" In *Latin American Women Writers: Yesterday and Today.* Ed. Yvette Miller and Charles Tatum. Pittsburgh: Latin American Literary Review Press, 1977.

Toledo, Alejandro. "News of the Empire: Once Upon a Time There Was a Queen." *Voices of Mexico* 8–9 (June–Nov. 1988): 73–74.

Toledo, Francisco. *Lo que el viento a Juárez.* Mexico City: Ediciones Era, 1986.

Torre, Gerardo de la. *El vengador.* Mexico City: Joaquín Mortiz, 1973.

———. *Muertes de Aurora.* Mexico City: Ediciones de Cultura Popular, 1980.

Torre, Gerardo de la, with José Agustín and René Avilés Fabila. *De los tres ninguno.* Mexico City: Federación Editorial Mexicana, 1974.

Torres, Blanca. *Historia de la Revolución Mexicana.* Vol. 21, *1940–1952: Hacia la utopía industrial.* Mexico City: El Colegio de México, 1984.

Torres, Gerardo. "José Emilio Pasado." Review of *Las batallas en el desierto. La Onda,* May 31, 1981, 7.

Torres, Juan Manuel. "Hasta el fin de la esperanza." Review of *Hasta no verte Jesús mío. La Vida Literaria* (Apr. 1970): 15.

Torres, Vicente Francisco. "*Las batallas en el desierto.*" Review in *Tiempo,* June 8, 1981, 58.

Trejo Delarbre, Raúl. "Los sonidos del silencio." Review of *Fuerte es el silencio. Nexos: Sociedad, Ciencia, Literatura* (Mar. 1981): 49–50.

———. "The Three Faces of Mexican Television." *Voices of Mexico* 7 (1988): 41–44.

Trejo Fuentes, Ignacio. "Una novela polifónica." Review of *Palinuro de México. El Universal,* Aug. 17, 1981, 24.

———. *Segunda voz: Ensayos sobre novela mexicana.* Mexico City: Universidad Nacional Autónoma de México, 1987.

———. *Faros y sirenas.* Mexico City: Plaza y Janés, 1988.

Trejo Villafuerte, Arturo. "José Emilio Pacheco y la otra historia." Review of *Las batallas en el desierto. Nosotros* (June 1981): 20.

Ulloa, Berta, et al. *Historia general de México.* Vol. 4. Mexico City: El Colegio de México, 1976.

Urrutia, Elena. "Experiencias de organización." *Trabajadoras domésticas asalariadas en México: Lecturas seleccionadas de fem* (4.16 [1980–1981]). New York: Women's International Resource Exchange, n.d. 10–12.

Valencia, Tita. *Minotauromaquia.* Mexico City: Joaquín Mortiz, 1976.

Vallarino, Roberto. "*Las batallas en el desierto:* La narración que une el testimonio y la historia literaria." Review in *Uno Mas Uno: Sábado* (1981): 22.

Vásquez, Josefina Zoraida, and Lorenzo Meyer. *The United States and Mexico.* Chicago: University of Chicago Press, 1985.

Vera, Rodrigo. "Magnates y extranjeros se reparten lo que dejó Aeroméxico." *Proceso,* July 20, 1988, 14–15.

Verani, Hugo. "Disonancia y desmitificación en *Las batallas en el desierto* de José Emilio Pacheco." *Hispamérica* 42 (1985): 29–40.

———, ed. *José Emilio Pacheco ante la crítica.* Mexico City: Universidad Autónoma Metropolitana/Universidad Veracruzana, 1987.

Vicens, Josefina. *Los años falsos.* Mexico City: Martín Casillas, 1982.

———. *El libro vacío.* Mexico City: Ediciones Transición, 1978; Secretaría de Educación Pública (Lecturas Mexicanas), 1985.

Vidal, Hernán. *Poética de la población marginal. I: Fundamentos materialistas para una historiografía estética.* Minneapolis: Prisma Institute (Literature and Human Rights, 1), 1987.

Villena, Luis Antonio de. *José Emilio Pacheco.* Madrid, 1987.

Villoro, Juan. *La noche navegable.* Mexico City: Joaquín Mortiz, 1980.

———. *Albercas.* Mexico City: Joaquín Mortiz, 1985.

———. *Tiempo transcurrido (Crónicas imaginarias).* Mexico City: Fondo de Cultura Económica, 1987.

———. *Palmeras de la brisa rápida: Un viaje a Yucatán.* Mexico City: Alianza Editorial Mexicana, 1989.

———. "Pasaportes mexicanos." *Hispamérica* 53–54 (Aug.–Dec. 1989): 113–118.

Volkow, Verónica. "Crónicas del silencio." Review of *Fuerte es el silencio* by Elena Poniatowska. *Revista de la Universidad de México* 36.4 (1981): 41–42.

———. *Diario de Sudáfrica.* Mexico City: Siglo XXI, 1988.

Willis, Susan. "El 'consumidorismo' y las mujeres." In *Las mujeres.* Ed. Margaret Randall. Mexico City: Siglo XXI, 1970. 52–64.

Woodyard, George. "Language and Tension in José Agustín. *Hispania* 63.1 (1980): 31–37.

Young, Dolly. "Mexican Literary Reactions to Tlatelolco 1968." *Latin American Research Review* 20.2 (1985): 71–85.

Young, Kate. "The Creation of a Relative Surplus Population: A Case Study from Mexico." In *Women and Development.* Ed. Lourdes Benería. London: Praeger, 1982. 149–175.

Zapata, Luis. *Las aventuras, desventuras y sueños de Adonis García, el vampiro de la colonia Roma.* Mexico City: Grijalbo, 1979. Translated as *Adonis García.* San Francisco: Gaysunshine Press, 1981.

Zepeda, Eraclio. *Asalto nocturno.* Mexico City: Joaquín Mortiz, 1974. (Awarded the Premio Nacional de Cuento.)

———. *Andando el tiempo.* Mexico City: Martín Casillas, 1982.

Zermeño, Sergio. *México: una democracia utópica—el movimiento estudiantil de 1968.* Mexico City: Siglo XXI, 1978.

Agustín, José

Narrative

La tumba. Mexico City: Ediciones Mester, 1964.
De perfil. Mexico City: Joaquín Mortiz, 1966.

Inventando que sueño. Mexico City: Joaquín Mortiz, 1968.
Se está haciendo tarde (final en laguna). Mexico City: Joaquín Mortiz, 1973.
With René Avilés Fabila and Gerardo de la Torre. *De los tres ninguno.* Mexico City: Federación Editorial Mexicana, 1974.
La mirada en el centro. Mexico City: Joaquín Mortiz, 1977.
El rey se acerca a su templo. Mexico City: Leo-Mex, 1977.
Ciudades desiertas. Mexico City: Edivisión, 1982. (Received the Premio Latinoamericano de Narrativa Colima–INBA, 1983.)
Confrontaciones. Mexico City: Universidad Autónoma Metropolitana, 1984.
Cerca del fuego. Mexico City: Plaza y Janes, 1986.
"Mientras más rápido vamos más redondos nos ponemos." *La Cultura en México: Suplemento de ¡Siempre!* July 22, 1987, 38–39.
Amor del bueno, juegos de los puntos de vista. Toluca: Gobierno del Estado de México, 1987.
No hay censura. Mexico City: Joaquín Mortiz, 1988.

Theater

Abolición de la propiedad. Mexico City: Joaquín Mortiz, 1969.
Alguien nos quiere matar. 1969.
Círculo vicioso. Mexico City: Joaquín Mortiz, 1974. (Received the Juan de Ruiz de Alarcón Prize.)
Luz externa. 1973.

Screenplays

Cinco de chocolate y uno de fresa.
Ya sé quién eres (te he estado observando). 1970.
El apando (collaborator).
Bajo el volcán (collaborator).
The Devil's Elixir (collaborator).
La viuda de Montiel (collaborator).
With José Buil and Gerardo Pardo. *Ahí viene la plaga.* Mexico City: Joaquín Mortiz, 1974/1985.

Essays

Autobiografía. Mexico City: Empresas Editoriales, 1966.
Three Lectures. Literature and Censorship in Latin America Today: Dream within a Dream. Denver: University of Denver (Occasional Papers, No. 1), 1978.
"*Las batallas en el desierto:* Noveleta impecable." *Excélsior* June 30, 1981, 2.
La nueva música clásica. Mexico City: Editorial Universo, 1985.

El rock de la cárcel. Mexico City: Editores Mexicanos Unidos, 1986.
Tragicomedia mexicana. Vol. 1. Mexico City: Planeta, 1990.
Contra la corriente. Mexico City: Editorial Diana, 1991.

Interviews

"Entrevista." Interview with L. Guerra-Cunningham, M. Paley Francescato, and Inma Minoves-Myers. *Hispamérica* 8.22 (1979): 23–40.
"Entrevista con José Agustín." Interview with John Kirk. *Hispania* 63.3 (1980): 588–591.
"José Agustín habla sobre la literatura latinoamericana." Interview with John Kirk and Donald L. Schmidt. *Chasqui* 9.2–3 (Feb.–May 1980): 65–70.

Pacheco, José Emilio

Narrative

La sangre de Medusa. No. 18. Mexico City: Cuadernos del Unicornio, 1958; 2nd ed., Editorial Latitudes, 1978 (Col. El Pozo y el Péndulo).
El viento distante y otros relatos. Mexico City: Ediciones Era, 1963 (Col. Alacena); 2nd ed., rev. and enlarged, 1969.
Morirás lejos. Mexico City: Editorial Joaquín Mortiz, 1967 (Serie del Volador); 2nd ed., 1977; Barcelona: Editorial Montesinos, 1980; Mexico City: Origen/Planeta, 1985; Mexico City: Secretaría de Educación Pública and Editorial Joaquín Mortiz (Lecturas Mexicanas No. 65), 1986. (Received the Magda Donato Prize, 1967.)
El principio del placer. Mexico City: Editorial Joaquín Mortiz, 1972 (Serie del Volador). (Received the Xavier Villaurrutia Prize, 1973.)
Las batallas en el desierto. Mexico City: Ediciones Era, 1981.
Battles in the Desert and Other Stories. Trans. Katherine Silver. New York: New Directions Books, 1987.
La sangre de Medusa y otros cuentos marginales. Mexico City: Ediciones Era, 1990.

Poetry

Los elementos de la noche. Mexico City: Universidad Nacional Autónoma de México, 1963; 2nd ed. rev., in *Tarde o temprano,* 1980; 3rd ed., Ediciones Era, 1983.
Arbol entre dos muros. Mexico City: Universidad Autónoma Metropolitana, 1963. Trans. Ed Dorn and Gordon Brotherson as *Tree Between Two Walls.* Los Angeles: Black Sparrow Press, 1969.
El reposo del fuego. Mexico City: Fondo de Cultura Económica (Col. Letras Mexicanas), 1966; 2nd ed., rev., in *Tarde o temprano,* 1980; 3rd ed., Ediciones Era, 1984.

No me preguntes cómo pasa el tiempo. Mexico City: Joaquín Mortiz, 1969. National Poetry Prize, 1969. Trans. Alistair Reid as *Don't Ask Me How the Time Goes By.* New York: Columbia University Press, 1978; 2nd ed., rev., in *Tarde o temprano*, 1980; 3rd ed., Ediciones Era, 1984.

Irás y no volverás. Mexico City: Ediciones Era (Letras Mexicanas), 1973; 2nd ed., 1976; 3rd ed., Ediciones Era, 1985.

Al margen. Paris: Colección Imaginaria, 1976 (twenty-two poems incorporated into *Desde entonces*).

Islas a la deriva. Mexico City: Siglo XXI, 1976; Ediciones Era, 1985.

Ayer es nunca jamás. Ed. José Miguel Oviedo. Caracas: Monte Avila, 1978 (anthology).

El jardín de niños (with serigraphs by Vicente Rojo). Mexico City: Ediciones Multiarte, 1978 (poems incorporated into *Desde entonces*).

Desde entonces. Mexico City: Ediciones Era, 1980; 2nd ed., 1983.

Breve antología. Ed. Rafael Vargas. Mexico City: Universidad Nacional Autónoma de México, n.d. [1980].

Signals from the Flames. Trans. Thomas Hoeksema. Pittsburgh: Latin American Literary Review Press, 1980.

Tarde o temprano: Obra poética reunida. Mexico City: Fondo de Cultura Económica, 1980.

Prosa de la calavera (with engravings by Miguel Cervantes). New York, 1981.

Los trabajos del mar. Mexico City: Ediciones Era, 1982; Madrid: Cátedra, 1984.

Fin de siglo y otros poemas. Mexico City: Fondo de Cultura Económica, 1984 (anthology).

Aproximaciones. Comp. Miguel Angel Flores. Mexico City: Editorial Penélope (Libros del Salmón), 1984.

Alta traición: Antología poética. Ed. José María Guelbenzu. Madrid: Alianza Editorial, 1985.

Miro la tierra. Mexico City: Ediciones Era, 1986.

Selected Poems. Ed. George McWhirter. New York: New Directions Books, 1987.

"Los vigesémicos." *Nexos: Sociedad, Ciencia, Literatura* (Dec. 1987): 73.

Ciudad de la memoria. Mexico City: Ediciones Era, 1989.

Essays

"José Emilio Pacheco." *Confrontaciones: Los narradores ante el público,* Serie 1. Mexico City: Instituto Nacional de Bellas Artes y Editorial Joaquín Mortiz, 1966. 241–263.

"Noticias del imperio." Rev. *Proceso*, Jan. 4, 1988, 50–51.

Talk at the University of Washington, Seattle, Apr. 6, 1988.

"Cien años de Julio Torri." *Proceso* 660, June 26, 1989, 56–57.

del Paso, Fernando

Poetry

Sonetos de lo diario. Mexico City: Colección "El Unicornio," 1958.
De la A a la Z por un poeta (poems for children), 1988.

Narrative

José Trigo. Mexico City: Siglo XXI, 1966. (Awarded the Xavier Villaurrutia
Prize.)
Palinuro de México. Madrid: Ediciones Alfaguara, 1978; La Habana, Cuba:
Casa de las Américas, 1985; Mexico City: Joaquín Mortiz, 1980. (Received
the Novela México International Prize, 1975; Rómulo Gallegos Inter-
national Novel Prize [Caracas, Venezuela], 1982; and the Médecis Inter-
national Prize [Paris, 1985].)
Noticias del imperio. Mexico City: Editorial Diana, 1987. (Awarded the
Mazatlán Literary Prize, 1987.) 2nd, illustrated ed., 1989.

Art Exhibitions

Institute of Contemporary Arts, London, 1973.
Galería Juana Mordó, Madrid, 1980.
"Fernando del Paso: Visiones de un escritor." Museo de Arte Carrillo Gil,
Mexico City, 1981.
Centro Cultural Mexicano, San Antonio, Texas, 1982.
University of Notre Dame, Indiana, 1983.
"Demonios y maravillas. Pinturas de América Latina." Ivry-sur-Seine,
France, 1986.
Maison de l'Amerique Latine, Paris, 1989.
"Fernando del Paso: Visiones de un escritor." Mexico City: Instituto Na-
cional de Bellas Artes, 1990.

Catalogs and Reproductions of Art

"Fernando del Paso: Visiones de un escritor." Instituto Nacional de Bellas
Artes y Museo de Arte Carrillo Gil, 1981.
"Fernando del Paso: Visiones de un escritor." Consejo Nacional para la
Cultura y las Artes, Instituto Nacional de Bellas Artes y Museo de Arte
Moderno, 1990.
"Obra gráfica de Fernando del Paso." *Tierra Adentro* 47 (May–June 1990),
insert.

Essays

"La imaginación al poder: El intelectual y los medios." *Revista de la Universidad de México* (Oct. 1979): 15–16.

"Mi patria chica, mi patria grande." *Casa de las Américas* 23.136 (1983): 154–160.

Interviews

Personal interviews (oral and written), Mexico City, Aug. 17–20, 1981.
"Entrevista con Fernando del Paso." Interview with Ignacio Trejo Fuentes. *La Semana de Bellas Artes*, Aug. 19, 1981, 2–4.
"Las visiones de un escritor y la pasión por el exceso (Entrevista con Cristina Pacheco)." *Unomásuno: Sábado*, Aug. 22, 1981, 7–8.
"Autoentrevista." *Revista de Bellas Artes*. 3rd ser. 1 (1982): 26–31.
"Entrevista binaria con Fernando del Paso." *Cuadernos de Marcha* n.s. 3.17 (1982): 23–28.
"La locura de Carlota: Novela e historia." Interview with Juan José Barrientos. *Vuelta* (Apr. 1986): 30–34.
"Diálogo de Fernando del Paso con Angeles Mastretta." *La Jornada*, July 9, 1988, 18.
"Entrevista" with Gerardo Ochoa Sandy. *Sábado* (supplement to *Unomásuno*), July 23, 1988, 2.
"La cabeza de Carlota, el único castillo en el que estuvo encerrada." Interview with Armando Ponce. *Proceso* 613, Aug. 1, 1988, 50–51.
"Ecos del imperio: Una conversación de Fernando del Paso y Angeles Mastretta." *Nexos* 138 (June 1989): 5–11.

Poniatowska, Elena

Narrative

Lilus Kikus. Mexico City: Los Presentes, 1954; Grijalbo, 1982; Ediciones Era, 1985.
Hasta no verte Jesús mío. Mexico City: Ediciones Era, 1969. (Awarded the Mazatlán Prize, 1970.)
La noche de Tlatelolco, testimonios de historia oral. Mexico City: Ediciones Era, 1971. (Awarded the Xavier Villaurrutia Prize, which the author rejected, 1970.)
Querido Diego, te abraza Quiela. Mexico City: Ediciones Era, 1978.
De noche vienes. Mexico City: Grijalbo, 1979.
Gaby Brimmer (with Gaby Brimmer). Mexico City: Grijalbo, 1979.
Fuerte es el silencio. Mexico City: Ediciones Era, 1980.
La "Flor de Lis." Mexico City: Ediciones Era, 1988.
Nada, nadie: Las voces del temblor. Mexico City: Ediciones Era, 1988.

Theater

Melés y Teleo (apuntes para una comedia). Panoramas 2 (1956).
"Un libro que me fue dado." *La Vida Literaria* (Apr. 1970): 3–4.
"Hasta no verte Jesús mío." *Vuelta* (Nov. 1978): 5–11.

Interviews by the Author

Palabras cruzadas. Mexico City: Ediciones Era, 1961.
Domingo siete. Mexico City: Editorial Océano, 1982.
Todo México, Vol. 1. Mexico City: Editorial Diana, 1990.

Essays

Todo empezó en domingo. Colección Vida y Pensamiento de México. Mexico City: Fondo de Cultura Económica, 1963.

Unpublished transcriptions of interviews with Josefina Bórquez (1964) and various manuscripts of *Hasta no verte Jesús mío.*

"La literatura de las mujeres en América Latina: México." Wellesley College Conference, "Breaking the Sequence: Women, Literature and the Future." Wellesley, Massachusetts, Apr. 30–May 2, 1981 (unpublished paper).

El último guajolote. Colección Memoria y Olvido: Imágenes de México, 10. Mexico City: Secretaría de Educación Pública y Martín Casillas Editores, 1982.

"Presentación al lector mexicano." *Se necesita muchacha.* Ed. Ana Gutiérrez. Mexico City: Fondo de Cultura Económica, 1983. 7–86.

"Testimonios de una escritora: Elena Poniatowska en micrófono." *La sartén por el mango: Encuentro de escritoras latinoamericanas.* Ed. Patricia Elena González and Eliana Ortega. Río Piedras, Puerto Rico: Ediciones Huracán, 1984. 155–162.

"Prólogo." *Meditación en el umbral: Antología poética,* by Rosario Castellanos. Ed. Julian Palley. Mexico City: Fondo de Cultura Económica, 1985.

¡Ay, vida, no me mereces! Mexico City: Joaquín Mortiz, 1985.

"Día de muertos." *La Jornada Semanal,* Jan. 10, 1988, 5–7.

"Introduction." *Cartucho and My Mother's Hands,* by Nellie Campobello. Austin: University of Texas Press, 1988. xii–xiv.

"Bewitched by Words" and "Words that Bewitch Us." Occasional Papers, Department of Romance Languages, University of Washington, June 1989.

"A Question Mark Engraved on My Eyelids." Trans. Cynthia Steele. *The Writer on Her Work,* II. Ed. Janet Sternburg. New York: Norton, 1990.

Prologues and Texts for Books of Photographs

La casa en la tierra, by Mariana Yampolsky. Mexico City: Instituto Nacional Indigenista–FONAPAS, 1980.

La raíz y el camino, by Mariana Yampolsky. Mexico City: Fondo de Cultura Económica, 1985.

Estancias del olvido, by Mariana Yampolsky. Pachuca: Centro Hidalguense de Investigaciones Históricas, 1987.

Tlacotalpan, by Mariana Yampolsky. Veracruz: Instituto Veracruzano de Cultura, 1987.

Hablando en plata: Ensayo fotográfico sobre minería en Real del Monte y Pachuca, Hidalgo, by David Maawad. Pachuca: Centro Hidalguense de Investigaciones Históricas, 1987.

La hacienda en México, by Daniel Nierman and Ernesto H. Vallejo. Mexico City: Daniel Nierman and Ernesto Vallejo, 1988.

Juchitán de las mujeres, by Graciela Iturbide. Trans. Cynthia Steele and Adriana Navarro. Mexico City: Ediciones Toledo, 1989.

Mujer x mujer: 22 fotógrafas. Mexico City: Consejo Nacional para la Cultura y las Artes and Instituto Nacional de Bellas Artes, 1989.

Compañeras de México: Women Photograph Women. Riverside: University Art Gallery, University of California, Riverside, 1990. Trans. Irene Matthews and others.

Romualdo García: Retratos. Guanajuato: Archivo Romualdo García, Museo de la Alhóndiga de Granaditas, Instituto Nacional de Antropología e Historia, 1990.

Interviews with the Author

"Elena Poniatowska: Hasta no verte Jesús mío." Interview with Margarita García Flores. *Hojas de Crítica: Suplemento de la Revista de la Universidad de México* (Oct. 1969).

"Con Elena Poniatowska." Interview with Cecilia López Negrete. *La Vida Literaria* (Apr. 1970): 16–21.

"Interview with Elena Poniatowska." With Beth Miller. *Latin American Literary Review* 4 (1975): 73–78.

"Entrevista a Elena Poniatowska." Interview with Margarita García Flores. *Revista de la Universidad de México* (Mar. 1976): 25–30.

"A diez años de la noche triste de Tlatelolco: En charla con *Siempre!*, Elena Poniatowska revive las horas más sombrías de México." Interview with Cristina Pacheco. *Siempre!*, Oct. 11, 1978, 30–31, 58–59.

"Entrevista con Elena Poniatowska." Interview with Margarita García Flores. *Elena Poniatowska* (Material de Lectura No. 10). Mexico City: Universidad Nacional Autónoma de México, 1983.

"Entrevista con Elena Poniatowska, octubre de 1983, en su casa de Coyoacán." *Historias íntimas: Conversaciones con diez escritoras latinoamericanas*. Magdalena García Pinto. Hanover: Ediciones del Norte, 1988. 174–198.

"La muchacha de la leña: Elena Poniatowska." Interview with Amílcar Leis Márquez. *La Plaza* (Guadalajara) n.s. (Sept. 1987): 8–11.

"¿Mil miradas? Mil oídos y una sonrisa: Elena Poniatowska." Interview with Beatriz Zalce. *La Plaza* (Guadalajara) n.s. (Sept. 1987): 5–7.

"Los muchachos de entonces." Interview. *Nexos: Sociedad, Ciencia, Literatura* (Jan. 1988): 101–102.

"Entrevista." Interview with Cynthia Steele. *Hispamérica* 53–54 (Aug.–Dec. 1989): 89–105.

Personal interviews. Mexico City, July 1983, Aug. 1984, July 1987, Sept. 1988, May 1989; Seattle, Oct. 1987.

Index